Included in E
Learning Climates ~~that~~ ~~cultivate~~
Racial and Ethnic Diversity

Shelli B. Fowler and Victor Villanueva, editors

Carolyn Vasques-Scalera, AAHE project editor

A publication of

AMERICAN ASSOCIATION
FOR HIGHER EDUCATION

Published in cooperation with the National Council of Teachers of English

Published in cooperation with the National Council of Teachers of English

The National Council of Teachers of English is devoted to
improving the teaching and learning of English and the language arts at all
levels of education. Since 1911, NCTE has provided a forum for
the profession, an array of opportunities for teachers to continue their
professional growth throughout their careers, and a framework for
cooperation to deal with issues that affect the teaching of English.

National Council of Teachers of English
1111 W. Kenyon Road, Urbana, IL 61801-1096
800-369-6283 or 217-328-3870
www.ncte.org

Included in English Studies: Learning Climates That Cultivate Racial and Ethnic Diversity
Shelli B. Fowler and Victor Villanueva, editors
Carolyn Vasques-Scalera, AAHE project editor

AMERICAN ASSOCIATION FOR HIGHER EDUCATION
One Dupont Circle, Suite 360
Washington, DC 20036
ph 202/293-6440, fax 202/293-0073
www.aahe.org

10 9 8 7 6 5 4 3 2 1   ISBN 1-56377-056-3

Contents

Foreword: AAHE

The American Association for Higher Education is pleased to publish this most timely volume, *Included in English Studies: Learning Climates That Cultivate Racial and Ethnic Diversity*, the third of three volumes that showcase innovative teaching and learning strategies, provide faculty in selected disciplines examples from their peers as to how they can make a difference in the success of students of color in introductory and gateway courses, and promote conversations in departments across the nation about the importance of diversity and the opportunity it brings to explore innovative pedagogy and revitalize learning in classrooms.

The 21st century is the time for higher education to rise to the occasion to serve the most diverse student population in history. For more than 30 years, AAHE has been the premier higher education association to lead faculty to achieve teaching and learning excellence. For the past decade or so, colleges and universities around the country have been trying to determine the impact of diversity on curricular and cocurricular life. In 1999, AAHE's Board of Directors officially adopted a statement on diversity in which they pledge: "AAHE will continue through its projects, conferences, and publications to assist campuses to increase access and diversity for students, faculty, and staff, as well as in curricula and programs." This publication builds on that pledge.

The three volumes (in communication, sociology, and English studies) also represent AAHE's continuing commitment to collaboration on two levels. First, they bring together AAHE's own work in assessment, faculty roles and rewards, teaching and learning, and diversity in new ways. Second, AAHE is also collaborating with disciplinary associations — the National Communication Association, the American Sociological Association, and the National Council of Teachers of English, respectively. All three books are produced under the leadership of Dr. Carolyn Vasques-Scalera, AAHE's director of diversity initiatives, and disciplinary colleagues, with funding from the Knight Foundation.

Research shows that the success of students of color ultimately depends on the transformation of faculty who teach them, as well as institutional and departmental climates that value the presence of diverse students. AAHE as a praxis organization is committed to taking research and operationalizing it through exemplary practice, as modeled through this publication.

Yolanda T. Moses
President, American Association for Higher Education

Foreword: NCTE

Students of color in gateway courses compose their individual narratives on paper, sometimes — and always compose narratives in their heads. Sometimes their narratives include the communal support needed to fuel the individual efforts that will one day lead to a measure of success, the community enabling the student to deal with the continual challenges faced by people of color. My own story is such a tale. I entered postsecondary education in a community college and made it through graduate school to a professional position of relative influence and creativity. I exerted great effort and made some great personal sacrifices. I also had tremendous communal support within the institution that I attended. Since then, I have still not arrived at some trouble-free life that without literacy I would not have been able to reach. This is not Nirvana, heaven, or the true meaning of the democratic ideal, after all. But I have arrived at a better positioning with which to grow further, with which to support my family and to contribute to the communal effort of others on this path.

Whatever is unique about my story, though, it is part of a larger narrative. The autobiographic tradition within the African American literary canon and the more recent phenomenon of autobiography among teachers and education scholars share common elements. Many of the from-there-to-here narratives from this tradition reflect what Cornel West once referred to as "the grand tradition of struggle." It is a struggle for Self within and for a broader communal good. While self-effort, exertion, and personal sacrifice are of course part of the story, communal support and effort on behalf of the protagonist is an equally, if not more important, part of such narratives. Not all African American autobiography relate a tale of triumph through work and support to overcome life's travails. Some are efforts to explore the tensions between individuality and group identity. Others are constructed in order to assert the importance of an integrationist or separatist ideology. However, narratives that do offer a tale of personal and social development and triumph, even while admitting to the ongoing struggle against racist efforts that seek to assault and destroy personal and social gains, offer common elements identifiable as the means for "overcoming."

The recipe of self-sacrifice and consistent effort is fairly clear. There are traditional and contemporary African American proverbs and expressions that testify to this "keep on keeping on." The road less traveled in much public dialogue about education highlights and explores the communal effort, especially when the discussion concerns academic achievement among probationary students of color. For some, this book begins the dialogue on communal responsibility; for others, it is a continuation, a nuancing, or a refining of the discussion. In both cases, the effort goes beyond simply asserting the now almost cliché that "it takes a village."

The communal vision transcends the individual protagonist, enabling all involved to see him or her as part of a collective moving forward, albeit often in recursive fashion. Members of the community inspire, cajole, mentor, and support the protagonist either throughout his or her efforts. The narrative tradition within African American literature, from classic narratives such as those written by Fredrick Douglass and Malcolm X, up to more contemporary autobiographies including those written by Nathan McCall and Brent Staples, continues to resonate with these messages, messages of the need for communal support.

In the pages that follow you will meet a community of writers, scholars, mentors, and teachers gathered to offer a call to educators to see themselves as part of a community that is responsible for the students before them. Rather than guardians of the gate who prevent the masses from entering, advancing, achieving, the writers in this volume call upon educators to see themselves as gatekeepers, even as gates, portals through which they can usher students onward to the next stage in their academic, personal, and social development. NCTE and AAHE join together in advancing the narratives of those who have been through the gates and of those who form the community that sometimes enables new narratives to be written.

Dale Allender
Associate Executive Director, National Council of Teachers of English

The Diversity Framework Informing This Volume

Carolyn Vasques-Scalera

This volume is one of three in a project funded by the Knight Foundation. Each asks the question how can we create learning climates (in English studies, in communication, and in sociology, respectively) that cultivate racial and ethnic diversity and promote the success of *all* our students?

The concept for these disciplinary monographs emerged from two important realities. First, despite gains made in access to higher education, numerous studies show that students of color remain underrepresented at every degree level and in many disciplines. Second, despite all we have learned about effective teaching and learning and about the importance of diversity in general, we haven't done enough to translate that general knowledge into specific disciplinary and teaching practices. These volumes are an attempt to make more intentional the connections between diversity and teaching/learning and to provide faculty with concrete strategies for enacting those connections in their discipline. To that end, there are several critical questions that must be considered:

What are our assumptions about who learns and how? Do we enact practices that suggest that there is only one way to teach and learn and belong to a disciplinary community? Do we send the message that only some students are capable of learning; that students are somehow deficient if they fail to learn under the conditions set explicitly or implicitly by the discipline? Do we adhere to elitist "weed-out" notions of success, that students who fail to succeed simply did not belong? Do we think of diversity in terms of excellence, or diminishment? Why should disciplines care about diversity?

The Framework's Elements

"Diversity" is a term that has been used widely and loosely with very different meanings and implications for practice. The questions posed above reveal some important insights about the particular diversity framework informing this volume and its companion two volumes.

1

These volumes challenge the deficit model of diversity, in which difference is equated with deficiency and seen as a challenge rather than as an opportunity for learning. *All* students and faculty bring a wealth of tradition, information, and experience to their understandings of the world, and that wealth can contribute in meaningful ways to the learning process. Furthermore, to focus on how some students are different, or to assume that *different* means "deficient," is to leave unexamined how the learning experience is set up to the benefit of particular groups by rewarding their culture-specific ways of knowing and doing.

2

These volumes move beyond a singular focus on access and representational diversity — the *numbers* of students of color in our classes and campuses — to examine the experiences students face once there. It's not enough to recruit diverse students if we do nothing to retain them; that is, if we don't offer a teaching/learning environment where they are genuinely included and are expected to succeed.

3

In thinking about students' experiences, these volumes expand the conversation beyond the usual focus on content — *what* we teach — to a discussion about the impact on students of process — *how* we teach. The volumes don't advocate an additive approach to curriculum, in which diverse perspectives are simply tacked on to the content of courses. Rather, they prompt us to think deeply about what it means to be included in classroom and disciplinary communities, and the ways in which we create, intentionally or not, barriers to meaningful student learning and participation in those communities. The volumes ask faculty to examine the hidden messages in our pedagogy, and they provide some alternate ways of teaching that are more inclusive and conducive to the success of diverse students.

4

These volumes challenge the notion that diversity is solely or primarily the responsibility of certain faculty (usually faculty of color); involves particular students (usually students of color); and is relevant only to certain areas of the campus (student affairs) or to specific disciplines (humanities and social sciences). The issues they raise and the practices they advocate illustrate not merely the relevance but the absolute *centrality* of diversity to teaching and learning. Their essays challenge not merely pedagogical practices but the epistemological foundations upon which each discipline rests. Each volume makes diversity relevant to that disciplinary context and raises important questions about what it means to engage in a disciplinary community that truly values diversity. They make clear that teaching and learning *about* diversity is not the same as engaging diversity and diverse learners in the learning process. As such, they model for other disciplines how to take up these issues.

5

While these volumes primarily address students of color and gateway courses, the issues raised apply to other forms of difference; the practices described transcend specific courses; and because the volumes are essentially about enhancing pedagogy and engaging diversity, the benefits extend to *all* students. An important theme concerns not simply making curriculum and pedagogy more relevant to students of color, but helping all students (and indeed, faculty) become more culturally aware and multiculturally competent. A growing body of research documents the benefits of having diverse learners and of engaging diversity issues — not just for the success of students of color, but for all students.

6

Finally, while the focus is mainly on classrooms, these volumes include essays and instructional practices that situate the classroom within its larger departmental, institutional, and disciplinary contexts. A meaningfully diverse classroom climate is a necessary but insufficient criterion to achieving the goals outlined above. Students also need to see themselves reflected in the curriculum and in the faces of faculty and administrators. Students need to experience an inclusive campus climate and disciplinary community. Individual faculty members enacting good practices in their classes is not enough; we need departmental, institutional, and discipline-wide support for diversity.

A Prompt for Conversation and Change

Thus the title of the volumes, *Included in* — which reflects that it is not enough to recruit students of color into higher education and into the disciplines if, once there, their progress is blocked by teaching/learning practices that exclude them. Nor is it enough to focus on persistence and success if, by that, we mean success only in the academy's dominant ways of thinking and learning. To their credit, many students of color have succeeded in higher education and will continue to succeed despite too-often unwelcoming climates and other barriers. But the title reflects the larger outcome we all desire; that is, for students of color to feel *included* in a discipline, to feel a sense of ownership and empowerment in the learning process, the discipline, the academy. The subtitle — *Learning Climates That Cultivate Racial and Ethnic Diversity* — reflects the means for getting there, that we must intentionally *cultivate* diversity (in all its forms). To do that is not simply a matter of letting people in, it means opening up the knowledge-creation process. The result is a more vital and viable discipline.

The use of the word *cultivate* is very intentional. These volumes present a fundamental challenge to the weed-out mentality that says only some students can learn and those who fail don't deserve to be there. But neither do the volumes assume that to succeed, students simply need to learn better study skills. They are not about changing who students are or how they learn. Rather, these volumes are intended to encourage faculty to examine our assumptions about who students are and how they learn, and the ways in which our pedagogy either contributes to or inhibits the inclusion and success of all our students.

These volumes are not intended as the final or definitive word on cultivating racial and ethnic diversity in the disciplines. Nor are they meant to be cookbooks for doing so. We risk perpetuating the exclusion and marginalization of students of color if we equate *identity* with *learning style*, or apply unreflectively the instructional practices that work well in one context with one group of students to all contexts and groups. Instead, the volumes are intended as a resource for conversation and examining assumptions, and they provide some guidelines for practice. But we must think carefully about who our students are, and enact multiple forms of teaching and learning that provide opportunities for all students to be genuinely included.

Clearly the issues raised in this volume and the other two point to the need for more research in the scholarship of teaching and learning that explicitly investigates diversity questions. My hope is that you will find the monographs — individually and collectively — stimulating and empowering in furthering such work in collaboration with colleagues on campus, at your disciplinary meetings, and at AAHE events. I invite you to visit the AAHE website (www.aahe.org) for further resources and for venues in which to share your progress.

These are issues about which I care deeply, and with which I continue to struggle in my own teaching. It is exciting and illuminating to learn how different disciplines are grappling with these issues and bringing discipline-specific research to bear on pedagogical practices.

Acknowledgments

I would like to express my thanks to the editors from English studies, Drs. Shelli Fowler and Victor Villanueva, of Washington State University, for their hard work in bringing this volume to fruition; also to our colleagues at the National Council of Teachers of English, particularly Dr. Anne Ruggles Gere, for her support of this collaboration. Many thanks to Bry Pollack, director of publications at AAHE, for her keen editorial eye.

This volume (and those in communication and sociology) would not be possible without the generous support of the Knight Foundation and the guidance of Rick Love and Julia Van.

Most especially, thanks go to the faculty members and students in English studies who willingly and ably raised some critical issues and shared exemplary practices by which we might create more-inclusive disciplines, and indeed a more-inclusive academy.

Introduction

Victor Villanueva and Shelli B. Fowler

A graduate student from Puerto Rico emails one of us, Victor. She asks why he self-identifies as a person of color. "Why not a Puerto Rican? . . . Or an AmeRican?" Victor answers that these really are his first self-labels — Puerto Rican, Nuyorican — but that in all the years away from his first home, Brooklyn, he has found that the problems of racism faced by the Puerto Rican are the same for the American Indian, the Asian and Asian American, the Latina and Latino, the African American, and a host of others whose histories are not rooted in Western Europe but who are here, in U.S. classrooms, nevertheless.

A message to the National Council of Teachers of English a decade back resonates. "Why does Victor refer to himself as a person of color? We are Mexican American" (the fellow having not read the book, obviously, but having come to some conclusions based on a Spanish surname). Victor explains that this is a matter of representation, of how we are cast, and of real social and economic circumstance and opportunity. Skin color is not the same as *of color*. Some of us are colored by the culture at large, no matter our melanin mix. Yet we (at least Americans) sort folks this way. Omi and Winant (1994) say that the second thing we do when we meet someone new is to come to some conclusion about the person's race (the first thing being to realize gender). Race is how we believe we know something about the person being introduced. Yet Victor is as much Italian, Jewish, Middle Eastern as he is Puerto Rican — at least to the eye. Whatever the conclusion, though, he is subject to racism, as are all whose physical characteristics are not Western European. Omi and Winant (1994) put it this way:

> The effort must be made to understand race as an unstable and "decentered" complex of social meanings constantly being transformed by political struggle. With this in mind, let us propose a definition: *race is a concept [that] signifies and symbolizes social conflicts and interests by referring to different types of human bodies.* Although the concept of race invokes biologically based human characteristics (so-called "phenotypes"), selection of these particular human features for purposes of racial signification is always and necessarily a social and historical process. In contrast to the other major distinction of this type, that of gender, there is no biological basis for distinguishing among human groups along the lines of race. Indeed, the categories employed to differentiate among human groups along racial lines reveal themselves, upon serious examination, to be at best imprecise, and worst completely arbitrary. (55)

And so the Irish were once something like *of color*, but the Irish were the colonized of another imperial center. If there's one thing we can hold in common as persons of color, it is a history of colonialism, so that as the U.S. sphere of influence extends to the globe, all of its colonies become subject to racism. The older colonialism provides America's people of color: the slaves of Africa, the slaves of the Caribbean and what has become the American West, the lands obtained from Spanish colonialism in the Caribbean, the American Southwest, and the Pacific. The newer colonialism extends *of color* to so many within U.S. borders, the victims of neocolonialism of the Southern Hemisphere, South Asia, Africa. With the influx of immigrants from Russian and Europe's northern and eastern climes, even *Caucasian* becomes colored (as those from the Caucuses are not the white folks of Western Europe). Racism is complex in its absurdity.

Racism — its end — then, is the overall goal. And to be able, somehow, to change the effects of racism through language and language instruction would be nice for us, those of us who have classrooms as our sites for political and social change. We want to believe Freire (in Freire and Macedo 1987), who says that if we can change the word, the world can be changed. We believe in the power of the word, know that Antonio Gramsci (1971) is right in suggesting that in order to act or change, we must have words for those actions or changes. If there is no word for a concept, then it cannot be, cannot assume life. Change the word — or add the words of those who haven't been sufficiently heard from — and the world might be changed.

Problem is, the job of a composition teacher or of anyone assigned to a gateway language course includes, even insists on, the inculcation of the accepted word, the conventions of a particular dialect (or grapholect). We teach conventions, or at least that's a part of our job. Convention does not equal change. Gateway too often equals gatekeeper. We wish heterogeneity; we teach homogeneity. That's hard to get around. But we must. We do have our utopian hope and utopian drive. The essays contained in the pages that follow depict the authors' struggles with the contradictions — convention and change.

We really don't know how to deal in the contradiction of our work — of wanting substantial critical engagement in a language that is ultimately assimilationist. Say what you will; just read like us. Ain't no change gonna happen no way *that* way. We've got stuff to figure out. Ishmael Reed (1998) (with help from Richard Robertiello through Daniela Gioseffi) writes about the problem of convention in larger terms, as matters of the common culture:

> The McIntellectuals and the black and brown Talented Tenth auxiliary insist that we embrace a common culture, and their consensus seems to be that this culture is Yankee, or Anglo. A genuine Englishman and scholar, A. Robert Lee, of the University at Kent, might dispute the notion that the culture of England is an Anglo culture. Anglos were only one tribe, he would claim, but the Anglo model for the American common culture persists, and it is the model that Lati-

nos, Asian Americans, African Americans, and even European
Americans are required to embrace. . . . Daniela Gioseffi quotes
Richard Robertiello: "Although a nation of ethnics, our established
ethic is WASPishness, the standard by which assimilation is judged,
while WASP conduct, for its part, was early on patterned on the
model of the British upper class. Altogether, this has proved to be a
very bad thing, making Americans WASP-worshippers, with an
attendant devaluation and dilution of ethnic pride." One might add
that the WASP ideal is also unfair to those Americans with Anglo
heritage. They must abide hurtful stereotypes and suffer the resent-
ment of those who resist the Anglo model, even though they had
very little to do with the establishment of the WASP ethic. (xvi-xvii)

We must conform, in other words, to a standard culture with its standardized language. Not to do so can have consequences. There is real power to the
assertion of a cultural assimilation, real economic power, even real global power,
as the language of the world's economic center becomes the lingua franca of the
globe. So we can't simply ignore convention. Students do have the right to their
own language, but that right is always already mitigated by economic verities. We
have contradictions to play out. From Sandra María Esteves (1991):

> We are a multitude of contradictions
> reflecting our history
> oppressed
> controlled
> once free folk
> remnants of that time interacting in our souls
>
> Our kindred was the earth
> polarity with the land
> respected it
> called it mother
> were sustained and strengthened by it
>
> The european thru power and fear became our master
> his greed welcomed by our ignorance
> tyranny persisting
> our screams passing unfulfilled
>
> As slaves we lost identity
> assimilating our master's values
> overwhelming us to become integrated shadows
> unrefined and dependent
>
> We flee escaping, becoming clowns in an alien circus
> performing predictably
> mimicking strange values
> reflecting what was inflicted

> Now the oppressor has an international program
> and we sit precariously within the monster's mechanism
> internalizing anguish from comrades
> planning and preparing a course of action. (186-187)

A course of action — providing the access that students need and desire, recognizing the power of particular ways with words, yet to the degree that we as teachers have any power at all, allowing entrée to those who have been traditionally excluded, disallowing gateway courses in language from remaining gatekeeping courses. That's the problem to be worked through, the task needing to be achieved for us whose sites of action are classrooms.

Herein, then, we have gathered a group of teachers to discuss their courses and their theories and research. They work in community colleges and in research universities, predominantly white institutions, overwhelmingly Latino institutions, and historically black institutions. In addressing strategies for working with students of color in gateway courses in English, the writers range through the world as well as the classroom, understanding that to know about ourselves, our students of color, or our classrooms, we must come to know something of our context, one quite literally global. We read what happens when teachers are white but students are black, when the student is black, the teacher is Puerto Rican, and the classroom is American Indian, Latino, international, when the teacher is black and the student is Latina, when the racialized mixes of our classrooms must confront convention yet set about creating change.

We begin with a research study that addresses the fundamental question — how do white teachers approach students of color, or more specifically, black male students? This has got to be the basic question of white teachers wanting to effect change, wanting to confront racism but fearing perceptions of being racist, recognizing the stereotypes to which Ishmael Reed refers. In the study by Lisa Gonsalves, we hear from teachers and from students. The first section of this book takes us further into the voices of those who sit in our classrooms. Arlette Ingram Willis and Ana Lucía Herrera explore the moments of connection and interaction in which we can learn directly from our students of color — even when we are ourselves teachers of color — what their experiences in the classroom are like.

Michelle Hall Kells begins by examining effective pedagogical practices for teaching composition to Chicana and Chicano bilingual college writers. Rhonda Grego argues that the ongoing marginalization of composition courses within most English departments continues to limit the kinds of rhetorical issues explored in first-year writing courses. In discussing the development of the Bridges Writing Program at the historically black institution where she teaches, Grego asks us to be attentive to the geopolitics of the specific location in which we teach and to "the material conditions of work" as we choose an appropriate composition pedagogy. Dan Melzer focuses on a pluralist practice that will engage African American vernacular English (AAVE) speakers and help to disrupt the gatekeeping aspect of first-year writing courses in open-admissions institutions. And Jaime Armin Mejía examines the connections between the collaborative aspects of the Chicana and Chicano cultural norm of "clustered extended families" and the collaborative ways that Chicana and Chicano students tend to compose in the writing classroom. In so doing, Mejía discusses both the usefulness and limitations of postprocess composition theory.

In the essays by Fowler, Pimentel and Pimentel, and Ong, Kim, and Graber, the attention shifts to the instructor in gateway courses. Shelli Fowler examines ways to engage students in systemic and structural analyses of diversity. In asking what difference race makes in interpreting African American literature, she explores the need for critically self-reflexive interpretive and pedagogical practices, and calls for teaching strategies that work to foster critical consciousness in all students — of color and not of color — in order to help dismantle the gated community of English studies. Charise Pimentel and Octavio Pimentel argue that by "voicing our political viewpoints, we begin to identify with and build coalitions with students who experience oppression on an ongoing basis." After providing a useful summary of critical pedagogy (invoked in so many of the essays in this collection), they advocate a strategy within the critical: a coalition pedagogy. Rory Ong, with Albert Kim and Dorothy Graber, brings our attention to what is often missing in the literature on multiculturalism — a "critically complex articulation of culture, given the current concerns over globalization." Ong engages us in the pedagogy; two of his students, Kim and Graber, demonstrate what can arrive from that pedagogy.

The remaining essays broaden the discussion by exploring the role gateway English courses play in helping students in general, and students of color in particular, adjust to postsecondary academic work. In "The Color Line," Janet Bean brings our attention to the inaccuracies various word-processing grammar checkers routinely include. Her essay argues that word-processing skills have become "an invisible literacy" that affects students unequally across the digital divide. Bean suggests that the text-editing tools included in software should be "interrogated" in the writing classroom, asserting that the grammar checkers are correct less than half the time and are a particular problem for AAVE speakers, as the language bias of the grammar checkers marks the written patterns of their speech as "error." Marcia Ribble discusses the need to address retention for working-class students of color. She provides a sample diversity assignment that mentors students in imagining the transition from precollege to postdegree successfully. Jennifer Young provides us with an example of a practical application of classroom assessment techniques (CATs) to enhance the critical engagement of students of color in interdisciplinary literature courses, and Judy Massey Dozier stresses the importance of allowing African American literary texts to "enter our courses using their own voices and culture." She argues that the literature must be read within the historical and cultural context of African Americans and asserts that white teachers should not overlook (and inadvertently disrespect) the use of black dialect in the fiction and poetry of African American writers.

For all the differences among the essays, politically and pedagogically they come together in the common assumption that racism is untenable and that we are obliged, as believers in the epistemological function of language, to address the untenable and to nullify its effects. Our hope is that the pages that follow will be not only informative but also provocative, provoking us into lessening the contradictions of our profession.

References

Esteves, S.M. (1991). "From Fanon." In *Puerto Rican Writers at Home in the USA: An Anthology*, edited by F. Turner, pp. 186-187. Seattle: Open Hand.

Freire, P., and D. Macedo. (1987). *Literacy: Reading the Word and the World*. South Hadley, MA: Bergin & Garvey.

Gramsci, A. (1971). *Selections From the Prison Notebooks*, edited and translated by Q. Hoare and G.N. Smith. New York: International.

Omi, M., and H. Winant. (1994). *Racial Formation in the United States: From the 1960s to the 1990s*. New York: Routledge.

Reed, I., ed. (1998). *MultiAmerica: Essays on Cultural Wars and Cultural Peace*. New York: Penguin.

The Dance of Safety

Examining the Stances Taken by White Faculty in Relation to
Black Males in the College Classroom

Lisa M. Gonsalves

I have been teaching composition in urban colleges and universities for the last 14 years. As a black woman in this role, I am often approached by white colleagues for advice about the writing skills of black students, particularly black males. Because of these discussions, I have become increasingly concerned with the relationships that develop, or do not develop, between my white colleagues and the students of color on campus. This concern arose because of the disparities I have seen in the cross-racial interaction stories that have been shared with me over the years.

These divergent reports piqued my curiosity and led to the study reported here. In this study, I focused exclusively on the interactions between white faculty and black male students for the following reasons: First, the white faculty who approached me were predominantly concerned with their black male students. It seemed that their most difficult and perplexing teaching situations involved these students. Second, I have always been distressed by the lower retention rates of black male students, particularly those males who enter college from urban public high schools. Knowing how important faculty-student relationships are to student success (see, e.g., Endo and Harpel 1982; Grant-Thompson and Atkinson 1997; Kobrak 1992; Pascarella and Terenzini 1977; Wilson et al. 1975; Word, Zanna, and Cooper 1974), I decided to investigate the following question: *What stances are taken by white faculty when confronted with students of color, specifically black male students, in the classroom?*

I researched this question by conducting qualitative interviews with the participants. The sample for this study was drawn from two groups: black male students and white faculty recruited from three urban educational institutions. Ten students, who ranged in age from 20 to 36, were asked to participate in this study. Half of the students were recruited as a sample of convenience identified through snowball selection; that is, previous student participants were asked to suggest other students they knew who might want to participate. The remaining students were recruited from black student centers on the various urban campuses. Nine of the students attended urban public high schools; two of them dropped out of high school and later earned their GED. One student grew up in a suburban community and attended a predominantly white high school.

Twelve white faculty were asked to participate in this study — eight men and four women. Faculty were recruited in two ways. First, those faculty who demonstrated an awareness of the particular issues faced by minority students were invited to participate. They were faculty who were known, to myself and others on campus, as individuals who strove to act in nonracist ways with their black students. These faculty were selected based on the assumption that because they had already exhibited caring behavior toward black students, they would be more likely to participate openly and honestly in all stages of the research.

The second method of faculty recruitment was based on student participants' recommendations. All the recommended faculty agreed to participate. About one-third of the faculty participants were recruited in this manner. These faculty differed from the other faculty participants in that I was not previously aware of their attitudes toward, and work with, black students. All the faculty participants had between five and 20 years of teaching experience in urban institutions, and all but one of them had tenure. The faculty taught courses ranging from the humanities to math and science.

Rather than ask the participants to talk with me directly about their experiences, I developed vignettes, or short cases, depicting real-life scenarios that were representative of the types of interactions that had been described to me in the past. The vignettes used for this research were designed to uncover the opinions, reactions, and perspectives of the participants. Each participant was asked to respond to four of the vignettes, two of which depicted in-class interactions and two of which depicted one-on-one interactions between faculty member and student. The participants were asked to explain what they saw happening in the vignettes. After the participants explained their observations and perceptions fully, other, more pointed questions were asked. For example, if race was not mentioned as a factor in the interaction, the participant was asked more directly whether or not he or she felt that race had any bearing on what happened in the vignette. An added bonus of this approach was that the vignettes, presumably because they were also stories, prompted many of the participants to tell stories of their own cross-racial interactions with white faculty or black students. Some of those narratives, as well as participants' overall reactions to the vignettes, are represented in the following discussion of the findings.

Research conducted over the last 20 years has demonstrated that both in-class and out-of-class interactions with faculty improve student retention (Endo and Harpel 1982; Grant-Thompson and Atkinson 1997; Kobrak 1992; Pascarella and Terenzini 1977; Wilson et al. 1975; Word, Zanna, and Cooper 1974). Wilson et al. report that students who had such interactions expressed greater satisfaction with their overall college experience. However, these same studies report that faculty-student interactions on many campuses tend to be infrequent.

Those studies that specifically examine faculty-student interactions among mixed-race pairings point out that race does indeed influence how the interaction turns out (Feldman and Saletsky 1986; Grant-Thompson and Atkinson 1997;

Kobrak 1992). For example, Grant-Thompson and Atkinson (1997) found that white faculty can work successfully with black students if the faculty members exhibit culturally sensitive behaviors. They found that one behavior that has a large impact on the responsiveness of African American males is when white faculty respond to the cultural content of the comments the students make rather than ignoring or "not hearing" those comments. (For example, white faculty advisers who empathetically acknowledged the "importance of ethnicity and cultural values" in a black male student's decision to transfer to a predominantly white institution were rated higher than were white faculty who did not acknowledge the role of ethnicity and culture.)

Other researchers support the assertion that it is possible for white faculty to work well with black students. Allen, Epps, and Haniff (1991) point out that the most supportive relationships that develop between black students and white faculty grow out of genuine caring on the faculty member's part rather than from specific programs designed to bring black students and white faculty together. They conclude that white faculty who exhibit caring behavior toward black students do go a long way toward combating the racism these students encounter in other parts of the university. Also, those black students who are able to interact with white faculty on a regular basis report being more content with their educational and personal development than do black students who do not interact with white faculty at all (Nettles 1988).

The present study was conducted in urban colleges and universities because faculty who choose to teach in these settings exhibit characteristics that set them apart from those in nonurban institutions. For example, given the wide disparity in student preparedness at many urban institutions, faculty tend to emphasize teaching more, seeing their role as facilitating critical thinking and the acquisition of skills rather than as simply passing on subject matter to students (Elliot 1994).

My data suggest that when faced with students of color, particularly black male students, white faculty take one of three distinct stances in relation to those students. Faculty (1) *deemphasize the effect of racial differences,* (2) *become overly hesitant or, in some cases, paralyzed by their awareness of racial differences,* or (3) *demonstrate a special awareness of the effect racial differences have on students of color.* These stances influence the interaction patterns of white faculty in their work with black students, which in turn impact those students in specific ways. It is my hope that naming these stances will provide white faculty with a framework for reflecting upon their own classroom interactions with black students in new ways.

Deemphasizing Racial Differences

Those faculty who deemphasize racial differences tend to stress the importance of not seeing or of not acknowledging a student's racial identity. Faculty who take this stance strongly believe that acknowledging a student's race is calling attention to a false marker. Because of this, they are less likely to pay particular attention to the black male students in their classrooms; to do so would contradict their philosophy about not attending to race. As the following faculty talked about their experiences with students in general, I asked whether they had had similar experiences with *black* students. This question elicited the following responses:

> I really don't care [about race]. A student is a student, as far as I am concerned. The fact that a student is African American, to me, would be immaterial. If they work hard, I don't see it that way. I've got just a different upbringing I guess. . . . I went to a high school where we didn't look at people. "I like this person, I don't like this person," but race wasn't involved. But I think there are a lot of people out there who would be influenced [by race]. I think people preconceive, preconceive, preconceive, preconceive. (Dr. Alpert, white male faculty member)

> This is not me trying to be PC (politically correct), but I really can't say I have seen any difference between white students, Latino students, African American students, and black students who are not African American — it's just. . . . (Dr. Delta, white female black studies faculty member)

In these comments, the faculty declare strongly that it is "proper" *not* to see or acknowledge a student's race. They equate seeing color with confirming differences and thereby creating inequalities. For them, to acknowledge a student's color or race is to acknowledge that the student is somehow different. This causes psychological discomfort for some white faculty, because once they acknowledge that black students might be different, they have to explain, at least to themselves, the ways in which they are different. These data suggest that for these faculty, difference means inferior. When Dr. Alpert says, "I think there are a lot of people out there who would be influenced [by race]. I think people preconceive," it suggests that he believes that when others acknowledge race, they display negative preconceptions of what black people are like rather than positive ones.

The beliefs articulated by these faculty are not simply about the fear of acknowledging that black students might be inferior. These participants also believe that not acknowledging a student's race is the *right* thing to do, evident in Dr. Delta's statement, "This is not me trying to be PC." Clearly, these individuals personally subscribe to the belief that this is the proper way of dealing with racial difference, even though it might also be seen as politically correct.

Faculty who deemphasize the impact of racial difference focus on bringing students in the classroom together by promoting unity among all students. However, for these faculty, a safe classroom is one without conflict or discomfort. Dr. Griffith, a white male music faculty member, explains his strategy for promoting unity in the classroom:

> Rather than emphasizing the blackness of the [content], I would rather emphasize the [content]. But not to the point that we are not

saying where it came from and understanding that. We have to do that, but to put [race] right up at the top seems to me to set up confrontation possibilities, to set up difficulties, when really the goal in my classes is to get people, all of us, to work together. Rather than this straight-out point. No. That's a way of dividing, it seems to me. What the great black artists can do for us is we're not viewing them as black in particular, but just as part of the big picture. They're, for most people, they're human beings and they're artists. Artists is what they are most of all to students, and that's what's exciting about these people.

Dr. Griffith's approach reflects his desire to maintain unity in the classroom by suppressing the discussion when race or other uncomfortable subject matter is raised by a student's question or through class discussion. This is illustrated at another occasion when Dr. Griffith says he would "rather work through [the racial aspect] of the content in another way, rather than [by] looking directly at it." The motivation for promoting unity is so that the class as a whole will feel like a safe place; however, deemphasizing racial difference ends up promoting safety mainly for the white faculty member.

Becoming Overly Hesitant or Paralyzed by One's Awareness of Racial Difference

A second group of white faculty in this study exhibits an awareness of racial difference in students, but they are so apprehensive about acting on that awareness that they become overly hesitant or paralyzed when faced with a black male student who is not performing well academically. In the following narrative, Dr. Collins, a legal studies professor, recounts his contact with a student after the two had a disagreement over the quality of the student's work.

He [the student] did poor work. I have three papers in my course, and each one of them he had to do again and each time he barely got it up to the level. All of my instinct from talking to him was that he was brighter than his papers. So I kept expecting more, and I kept telling him that I was expecting more, that I was disappointed. Then we got in a real tiff because I didn't give him a grade. The final paper came in and it was just like the other papers. I gave him an incomplete, and he was very unhappy about that. He was somewhat offensive at me, and I reacted by getting annoyed and saying, "Look, I don't need to be talked to that way; the work wasn't done. . . ." I'm not totally pleased with the way I reacted. He went off and complained to other people. I settled down and got upset a little bit with myself for having been, I thought, somewhat unprofessional with him, so I called him at home and said, "Look we didn't do this right. Can we back up two steps and start this conversation over?"

So he came in, [and] we redesigned another assignment because I thought he was in a kind of a rut. He was making the

same mistakes over and over again. In my judgment, [he was] mis-reading the same instruction the wrong way. And so I redid the assignment so that we would get out of the problem of just a bad read of the instructions. He seemed relieved. I certainly was. . . .
He said in our conversation at the very end that I had insulted him a couple of times during class, which I didn't know. He had not told me then. The insults were in the form of dismissing comments he made. He [said that he] made observations that he thought I didn't take seriously, classroom comments about subject matter. He would say something, and in his judgment I didn't respond seri-ously. I went to another student, or I didn't act as if that was the right answer. He felt that he knew a lot, and I wasn't being respect-ful of that, and I may well have not given that deference. I won't say I didn't do it, but I'm not quite sure why I would have wanted to dismiss him that way or be dismissive. It worries me mainly because had we not had the blowup around the paper, if I had given him a grade, I would never have known I'd ever done that, which leads me to wonder what are the other ones I don't know about.

Two levels of engagement are at work here: First, Dr. Collins and the stu-dent are directly engaged in issues about the student's written work; second, they are also silently engaged with each other during classroom discussion, as evi-denced by Dr. Collins's statement that the student confessed to feeling insulted by him.

If one were to speculate about how this silent engagement affected the stu-dent and his subsequent interactions with Dr. Collins, one might ask the follow-ing questions: Did the student attribute Dr. Collins's "insulting" behavior to racism? Was the student unconsciously, or consciously, resisting Dr. Collins's reac-tions to his work because of the perceived insult? Did he perceive Dr. Collins's reactions to his paper as another example of disrespect for his opinions? Although this narrative does not answer these questions, it is clear that Dr. Collins was not aware of the impact his classroom behavior had on the student.

It is through direct engagement and conversation that Dr. Collins is finally able to make a better assessment of what is causing the student's problem and design a more appropriate intervention. It is also at this point that the student tells Dr. Collins about the perceived insult. What motivated the student to make this revelation at the end? What does this reveal about the impact of meaningful inter-action between faculty and student? One motivation may have been the student's appreciation at being given another chance by Dr. Collins. Given an opening, the student was willing to talk with the professor about what was happening for him in class. Though the potential was there for Dr. Collins to relate in a very differ-ent way with this student from the beginning, he did not take the opportunity. Why not?

Unlike those who take a deemphasizing stance in relation to race, Dr.

Collins does acknowledge the particularized experiences of some black students when he says at another point in the interview in reference to the notion of pushing students to succeed academically:

> Am I reinforcing a message of "you ain't smart"? Since I know that's out there, I know that's in their heads from any number of spots, whether how they did in high school or their comparisons with students in the class here or any number of things. I'm very worried about playing into that, and that may inhibit me from pushing hard.

However, also unlike faculty who directly acknowledge racial differences, he is uncertain and apprehensive about the consequences of taking such a stance with students in the classroom. He says in the interview:

> Perhaps my thick-headed way is that I don't see the racial issue there. Or, to put it differently, I think there are so many issues there I'm not sure why I want to identify that one. . . . I think it carries risks. I think you have to ask yourself what the costs are of doing that. I mean something can explode. One of the things you always worry about is that someone's going to say "racist," and for a white person sitting there the issue is: [first], "No, I'm not"; second, "Maybe I am"; third, "Where's this going?" So the instinct to want to keep it in the bottle is pretty substantial when you're dealing with something that can go off in lots of directions, including inside yourself. My point is it's got to get recognized as hard, not because somebody's a jerk; it doesn't have anything to do with whether you're a jerk. Well, these are hard problems because you can — people can — get hurt. The risks are real for all sides.

Dr. Collins poignantly describes the dilemma for white faculty in these situations: the awareness that acknowledging racial differences can potentially open them up to charges of racism. This is personally risky, and some white faculty don't really know what to do in this situation. Fortunately, faculty such as Dr. Collins clearly have not opted out of the dilemma completely, but neither are they able to openly communicate their understanding to black students or to themselves.

In this next narrative, Dr. Wisler, a white female faculty member who teaches English, falls into the same traps as Dr. Collins in her work with a black male student. First, the student's writing difficulties became evident from a poorly completed assignment, in this case the midterm exam. Second, Dr. Wisler becomes very frustrated because the student appears to be misunderstanding the directions for the assignment. About the student's midterm exam, she says:

> He just didn't understand the instructions. He just didn't do it. He wrote hardly anything, and he just completely misunderstood. So after I passed the midterm back, I said, "Look, some people didn't do so well, and I'd like to give people a chance to do well here. So, I'm going to offer the option of doing an extra-credit paper to kind

of make up for the essay section of the midterm." So, he did that.
He did it, but he completely misunderstood again. He didn't do
what he was supposed to do. So then the final came along and he
screwed that up. Well, he ended up with a C- in the course, which
is the best I could do for him, but I felt badly about it.

Like Dr. Collins, Dr. Wisler has knowledge about the educational pitfalls that hinder black students' progress and an understanding of what might be needed to help black students succeed.

You know the Claude Steele [1992] article? That article really revo-
lutionized my thinking this past year about the point of trying to get
people to make an identification with the academic enterprise.
That the way to retain people is to get them to feel like they're part
of this, that they aren't outsiders looking in. So I keep thinking
about how to do that with people.

In this case, Dr. Wisler's awareness of the social situation and educational needs of black students gets translated into worry and concern about protecting this particular student from a perceived lack of confidence rather than into an ability to motivate the student to meet the academic challenge of the class. When asked why she did not talk directly with the student about his writing difficulties after the first midterm, Dr. Wisler explained, "To single him out — I mean, people are hanging around my desk afterwards. So, for me to say, 'Hey, _____ , wait a minute. Let me talk to you,' and a bunch of other people are hanging around. I don't want to embarrass him."

She articulates her fear as not wanting to "embarrass" the student. But Dr. Simms, an education and philosophy professor, articulates it differently in a discussion of the difficulties white faculty experience when race and academic standards intersect: "A lot of white faculty feel like somehow if they engage with the black student, they are playing into the stereotype that the black student is inferior, or they are worried about avoiding that." In other words, behind Dr. Wisler's fear of embarrassing the student is a fear that if she engages with him over his failure after class, in front of the other, white students, she will be "playing into the stereotype" of black inferiority. In an attempt to avoid this, she hesitates to really call attention to his weaknesses, not only in front of the other students after class but also between the student and herself, as indicated by her failure to require a meeting outside class. Unfortunately, the black male student loses out in this situation, not because Dr. Wisler is not concerned or does not care but because she has become paralyzed by her awareness of the student's racialized position in relation to herself and the rest of the class. Such paralysis prevents white faculty from really pushing black male students to succeed academically.

The narratives of Dr. Collins and Dr. Wisler demonstrate how faculty confusion and paralysis stem partly from self-protection (Will I be called a racist if I push him too hard on this?) and partly from a belief about what is best for the black student (I will damage his self-esteem if I push him too hard on this.). These two bases for action get conflated in these situations.

Unlike faculty who deemphasize racial differences, faculty who hesitate or find themselves paralyzed in the face of possible black student–white faculty conflict, such as Dr. Collins and Dr. Wisler, end up trying to promote safety for both themselves and the black students. Unfortunately, they are seldom successful on either score. Rather than having clear strategies for dealing with the issues that arise for black students when they come up, they get caught off guard, which sets off a variety of conflicting feelings within them, as well as an often unsuccessful scramble to help at the last minute.

These types of experiences can have a detrimental effect on faculty over time. Experiencing the repeated loss or failure of black male students in their own classroom causes those faculty who attempt to be cognizant of racial dynamics to further question their own abilities to work well with these students. Rather than easing future situations with black students, these incidents further complicate them. Dr. Wisler articulates the emotional impact this can have on faculty: "I felt badly about it. I thought, 'What is it that is making him be the one person in the class who gets a C-?' He got the lowest grade in the class and I felt badly about it, but you know, it's hard."

Demonstrating an Awareness of Racial Differences

Faculty who demonstrate an awareness of racial difference are motivated by the same goal as the faculty described above: maintaining a safe classroom atmosphere. For those who openly demonstrate an awareness of racial difference, a safe classroom is one where all students can feel comfortable and protected in the airing of conflictual feelings and beliefs. Dr. Spencer, a white male faculty member in sociology, acknowledges race and racial differences in an attempt to make the classroom safe for black students:

> In my experience, the black males in the class sort of sit there for a long time without feeling like they ought to participate. They're sort of judging and psyching out the situation and waiting before they feel comfortable to jump right in. The black females seem to be much more willing, right from the beginning, to be involved in the discussion, but the black men sort of sit there. They're listening, and they're waiting, and they are going to pass judgment about whether they think that they should participate or not.
> I mean, every class has its wallflowers, the people who don't participate. I think it's a prevalent phenomenon. The fact that there's a few black faces among the wallflowers doesn't strike other [white] faculty as being all that odd, but I see something more. A quiet person, who is just naturally quiet, that is one thing. But if I see somebody who is normally an outspoken extrovert, and he or she becomes an introvert in a classroom situation, that's something different. That's not just somebody who's naturally intro-

verted or not willing to participate. This is somebody who is saying, "I am in a classroom now. I'm on my guard. I got to wait until there is a clear signal that what I am going to say is going to be appreciated." I am aware of that and I think that that is a subtle difference, a subtle enough difference that the students of color pick up on it and are willing to open up a little bit more.

For Dr. Spencer, the implication here is that the black males are judging not only the classroom atmosphere but also him as the white professor. Faculty who demonstrate an awareness of racial difference have an ability to tolerate and reflect upon the various ways that black students might be judging them. Other white male faculty members describe similar feelings of being judged.

I have a few [black males] in my class now and there was some coldness; I felt some coldness. Like, when I came up with some ideas for discussion questions, I saw eyes rolling. I said to myself, "Oh, I'm not connecting; we're not connecting." Whereas most of the other students were connecting. [The black males] were kind of in a corner, and I was like, "Oh man, I don't want to lose them." (Dr. Ford, English)

The first class I regard as absolutely crucial. If I can win them over with my wit, with my humor, with the things I say in that class, that's a good start. The most important thing is whether I can get them [the black students] to see me as somebody who wants to help them. I think I go especially far in that because I'm dealing with students [who] aren't from my race. Given the particular history of racism in the United States, it's not just that we're different, it's that I'm white and . . . they're not. I realize that I've got a selling job to do from class one. (Dr. Scott, mathematics)

Whether student behavior is framed as "psyching" the situation out, as a "lack of connection," or as a selling job for the teacher, these faculty have acknowledged to themselves the effect of race and racial differences on those in the classroom. Data collected from the student participants appear to corroborate the faculty perceptions. One student says:

A person like me, I would just sit back and watch, because you can see where a person is really coming from under the protection of "this is class." The difficulty lies in the fact that if my defenses were weak, I could really feel intimidated being surrounded . . . just the [discomfort] of that. . . . Most of the time, I'm just as intelligent or more intelligent than anyone else in the room, so I can participate and pull back as much as I need to based on what's going on. (Mr. Douglas)

What these participants seem to be describing is what I call a "dance of safety" that takes place between black male students and white professors. Mr. Douglas describes the students' part in the dance. In response to the students' behaviors, Dr. Spencer, Dr. Ford, and Dr. Scott have developed corresponding steps designed to demonstrate their own special awareness of the fact that being racially different in the classroom affects black male students. Dr. Spencer describes the particular steps he takes in the dance of safety:

> I sort of set the stage in such a way that the typical minority student feels I am sympathetic, and I understand some of the things that they have to deal with. That is enough to encourage them, really, to participate more actively and feel like if they do have problems with a paper or whatever, they can come to me.
>
> I deal with it by trying to . . . sort of introduce the idea of the general level of harassment that minority people still face. . . . Once I state that general opinion, my sense is that the minority students feel like I understand their side of it a little bit more, and they are more willing to come and talk to me as though I am an understanding person.

Dr. Collins, on the other hand, was not aware of this dance of safety. He was not aware of the ways in which the student might have been judging him. This lack of awareness about how it might feel to be a black male in a predominantly white classroom prevented Dr. Collins from, as Dr. Spencer says, "creating a general atmosphere that is conducive to" the student's coming to him if problems arise.

Dr. Spencer's methods represent just one way of demonstrating a special awareness of racial differences in the classroom. Dr. Ford takes a more personal approach. First, he discusses the difficulties he has in attempting to connect with black male students:

> For African American males who have lived in this town most of their lives, there's always one barrier after the next. I think that they probably haven't connected with many white males before. The black males who do come up and make a connection with me right away, after I get to know them, I've found that they had some white teacher in high school that might have had a connection with.
>
> I do have faith that [the connection] can happen, but there are so many layers to get through, to kind of cut through all the layers of misunderstandings and mistrust that have developed over centuries. I think I have gotten through . . . some of them, some of those barriers. It doesn't happen a lot. I'm not sure if the trust is completely there, but . . . I think they appreciate that I'm at least a little bit aware and that I try to be fairly honest. But the race issue always comes up. It always comes up. And I'm not afraid of it anymore. . . . I've found humor, a kind of self-deprecating humor, helps cut through the tension when it comes up.

Dr. Ford sees two things as influencing his difficulties in connecting with black male students: the differences in their personal backgrounds and the history of race in America. He understands that some black males may have trouble connecting with him as a result of their lack of experience with white males in general.

These comments suggest that Dr. Ford is aware of the historical context in which his classroom is situated. Other participants also referred to the racial history in America when attempting to explain black male behavior and how this history affects students personally. This illustrates that the historical experiences of black males shape not only their own perceptions but also the perceptions of white faculty, as well. It's important that faculty not divorce black male students' actions in the classroom from their collective historical and social experiences.

Cultivating Relationships With Black Male Students

The stance of demonstrating an awareness of racial differences provides an example of how white faculty can make cross-racial, faculty-student relationships work for both themselves and the students. In taking this stance, these faculty are cultivating supportive relationships between themselves and black students. To cultivate relationships with individual students is to foster their personal and intellectual growth by seeking their acquaintance and nurturing them as they proceed through the academy.

Two main characteristics define the cultivating relationship. First, faculty who cultivate relationships with individual students attempt to connect personally with them. Connecting personally with students means (1) discovering their "story" in an attempt to understand their early educational experiences, (2) discussing their educational and future goals and their out-of-school life as it pertains to those goals, and (3) serving as their connection or "lifeline" to the institution. The second characteristic of cultivating relationships with students is to support them academically, in one's own and their other classes. The main support faculty offer in these situations is to remain open about hearing how personal circumstances affect the student's educational endeavors and offering support when possible to alleviate some of the stress of those circumstances.

The following participant, a white male who has been teaching in an urban university for the last 20 years, talks about how he works to cultivate relationships with the black students in his classes:

> I do, I think, pay more attention to African American students. While trying to, you know, not give them special breaks or anything, I do sort of feel it's my responsibility to correct some of the inequities of society by helping this particular group that has suffered those disadvantages more than other groups. I also feel that white teachers have to not feel there's a barrier there [that] might not exist with the white students, and I want to make sure I bridge that barrier as best as I can. So, I do give them extra time in the following ways.
>
> I'm more likely to encourage a student to come to see me, or even require a student to come see me, and then try to find out something about how they're doing and what's going on in their life. It's not always totally focused on their work in the course.

> Sometimes it is a more general just keeping out a lifeline. I think that for one or two students, I have sort of served as their major sense of being connected to the institution.
>
> I would call them to come into the office, but in a nice way fairly early on, but not like right away. If you do it right away, it's like "How come you singled me out?" It's actually better if you do it as sort of a sign-up sheet, where a lot of people were coming in, so that the student wouldn't feel singled out. I sometimes do it, but I sometimes don't have time to do it. But even if you didn't, I would just in a sort of amiable way that is not laying guilt upon the student, just to kind of ask them how school is going. I wouldn't start, once I was sitting down with the student, I wouldn't hit them immediately with "You sit in the back and you don't seem at all interested." I would sort of try to make a connection with the student. "How are things going for you? How do you like this college? What else do you do with yourself, and where do you see yourself headed with your education?" and then kind of bring it down, find some hook in the thing that they said to connect it to their behavior in class. (Dr. Simms)

Dr. Simms deliberately sets up a situation early on that will give him an opportunity to connect with the student. The deliberate nature of cultivating is evident here. Dr. Simms is aware of the student's feelings. He knows it should not seem like he is singling the student out, even though that is what he's doing. Cultivating a relationship with a particular student is a conscious decision made by the faculty member about how closely to relate to a student for the purposes of helping him succeed academically. Because cultivating relationships with students is a deliberate strategy for fostering student success, the responsibility lies with the faculty member to make and sustain contact with the student.

Dr. Simms is also aware of the barriers faculty face in their attempts to connect with black students in particular:

> The key thing for students is having some sort of personal contact, but you've got to have white faculty comfortable that they could do that with black students. . . . If you sort of alert white faculty to some of the reasons that they might not be getting a response from the black students, both understanding what those barriers are but also understanding that you can overcome them through just trying again, really wanting to do it.

His point here about understanding both what the barriers to white faculty–black student connections are, and that they can be overcome with a little persistence, is an important one. Part of the difficulty encountered by Dr. Collins and Dr. Wisler was that they did not seem to understand what the barriers to communication were; therefore, they could not help the students or themselves through those barriers. The extra complexity in these cases for white faculty is that understanding the barriers to communication means understanding something about their own racial identity and racial awareness as a white person.

As these narratives illustrate, white faculty who can demonstrate their own awareness of the impact of racial difference on black students in the classroom are in a better position to motivate those students to succeed. This demonstration of one's awareness of racial difference serves to make the classroom atmosphere safe for both faculty and student, and by extension lays the groundwork for the professor to form a relationship with the student. Once this groundwork has been laid, the faculty member is in a much better position to cultivate a relationship with his or her black male students.

Those faculty who deemphasize or become paralyzed by their awareness of racial difference need assistance in examining their own racial beliefs and in seeing how those beliefs manifest themselves in specific classroom behaviors. What these faculty need is more certainty and self-confidence that they can survive racial conflicts in the classroom. They also need more experience in talking about difficult or confusing cross-racial interactions they may have had in the classroom.

The solution for these teachers is not more workshops about diversity, nor can this issue be handled by administrators in a top-down fashion. Strategies to increase self-awareness might be better received if they come from the very colleagues who are better at demonstrating their awareness of racial differences in the classroom. My research suggests that dialogue between groups of white faculty who are at different levels of racial and self-awareness, as well as cross-racial dialogue between white and black faculty, might contribute to helping white faculty see how certain classroom behaviors, although undertaken with racial considerations in mind, impact black students.

Such dialogue needs to take place in supportive environments, where faculty might feel less inhibited about revealing their vulnerabilities around race. The collegial connection is vital here. Having consultants come in from outside the institution can have one type of impact, but listening to and talking with the people, the colleagues, one sees every day is more likely to go further in altering actual classroom behavior among faculty. One of the biggest benefits of talking with one's colleagues about racial issues in the classroom is that it increases white faculty experience of the issue. Just as administrators and white faculty look to their black colleagues for solutions about how to improve the educational experiences of black students, they must look to those white colleagues who have a reputation on campus for success in dealing with issues of diversity for help in changing classroom practices. However, self-selection cannot be the only method undertaken if we are going to improve the educational experience for black males. There needs to be some knowledgeable recruitment of white faculty who have personally demonstrated approaches with students like those described above.

This research suggests that institutions must work with white faculty in ways that promote self-reflection and self-awareness around racial issues. They must move beyond those programs that promote racial awareness to programs that promote racial self-understanding and self-awareness and methods for acting on that awareness. Only then will we be able to build real confidence and trust throughout our educational institutions, not only between white faculty and black students but also among cross-racial colleagues.

References

Allen, W.R., E.G. Epps, and N.Z. Haniff, eds. (1991). *College in Black and White: African American Students in Predominantly White and in Historically Black Public Universities.* Albany: State University of New York Press.

Elliot, P.G. (1994). *The Urban Campus: Educating the New Majority for the New Century.* Phoenix, AZ: Oryx Press.

Endo, J.J., and R.L. Harpel. (1982). "The Effect of Student-Faculty Interaction on Student's Educational Outcomes." *Research in Higher Education* 16(2): 115-137.

Feldman, R.S., and R.D. Saletsky. (1986). "Nonverbal Communication in Interracial Teacher-Student Interaction." In *The Social Psychology of Education*, edited by R.S. Feldman. Cambridge, Eng.: Cambridge University Press.

Grant-Thompson, S.K., and D.R. Atkinson. (1997). "Cross-Cultural Mentor Effectiveness and African-American Male Students." *Journal of Black Psychology* 23(2): 120-134.

Kobrak, P. (1992). "Black Student Retention in Predominantly White Regional Universities: The Politics of Faculty Involvement." *Journal of Negro Education* 61(4): 509-530.

Nettles, M.T., ed. (1988). *Toward Black Undergraduate Student Equality in American Higher Education.* New York: Greenwood Press.

Pascarella, E.T., and P.T. Terenzini. (1977). "Patterns of Student-Faculty Informal Interaction Beyond the Classroom and Voluntary Freshman Attrition." *Journal of Higher Education* 48(5): 540-551.

Steele, C. (April 1992). "Race and the Schooling of Black Americans." *Atlantic Monthly:* 68-77.

Wilson, R.C., J.G. Gaff, E.R. Dienst, L. Wood, and J.L. Bavry, eds. (1975). *College Professors and Their Impact on Students.* New York: Wiley-Interscience.

Word, C.O., M.P. Zanna, and J. Cooper. (1974). "The Nonverbal Mediation of Self-Fulfilling Prophecies in Interracial Interaction." *Journal of Experimental Social Psychology* 10: 109-120.

My Story, Her Story, Our Story

Arlette Ingram Willis and Ana Lucía Herrera

> The people who come to us bring their stories. They hope they tell
> them well enough so that we understand the truth of their lives.
> They hope we know how to interpret their stories correctly. We
> have to remember that what we hear is their story. (Coles 1989)

Our narrative is informed by a growing body of theories that highlight the importance of narrative (see, e.g., Casey 1995; Clandinin and Connelly 1994; Henry 1995). Drawing on this research, we both are participants and observers, learners and teachers, readers and writers, researchers and producers, and articulators and interpreters of the individual and joint stories of process and product known as narrative. Bateson observes that "narratives reflect the purpose for which they have been constructed, for self-understanding always includes a dimension of justification, not only 'what I did' and 'what happened' but how and why I chose to understand it, and a readying of the self for the tasks that lie ahead" (1997: viii). Given these parameters, this narrative is a glimpse of our ongoing understanding, not a beginning or an end but a place in time and space and in our hearts and minds.

The recent rise in autobiographical and personal essay forms of narrative by university professors suggests that there is a need in the academy to share and learn from our experiences. Neumann and Peterson offer the following rationale for using narratives to inform themselves and others about life within and outside the academy and about the connections between women's lives and their research interests:

> Autobiography helps us see and understand the hurtful aspects of
> institutional existence in academe through the eyes of those who
> may have suffered in silence through subtle and overt discrimina-
> tion or neglect. It also helps us see, appreciate, and support the
> informal structures that help people heal from and resist the hurtful
> features of organizational existence. (1997: 7)

We add our voices and experiences to other women who have embraced narrative as a means of understanding their experiences and knowledge building. In doing so, we bring our culturally specific ways of knowing and institutional histories in a collaborative approach to writing narrative.

A casual review of the literature finds an increasing number of narratives that explain the importance of creating a warm, welcoming, safe classroom environment where issues of difference can be shared, learned, and affirmed. Most, however, detail the experiences and enlightenment of white teachers and teacher-

23

educators who are beginning to understand and appreciate notions of difference — race, class, gender, language, ability, and sexual orientation. Among these narratives are examples of white students and students of color within these environments that range from chronicles of events to confessionals of ignorance. What is unique about our narrative is that we are two women of color — one African American, one Latina — living and learning in spaces (U.S. racialized society, a university classroom, a national conference) dominated by white mainstream viewpoints and the rhetoric of inclusivity.

Experts such as Clandinin and Connelly argue that narrative inquiry

> is collaboration between researcher and participants, over time, in
> a place or series of places, and in social interaction with milieus.
> An inquirer enters this matrix in the midst of progresses in this
> same spirit, concluding the inquiry still in the midst of living and
> telling, reliving, and retelling, the stories of the experiences that
> make up people's lives, both individual and social. . . . Narrative
> inquiry is stories lived and told. (2000: 9)

We have tried to stay mindful of the milieu in which our stories emerged. Thus, we begin by describing how our individual stories (my story, her story) are framed in this narrative. The individual stories are woven together to produce our story. Their interwoven format is what we call *narrative dialogue* — descriptions of events (or series of events) and explanations of the interconnectedness among events that chart our experiences and discoveries. Herein we share with the reader our understanding of the process of teaching, learning, and communicating in a culturally diverse classroom.

The "I" is Willis in my multiple roles as researcher, teacher-educator, author, and woman of color. As the researcher and teacher-educator of the pre-service literacy course in which the narratives arise, I offer my story to contextualize and situate both narratives. I also use this space to describe the theoretical underpinnings of the course and my goals for students. Next, Ana, a student of color, chronicles and describes several significant experiences she had in the course. (Throughout, Ana's individual part of the narrative is set off by indenting.) The narrative dialogue concludes with authorial reflections that offer hope for classrooms to become welcoming, safe, empowering learning environments for all learners, with a special focus on the concerns of students of color.

Telling Our Stories: Negotiating Textual Space and Form

As a researcher and coauthor of this chapter, the two most difficult roles for me have been writing myself into this space and situating the context for the reader. As I wrote myself into this space, I found it difficult to make public my thinking, which often ranges from moments of certainty to uncertainty, triumphs to failures (and their opposites), as teaching consists of planned and unplanned events. Although the profession of teaching is very public, it is masked by intrapersonal tension that teachers experience as they make multiple instantaneous decisions. In this narrative, I make public my unvoiced process. Throughout Ana's narrative, I weave my own as I offer explanations of their connections for the reader.

The connections among events seem so obvious to me because I was also a participant in the course as a learner/teacher. Constructing this narrative, however, has caused me to wonder whether recasting and deconstructing the events for the reader somehow spoils the stories and their connections. In my memory, the events are a seamless set, yet in this textual space they have a somewhat different life — one that needs supportive commentary, analyses, and interpretation for the reader to grasp the central points and implications.

> As I walk into my college classes, I make no apologies for my Mexicanidad and I proudly describe my experiences. But while I could always speak as the Mexican college student, it wasn't until Professor Willis's class that I received the freedom to develop my creative essence. Professor Willis has found a way to make my words sound important. Though my class writings form the body of this essay, I have made a few comments. I think they are more of a response than a correction to the written narrative. I mention them to add to, not hinder, the writing.

We have collaboratively constructed this piece as part of our ongoing relationship that began in the course, was strengthened during our presentation [of our story at a national conference], and continues into an uncertain future. Thus, the reader will experience with us shifts in time and place, though the characters, Ana and I, are constants. Through revisiting, retelling, and writing our story, we have a greater appreciation of the need to deconstruct the process of inclusion, especially for students of color in mainstream settings.

My Story: Fall Semester 1997

The semester began as so many others had at the University of Illinois at Urbana-Champaign. A new class of students all eager to become English teachers — to save children from themselves, to squash all the creative juices and life out of young people by expounding the importance of grammar rules and literary terms along with endless assignments in American and British literature. After all, they want nothing more desperately, nor more radical, than to become their favorite high school English teacher. My dreams are different: I want my students to care and respect the people in their classrooms, beginning in my classroom and beginning with themselves. I want my students to leave willing and able to fight for social change, to bring about a more just society, and to teach English. Simply stated, I seek effective ways to impart through literacy education an appreciation of difference — race, class, gender, language, religion, and sexual orientation — and a respect for the histories and futures of each student.

My classes, which meet for six hours weekly each, are composed of a similar student population — white, female, upper to middle class, English-speaking, and suburban. Generally, they are undergraduates who have excelled academically in a system that benefits them and people like them disproportionately. On occasion I have one or two students of color, and in rare instances I have several students of color in my classes. My class might also include graduate students who were not admitted to the undergraduate education program but who are earning a master's degree along with secondary teacher certification. As an African American, middle-class, monolingual, female professor, I welcome the challenge of training young minds, but I especially appreciate the rare opportunities to work with students of color.

In fall 1997, I continued my ongoing self-study of teacher education. For several years, I have collected data (videotapes, artifacts, interviews, etc.) on student progress in my critically framed literacy course. I participate in the class as a co-learner with the students, as I believe that my participation increases students' engagement and the tenor of the class is much more professional. As a researcher, I vigilantly watch and learn from my students' oral, written, dramatic, artistic, and musical assignments. Especially helpful in this endeavor, however, are my students' writings. I eagerly collect everything with the hope of possibly using it in the future. (The first class includes an opportunity for students to voluntarily agree or refuse to sign a consent form allowing me permission to use their work — all artifacts — as part of my data. I do not have access to these forms until after grades are posted for the semester.)

Several days before the onset of the semester, I scanned my roster to find the names of a couple of African American and Latino/a students who I knew were in the English education program. Ana was one such student. Although Ana had been assigned to me as a master's advisee, she had managed not to come to me for advising. She seemed to prefer to interact with two faculty members who were fluent Spanish speakers, which was okay. Both colleagues had described her as a brilliant and talented student, one whose passion for issues of social justice was almost all-consuming. I was pleased to see she had enrolled in my section. Most of the students in the class were more typical. For instance, Able, Casey, Jerry, Marc, and Olivia (all pseudonyms) were among the majority of European Americans in the class.

What is intriguing about Ana's work in my class is that she chronicled the events of the course with pithy commentary and allowed me a rare opportunity to hear the voice of a young woman of color in an English education methods course. Excerpts from her writings represent her experiences and inner struggles as a student of color faced with negotiating for respect and voice with her European American classmates during small-group work. She shares conversations and interactions that I was not privy to until after the course. Obviously, others in the class may have experienced the course differently, but this is her story.

Ana's Story: Fall Semester 1997

> <u>Tuesday, September 2.</u> The first day of class was a pretty overwhelming day because we were given a rundown of all the requirements. There is a lot of work for this class and I am worried about my performance. . . . The people in the class seem to be pretty friendly and open to the use of multicultural literature. I am hoping that the American/white students that signed up for the course are interested in open dialogue about some of the books we will read. It sounds bad, but I was really excited to have blacks and Latinos in class. Usually I am the only minority in the class, and I get tired of always trying to explain to people the situation poor folks must endure.

On the first day of class, students are called upon to participate and become immediately involved in the process of community building. These activities are part of a miniunit on identity. They introduce themselves, answer several questions, and share information about their lives. Based on their responses, I use this limited information throughout the semester to place them into small working groups. The next class continues this emphasis, as students are required to share an artifact from their lives.

> <u>Thursday, September 4.</u> Today is the second day of class, and it started as a good day but ended horribly. We all brought in our memories to share and I took in a picture of myself with braids. I told the class about the taunting that went on at school for looking too Mexican. I elaborated on the treatment my sister and I endured as children — being called *wetbacks, aliens,* and being told that the *migra* (immigration) was after us. It is difficult to talk about these things, but I think it is important for students to realize that children can be very cruel to each other. I think that teachers should intercede for students that are being harassed. Teachers need to tell and show students that tolerance and mutual respect are not negotiable. A teacher can't make students like each other, nor can a friendship be forced, but at minimum a teacher is responsible for creating an unhostile and nonthreatening environment in which each student can learn. Everyone in the class shared a memory. And last, but not least, you spoke of your parents' wedding picture and you almost made me cry.

Ana's Memory and Artifact

> As the child of Mexican immigrants, I often heard taunts about being a wetback alien. My older sister, Blanca, and I had no idea what the kids were talking about. I even remember a few suspicious stares exchanged between us as we undressed for bedtime. I honestly worried that Blanca and I would grow tentacles and turn green. We were constantly beaten by swarms of kids yelling, *"La*

migra, la migra — run wetback, run." I thought their racial slurs were making reference to the intense perspiration that became visible through the backs of our T-shirts as we ran from the crowd of Mexican haters. I didn't know why they hated us, but I could feel their repulsion as they pulled me down to the cement floor by my braids. Now I realize that our yearly summer shopping spree in Mexico made us targets. My mom purchased our school clothes in Mexico because the dollar always went farther across the border. Our clothes did not look American and when we did get items that displayed American icons, they were distorted because Mexican merchants were not licensed to reproduce characters such as the *pitufos* (that's the little blue Smurfs in Spanish).

Blanca and I got entire ensembles, including a book bag with the *pitufos*. The day we went to school with our new outfits was no different than most others. We were pushed, pulled, and laughed at for having retarded Smurf shirts. I cried as they kicked my book bag clear across the street. I took my torn bag home. But in my childlike naíveté, each year I proudly sported my colorful dresses. I thought my new cool outfit and colorful bows and ribbons would win over new friends. But that didn't happen. It never happened.

Today, I have long curly hair and only occasionally do I braid it. Sadly, I have lost my flair for colorful ribbons, but that image of me is constantly present.

Ana had offered the class an intimate portrait of herself. I was very touched by her honesty and willingness to share her life. After everyone had shared their memories and artifacts, I placed students in small working groups. I constructed groups that I believed would support and challenge their membership. I created one group of males and one group of females to determine how students interacted based on gender. Other groups consisted of mixed races and genders. I selected Ana Lucía to be the only woman of color in her all-female group because she was a graduate student. I thought she would be a good example of a serious scholar and dedicated student to the undergraduate women in her group.

Thursday, September 4 (continued). We had to get into groups — that we will have for the entire year, which I don't think is fair. I know that you did this in a completely random way, but this one grouping is going to carry through for all of the books we have to read. The other groups were paired in such a way that there were at least two minorities together. (They are so lucky.)

I was completely ignored (in the group) when the picking of novels occurred. Everything I was interested in was rejected as too political or depressing. I got to the point where I did not want to even be in the class. Everything that my group picked deals with assimilation and transition into the mainstream. I was disappointed to see that my group just wanted to read fiction and pure fluff.

I thought *Lakota Woman* [Crow Dog and Erdoes 1990] would

be a good choice, but, no, it was seen as being "too heavy." I feel like I had nothing to do with the selection of books. And, granted maybe other "minorities" would not have been interested in reading what I wanted, but they were selecting many of the books I wanted to read. I just think that it will be hard to work with a group I do not feel a part of.

Well, I will just have to deal with it. I don't hate the selections, I just wanted exposure to things I had not read. And I was also offended when Casey said that we had to work really hard on *Their Eyes Were Watching God* [Hurston 1965]; I knew she was making reference to you being black and that book being our African American selection. I just get really angry when people make ignorant comments like that. People say color doesn't matter, but color always does and people make stupid assumptions about minorities.

Ana took objection to her placement in an all-female group. I had thought that as the only graduate student in the group, she would become a natural leader. However, from her point of view, issues of race and class surfaced early as members of her group exerted their alleged "privileged" status despite her academic/graduate status. Moreover, she observed that they responded in ways that were not as apparent to me in class discussions.

Ana had perceptively analyzed her group situation and identified comments made by some group members, most especially Casey's, as indicative of notions of entitlement and white privilege. Mary Louise Pratt calls such spaces the *contact zone*. She defines the zone as "social spaces where disparate cultures meet, clash, and grapple with each other, often in highly asymmetrical relations of domination and subordination — like colonialism, slavery, or their aftermaths as they are lived out across the globe today" (1992: 4). Ana's early experiences in this group caused her to perceive her role quite differently than I did, as she experienced being silenced by the members of her group. Nevertheless, she continued to be engaged in whole-class discussions by contributing to a larger audience.

Tuesday, September 9. Great, today we had to share autobiographies and I got stuck with my "best friend," Casey. I know how to be civil toward people, but she just needs to get off her high horse. I don't care what she has written and that she had a role in her production. Okay, I am being childish — I will stop now.

An Excerpt From Ana's Autobiography

My parents are from a small picturesque town, La Mazanilla de La Paz, that is located high in the mountains of Jalisco. Many years after the initial contact between the indigenous people of Mexico and the Spanish Conquistadors, this region attracted large numbers of French settlers. Unlike other parts of Mexico, Jalisco is known for its large concentrations of "white-skinned" people. You can travel throughout several areas of the state and think that one town is simply an extension of another because people throughout the state have very similar facial features. Many people have a stereotypical image of Mexicans as being dark, short, with black hair and basically unattractive, but Mexico has several shades of color and varying degrees of attractiveness. There are people of fair skin, green eyes, and golden-colored hair, and there are others with bronze-colored skin, tall, and with big beautiful brown eyes. I describe these ethnic markers because they tend to distinguish us from people of other states in Mexico, but all Mexicans are *pisas,* fellow countrymen. . . .

The earliest recollections of both my parents, my sister, and I are of this town. Both of my parents and my older sister were born in this town. When my sister, Blanca, was three, my dad came to the United States to work. A year later, my mother came to help my dad work so that the three of them could settle in the United States. However, my mom was not able to work for very long because she became pregnant with me. A few months later, arrangements were made so that Blanca could be smuggled into the country. Because of my U.S. citizenship, my parents were able to file for their residency papers, and we were able to travel freely between Mexico and the United States. . . .

As I look around at my younger cousins, I feel myself growing old. I find myself talking about life in general terms and giving the same advice I was once given. The traditions and values that my parents imposed in our house are still the foundations of my life, but just when I was comfortable with these ideas, my parents have started to alter their approach to child rearing. My dad was really strict with us. Blanca and I never stepped out the door without giving a full account of what we would be doing. But the little Mexico my parents created in our home has changed. Now my (younger) sisters listen to English music and speak English with each other. Blanca and I listened to ranchera music, and we were not allowed to speak English in the house. My mother was determined to not let us forget our native language, and besides she could not comprehend English very well back then. I think that my parents are much more at ease with their lives in the United States. . . .

After writing this autobiography, I am thinking that perhaps the most valued tradition in my family extends beyond the maintenance of our language and customs. Maybe what has kept my family together is our ability to weave our lives into stories that carry within them the flavor of each special smell that emanates from our mothers' kitchen.

University classrooms often are constructed to form unnatural boundaries between self and others. One of the goals of my course is to help students reflect upon and address their understandings of race, class, gender, sexual orientation, and language differences. Another goal of the course is to help students understand these issues within their own lives and the lives of their future students. These goals have been more successful in some classes than others. Excerpts of autobiographies were shared, depending on each student's comfort level. Ana shared nothing.

> <u>Thursday, September 11.</u> Okay, class was great — worth all the garbage of the last couple of days. I really enjoyed being taught to see the similarities and differences that we bring to our interpretations of the world. I know that we bring several different experiences, but this activity shows you that regardless of who you are, we all carry different interpretations of our different experiences.
>
> I was emotionally challenged today; when I saw the picture of the border, I got really sad and had to hold back the tears. People don't realize how hard it is to come to this country. It was funny to see that people were identifying the pictures in such stereotypical ways. The border picture was described as being a drug addict and a drug pusher. The jazz player was described as a pimp. All I could think was, Can't people of color be thought of as doing good? I was surprised that someone would admit that this was what they thought. When the border picture came up, I kept my mouth shut because I wanted to see what people said.
>
> I think that this activity nicely brings together the concepts by Paulo Freire [1999]. Everyone is constantly learning by listening/speaking, reading/writing, thinking/reflecting, etc. The quotation "reading the word and reading the world" speaks to our ability to communicate with each other as human beings.

I display 10 color transparencies of photos from the book *A Day in the Life of America* (1986). Students are given only a few seconds to write the first thing that comes to their mind when they see the overhead. Then we discuss each individual photo, and students share their initial impressions. This activity offers me a means of understanding how students "read" their world.

> <u>Tuesday, September 16.</u> Class got started right away today when we came into the room and simply got us writing out some definitions for *culture*, *dominant* and *minority culture*, etc. Then we got into groups that were supposed to agree on a group definition of these words. Well, that was really hard because Able did not agree that a dominant culture is aggressively imposing. He thinks that the American culture is dominant because people just accept it and its influence makes it dominant (without any negative elements). Able also made his point to the class when we were discussing our definitions. I am not sure what Able thinks is nonthreatening about the dominant culture, but I

think he is in denial.

We also went on campus to conduct a survey, and there was some interesting stuff happening. Able and Olivia only questioned white people. It took a lot of effort on my part — like walking away from them with the notes toward someone of color — to include students of color in the survey. It was also interesting to note that when a Latina answered with political knowledge, Able perceived her as hostile. I was not amused by the attitude and crap that some people said, but I wasn't surprised to see what people think about "minorities."

We also went over our results in class, and I felt that my group was unaware of the type of attitudes we were reporting on. I think that often we excuse bigotry as ignorance, and when someone is confident in saying that they would like to answer something that is going to make them sound racist, then they are obviously plagued by the reality of their racist attitudes. Yet my group felt that these people were being sensitive and did not want to offend me.

Ana's entry describes a set of activities I have students complete as we attempt to adopt a language we are comfortable with as a class for discussing issues of difference. The activity, as she describes it, includes personal, group, person-on-the-street, and expert definitions. Once we have arrived at some politically sanctioned language, we discuss notions of political correctness and political incorrectness. The latter refers to a class brainstorming session of the race, gender, and class expletives we have heard. No group is left out, though most students couch their responses by suggesting they do not use the terms.

Thursday, September 18. This class started with the issue of studying whiteness. Jerry said that he liked to think of himself as "Euro-American" because it made him be more tolerant of other cultures or multiculturalism. But why is it that he did not figure this out on his own without feeling threatened by others having affiliations to their cultures? I know Jerry did not mean to sound competitive about culture, but it just seems that white people are always doing things in response to the actions/beliefs that people of color expose. . . . I have always believed that white people would be less angry if they had a little pride in their backgrounds. However, I did not think that white cultural awareness would come about in reaction to a feeling of inadequacy. I think that cultural identification gives an individual of color the strength to put up with the racist garbage of our society.

There were other students that have no desire to identify with the history of whites. Casey and Able feel that we just need to move on from where we are and minorities need to stop thinking about the past. How can they think that anything can be better without acknowledgment? And I don't mean the type that people usually give, such as, "I am sorry about slavery, but now let's move on." White people do not understand that this approach is full of ignorance. White people want to just go into poor neighborhoods and care for poor children, but let's not talk about the exploitation of the poor. White people do not want to move on. They want things to stay the same, but they want to be able to feel good about themselves, so they go into our neighborhoods and help us — the poor children of the ghettos. I just think that moving forward can only be accomplished when whites commit to and implement a revisionist view toward history. Good-intending white people just do not understand this perspective; they think we want to make them feel bad, but we want something more important than pity — we want respect.

We also did a literacy survey on sixth through 12th graders. I think that the general characteristics are very general and may not reflect the lives and concerns of inner-city kids. I understand that there are characteristics that are universal, but I guess I would like to also talk about the pressures that my kids will be facing. I feel like my teacher education is so mainstream that I will not be prepared to address the concerns of my students. I think that we rarely get the opportunity to deal with some of the serious issues that face inner-city kids. Maybe everyone in the class should be required to read *Our America* [Jones et al. 1998] and *Savage Inequalities* [Kozol 1991]. I know people hate to hear about the lives of poor people, but it is such a reality check to see the differences in the high school experience between middle-class kids and low-income kids. Gangs, teenage pregnancy, drug use, and suicide are all more important than the homecoming game and prom. I think that it is useful to look for general trends, but I wonder what I will do when I lose my first student to something I lived but never really learned to deal with. I got out — that is why I am here — but how I got through those years is a mystery to me. I know that I am proof that teachers can make a significant impact on their students' lives.

I think you are the first professor that offered a useful suggestion after I stated that an activity had little or no relevance to my future students. I think it is encouraging to be shown how the two worlds (the ivory tower and the ghetto) can inform one another; there is something terribly life affirming in this perspective.

Ana's comments about issues of class, so often overlooked in discussions of diversity or subsumed as a part of some ethnic groups, challenged us all to look beyond the rhetoric of inclusivity and the assumptions and values that inform our literacy curriculum.

Part of what informs my decision making about changes to the course are the nonverbal actions and interpersonal relationships I observe during class. I note, without any scientific accuracy, the nonverbal actions and interpersonal relationships in whole-, large-, and small-group settings. I have found that the small-group settings yield the most insightful information about students.

To lighten the stress that some white students appeared to be experiencing and to offer students an interesting way to discuss the notion of perspective, I shared multiple versions of two children's stories. We read and discussed how Western our understanding is of the Cinderella fairy tale, and I offered historical information of its origin. We also described the many versions from other cultures. Then we read different versions of The Three Little Pigs (see Scieszka 1991). Most students had not read or heard the story from the wolf's standpoint. Most students seem to understand the point, but I make it very explicit anyway: There is more than one way to describe a situation.

For the next class, students were assigned to read three chapters in Delpit's book *Other People's Children* (1995). I divided students into three groups, attempting to form new groups by altering the group membership from earlier projects. Each group was to focus on its chapter and be prepared to lead a discussion of the key concepts and questions raised by the group. In addition, groups were to answer two questions: (1) How do we currently address issues of power in language arts classrooms? (2) What is it that you think Delpit wants teachers, parents, administrators, and future teachers to know and understand about issues of power?

> Thursday, October 2. I am so upset I can hardly write. You know what the danger is in a class like this — stupid white liberals walk away feeling like they have experienced being minorities and now they are the "voice of the community."
>
> These people can be such a danger because they think they have learned to understand people of color, but they haven't. This class just gives them an opportunity to claim empathy, and instead they still look at us as if we need their sympathy. I know that I should not assume that I can include "you" when I say "we," but you are the first teacher of color that I feel I can identify with. I hope I am not offending you and I don't want to be disrespectful in any way toward you, but I am going to share my true feelings right now so you may want to just skip this entry.
>
> In my heart I know that I am not a dog on the street that needs sympathy, and I am not ignorant. It makes me so sick to have someone be condescending toward me. Sometimes white people fail to realize that they are being paternalistic and demeaning toward people

of color. I know I can struggle and make it in spite of the shit, but what about all those that don't make it. They are me and I am them. I am not the rule; I am the exception. The day I forget that, I will become assimilated. I will be the mainstream. I don't ever want to forget the difficulty of life in this society. I do not want to be the type of person who ignorantly believes that anyone can make it in America. Not everyone does.

As indicated by Ana, the whole-class discussion of Delpit's work became quite heated as class members expressed their viewpoints. We were unable to complete the assignment in class and left knowing that we would regroup, refresh, and reconvene our discussion during the next class.

> Tuesday, October 7. Shame on you! Why did you make us get into our Delpit [the silenced dialogue] groups? Was I not tested enough in having to be the monitor in the first activity? Well, I think what you tried to explain just made Able keep his mouth shut because he would not dare say to you what he said to me, but I think he thinks it is all bull. What he was arguing with me about was that we complain about wanting the language and then we reject it when it is given to us. I don't think he understands. He would like to have the experiences of people of color in books, because he can close it when he is made uncomfortable. He can put us on a shelf and display us as his knowledge.

During this class period, we also began Writer's Workshop. I reviewed the steps in the process, offered a minilesson on flash fiction, and allowed students 20 minutes to write. We conducted a status of the class period afterward. Each student kept his or her drafts for the next class period. Students were informed that work written during this period could be submitted for a class book.

The next class meeting, students started teaching literacy lessons from selected novels; four out of five are written by authors of color. A group member taught a lesson each week, with the responsibility for supportive materials rotating among the group members. After each lesson, we discussed whether or not we would teach the selected novels. Students explained that they were adopting a new set of lenses by which to read novels. In the past, they read for literary quality or enjoyment; now they were reading with an eye toward teaching, or what they called *teachability*.

> Thursday, October 16. We discussed the "teach-ability" of our novels, and we did flash fiction for Writer's Workshop. I am not sure about my stance on the inclusion of culturally irrelevant novels (mainstream white, middle class). On the one hand, I want to, have to, and will include mainstream irrelevant materials because they are the canon, they contain the language of power, and they reflect societal

ideas that students need to understand. However, I feel that even though I am acknowledging the gatekeeping abilities of these materials, I am also perpetuating the judgments implicit in mainstream literature. I know that much of my concern will manifest into creative approaches to teaching mainstream literature, but I guess I will have to figure out those techniques as I develop as a teacher.

I think that it is important for teachers to remember that cultural relevancy is not equated with depressing stories about crime, drugs, and poverty. I was often annoyed when a teacher tried to relate the material to us by selecting pieces that exclusively addressed ghetto issues. I was especially annoyed when the articles in some way or other set forth a moral lesson that people of color should adhere to in order to rid "their" neighborhoods of criminal elements. When this occurred, I felt that my integrity, dignity, and intelligence were disrespected (and perhaps not even acknowledged).

<u>Tuesday, October 28.</u> Okay, today was the first time I [taught] a lesson, and I really regretted having critiqued my peers. It is so easy to look at a lesson and to see what can be better or improved once it has been put on [taught] by someone else. I felt so bad because I could see [everyone's] boredom and I wasn't able to make myself stop. I think I enjoyed the process much more than the application. But I am glad to see how miserably horrible a lesson can go if I don't shut up. I was so bummed out about my screw-up that I had a hard time keeping a cheerful face, but I forced myself to continue participating as a class member even though I felt horrible.

I wrote a poem. It was really nice to capture what I was thinking in just a few words. I think I could get used to thinking of words that capture such strong emotions. What I fear, though, is that my poem is too culturally imbedded and difficult for outsiders to understand.

Ana's Poem

Shrouded in truth and betrayals,
Voice of the colonizer
Cry of the conquest

La Virgen de Guadalupe — ultimate symbol of Browness survival to
    accept indigenous face
Historical acceptance of her throughout the world
Mother of the Americas
Brown and coppered glory
They, us, we, others

> The first contact
> The end of civilization and our beginning
> We are ignorant of those past cultures and civilizations
> Voice of the colonizer — only history found through writings of the
>   colonizer this is why I think
> A voice, but you can still hear the cry of the colonized through the texts

The opportunity to write and to experiment with forms of prose appeared to offer Ana an outlet for her thoughts. She continues to write poetry but has not submitted any of her writing to the class book.

> <u>Thursday, November 6.</u> I wrote another poem. Now I just have to get over my fear of people disregarding my material as trash. I think your encouragement has really influenced my willingness to expand on my creativity with writing. I knew positive [reinforcement] was good for everyone, but I guess down deep inside I thought it was for kids, but it's good for me, too. I guess I am developing into both a reader and writer.

Ana's Second Poem

> La Llorona
> Cry Malinche for your lost name
> Malintzin your children didn't die in vain
> Lover of Mexico
> Mother of el Mestizo
> Property of Cortez
>
> Not a betrayal, to obey Quetzalcoátl
> Your sacrifice corroded and decayed lives in the ruins
> La Llorna
> Cry Malinche for your lost name
> Malintzin your children didn't die in vain
> Keeper of Mexico
> Mother of el Mestizo
> Property of Cortez
> Follow your way to Teotihuacán
> There the voices of the ruins speak your fame
> Hear the singing of the Quetzal, the voices of the ruins know your name
> No lloners mas hear the Quetzal

Poetry seemed to be a natural outlet for Ana. She could include her wealth of historical knowledge, and she could be as passionate as she liked. Today is the last day for Writer's Workshop. I have encouraged all students to revise their drafts and submit some of their work for the class book. All the students have submitted something, except Ana. I am truly disappointed, as I believe she is the most talented writer. We have all been very impressed by her short fiction and poetry, but she seems scattered whenever I ask her about submitting.

Tuesday, November 11. There were several lessons taught on this day. Marc's lesson took me through such a whirlwind of feelings about death and my parents. It is hard to face mortality, but at some point you grow up and find that life will pass you by if you do not take advantage of the time you have today. Death is so unpredictable and haunting.

Casey's lesson took me back to a childhood memory — my milieu — and I plan to write the apartment story for our class book. I responded to my peer's contempt and her condescending attitude with the force of my words. On one particular day, Casey instructed us to write a paragraph describing our milieu in a lesson on *To Kill a Mockingbird* [Lee 1982].

When I asked her to define the word *milieu*, she turned to me and in an annoyed voice said, "Well, it's like, environment and cultural elements, you know, stuff like that. Ah, Ah, Ah, where something comes from, is that enough?"

It was humiliating. How stupid did she think I was? Where something comes from, okay, I thought. I'll show her how well I understood and I wrote the following story:

> My home was always an apartment. Often we spent our entire winters without heat. In those days we considered ourselves Mexicans, illegals without rights and powerless. We would have never thought of calling city offices to complain about the rats, roaches, dripping ceiling, or the broken pipes.
>
> Almost a decade we lived in that hell-hole. My mother would wrap her legs around us and try to warm me with her body, but the cold was a penetrating chill that entered your bones regardless of how many blankets you used. With a low voice my mother asked the landlord for heat when he came to collect the rent, but he laughed at her and made vulgar body gestures implying that she should fuck to keep warm.

Yes, I understood the definition of *milieu*, but could she understand the milieu that defined me? This, I could tell by the look on her face, was a much harder task.

I was surprised that Ana responded to Casey's invitation to share a milieu. When Ana finished reading of her milieu, it was clear that it was not what Casey had expected. It was not what any of us could have imagined. Casey continued her lesson, but we were all changed by Ana's description of her milieu. Again, I thought about how powerful her words were and wondered whether she would contribute this piece to our class book.

Thursday, November 13. I enjoyed my group's interest in the historically based account of La Llorona. I think it is interesting to see the variations that folktales take, but sometimes I feel that we lose a part of our stories in the remapping of events and locations. All of the variations are valid, but I lament the loss of the historical elements of La Llorona. I think history teaches us about the Mexican culture and it speaks to the Mexican's endless struggle to claim a homeland.

I selected the folktale of La Llorona to offer students a means of extending literature to drama. In a very loose adaptation of Reader's Theater, students were left to their creativity in the skits. Ana's historical knowledge greatly enhanced her group's performance, though others took the task less seriously than she did. The idea of using Reader's Theater resonated with her.

For the remainder of the semester, we continued to read and discuss young adult literature and issues of race, class, gender, language, sexual orientation, and power. The course ended with a final exam on December 16, 1997. My relationship with Ana and our story, however, continued.

Our Story

As a researcher, it was clear to me that my experiences with Ana were unique in higher education. There were many stories to be told of the course and of our relationship throughout the course and beyond it. I could write my story, that of a teacher-educator who learns from a student with incredible insight to be far more mindful when arranging groups, to listen more intently to the voices and silences of my students, and to monitor more closely small-group work. Obviously, I could have encouraged Ana to write about her experiences in the course, and I could have assisted her in finding a journal outlet. Instead, I approached Ana with the possibility of presenting our experiences at a national literacy conference. Our proposal was accepted and we entered a new phase: writing our story. As a way to begin, I suggested we independently construct a summative version of most significant events.

ANA'S REFLECTIONS

For Professor Willis, the first day of class was the day we all physically met, but for me the first day of class was the day I brought in a picture of myself in ribbon-braided pigtails. For the first three to four classes, we were engaged in several activities that in some way or other served as personal introductions. My picture told a big story. There had never been a forum for the voice of the child I once was.

By looking over the work I have done for this class, I realize that the content of the course has determined the process of our individual growth as thinkers, readers, and writers. However, the content serves as a prompt for our development, for the degree or extent of change is completely within our control. It is difficult to accept that, although multicultural literature and issues are discussed, they can still be rejected and misunderstood. Exposure to nonmainstream ideas is important, but unless students view the materials with the purpose of revising previously held views, then there will be no social benefit to people of color.

I think that my willingness to share my stories was largely due to what seemed like your appreciation of raw honesty. I usually don't test the "academic boundaries" (or a tolerated level of personal involvement), but I decided to tell my stories and wait for your reactions. I became more involved with my writing as I received more encouragement from you.

As the course progressed, I found that the reading materials required personal responses and commitment. Increasingly, I had to prepare myself for the defense of nontraditional literature and ideas. At times I was the marginal voice, but at other times I was silenced. Often I fought to have my voice heard, but it was disappointing to feel that I was being "allowed" to speak on a subject that I wasn't "truly knowledgeable of." I felt that (some of my peers) "granted" me permission to speak, but they still had dominance because they could make the choice to not really listen. I know that I am an aggressive voice, but I feel like I have to establish myself in this way or accept manipulation and subordination.

Throughout the semester I found myself compelled to write. I learned to approach writing for the sake of communication. My initial reluctance to orally share my stories was overcome by my extreme respect for the professor. I viewed silence as uncooperative and rude — this my parents have taught me, especially my father, the former teacher. He would say that teachers are second to your parents. This, compounded with the professor's efforts to create membership for everyone in our learning community, made me a participant. On occasion, when my emotions were especially challenged, I thought of myself as responsible to my future students of color as well as to my peers. There were days when I made myself speak even though I felt that I spoke soundless words to deaf ears. I spoke because I didn't want to be a hypocrite and want, in the future, to tell my students that they must never relinquish the right to use their voices. I also spoke because I believed that perhaps I could influence the views of my peers by demonstrating a portrait of myself, me — the often voiceless, faceless, unknown, low-income immigrant, "minority," statistic.

WILLIS'S REFLECTIONS

Ana's writing and sharing during Writer's Workshop impressed me as an instructor and as a researcher. Her writing was incredible. It evinced the kind of responsiveness that teachers desire and the data that researchers covet. Moreover, I interpreted her responsiveness as supportive of my pedagogical beliefs. However, as the semester drew to a close, I became nervous that Ana would not contribute her work to the class book, part of my ongoing database. Weekly, I encouraged all of the students to submit something to the book, but I did not receive anything from Ana. I was very disappointed. Eventually, I assembled the class book without a contribution from her.

Once the class book was complete, I spoke with Ana to share my disappointment. She left me a voicemail message, a response and justification for her decision not to contribute to the class book. It was her way to help me understand her point of view. Ana's stories were hers to share, or not to share, with others. The class book was my idea, and she did not have to contribute; it was voluntary. She felt that I needed to understand why she had elected not to share her stories. In my zeal to share her work and to collect amazing data, I needed to respect the fact that the stories were hers, as well as respect her willingness to share them in class but not in print. Her stance was not an accident, nor was it inappropriate. She was correct.

WILLIS'S CONFESSION

After the voicemail message, I wondered whether my zeal and status had overwhelmed Ana. I wanted to be certain that she understood that I accepted her position. Her stories were hers to share or not share. As the instructor, I was proud of her work; as the researcher, I wanted to share it with others. I also wanted to be sensitive to Ana as a person and to our growing relationship as I struggled with my desire to share her work with others as a part of my own research agenda. Ethically, however, I knew that I could not share her work without her complete approval and acceptance. Nor could I recapture the honesty, courage, and strength she displayed throughout the course — that was her story.

Epilogue

We shared our experiences as researcher and participant at the national conference. It was the first time that Ana had presented and I did not know what to expect. I watched in amazement at the courage of this young woman, who stood erect with shaking hands, reading her work with clarity and passion. Ana told the audience, "I see this as an opportunity to give her [Willis] one of my stories that I had held onto in class. In fact, it is also her story, because without her support, this story would have never been written. This experience has been as much a gift of herself as it [the story] has been of me. She helped give voice to who I was, so I could become who I am today."

Several months later, I suggested we consider writing about this series of events. But I did not wish to proceed without her input. When the opportunity to write this essay presented itself, we agreed it was time to publish our work. We also agreed that offering levels of analysis and interpretation was not part of our story. We have resisted the temptation to make implications for others; the readers will have to draw their own. What readers learn from our stories will depend on factors we cannot control. Our hope is that in reading about our experiences, others will consider how their lives and stories become part of the lives and stories of their students.

References

A Day in the Life of America. (1986). New York: Collins Publishers.

Bateson, M. (1997). "Foreword." In *Learning From Our Lives: Women, Research and Autobiography in Education,* edited by A. Neumann and P. Peterson, pp. vii-viii. New York: Teachers College Press.

Casey, K. (1995). "The New Narrative Research in Education." In *Review of Research in Education,* Vol. 21, edited by M. Apple, pp. 211-253. Washington, DC: American Educational Research Association.

Clandinin, D., and F. Connelly. (2000). *Narrative Inquiry: Experience and Story in Qualitative Research.* San Francisco: Jossey-Bass.

Clandinin, D., and M. Connelly. (1994). "Personal Experience Methods." In *Handbook of Qualitative Research,* edited by N. Denzin and Y. Lincoln, pp. 413-427. Thousand Oaks, CA: Sage.

Coles, R. (1989). *The Call of Stories: Teaching and the Moral Imagination.* Boston: Houghton Mifflin.

Crow Dog, M., and R. Erdoes. (1990). *Lakota Woman.* New York: Harper Perennial.

Delpit, L. (1995). *Other People's Children: Cultural Conflict in the Classroom.* New York: New Press.

Freire, P. (1999, orig. 1970). *Pedagogy of the Oppressed.* New York: Continuum.

Henry, A. (1995). "Growing Up Black, Female, and Working Class: A Teacher's Narrative." *Anthropology and Education Quarterly* 26(3): 279-306.

Hurston, Z. (1965, orig. 1937). *Their Eyes Were Watching God.* New York: Harper Perennial.

Jones, L., L. Newman, D. Isay, and J. Brooks. (1998). *Our America: Life and Death on the South Side of Chicago.* New York: Washington Square Books.

Kozol, J. (1991). *Savage Inequalities: Children in America's Schools.* New York: HarperCollins.

Lee, H. (1982, orig. 1960). *To Kill a Mockingbird.* New York: Warner Books.

Neumann, A., and P. Peterson, eds. (1997). *Learning From Our Lives: Women, Research, and Autobiography in Education.* New York: Teachers College Press.

Pratt, M. (1992). *Imperial Eyes: Travel Writing and Transculturation.* New York: Routledge.

Scieszka, J. (1991). *The True Story of the Three Little Pigs.* New York: Viking Press.

Histories, Ideologies, and Discourses of (Un)Identification

An Approach to Composition and Critical Pedagogy for Mexican American College Writers

Michelle Hall Kells

racks and fissures extend across the quad where grass no longer grows and reach beneath the thick twisted sidewalks that crisscross this South Texas campus. Inside the cool-tiled hallways, behind ochre plaster walls, they sit writing. There is silence as I turn off the video and TV monitor. Rows of dark-haired students rest bent in thought.

> I really don't know much about the Chicano Movement except that Chicanos are always known as second class citizens. It really puzzles me that it is hardly mentioned in textbooks. When a person usually opens a history book and starts reading it talks about war, the slave trade, or also how economics and population is changing and growing. Also it talks about presidents. I think it should talk more about the Chicano Movement. (Tina)

> Watching this film I discovered that Mexican Americans striked against their schools and stood up for themselves. Many times we read in our history books about prejudice, but to see it on film is different. In books we feel the hardship and the anger, but on film we see the lives it affected. (Julissa)

> Before this film, I didn't know anything about the Chicano Movement. I learned that discrimination was much worse in the 1960s. To know this hurts me and really makes me angry. We don't study this movement because discrimination still exists. Many white people don't think our history is important so that's why we go throughout our education learning about George Washington and other whites only. (Rosa)

Their texts echo a near unanimous reaction. For most, this moment is an occasion of realization. Although 75 percent of the more than 140 students in the eight sections of first-year composition participating in this experimental syllabus are of Mexican origin, few have ever heard about the Mexican American civil rights movement. These textualized voices depict a moment of rupture, fault lines that extend beneath the surface of the daily routine toward social, political, and cultural fissures more than 100 years old.

This South Texas university is located in the border region between the

United States and Mexico, where the per capita income remains the lowest in the nation (Maril 1989). More than 50 percent of first-year composition students fail this course. Most entry-level students must enter the university through the remediation program, often repeating developmental writing courses several times before ever reaching first-year composition. The lack of quality formal education for South Texas Mexican Americans perpetuates economic inequities. More than 50 percent of Mexican American adults in the lower Rio Grande Valley have not graduated from high school; shockingly, 35.9 percent of Mexican American adults in this region had altogether fewer than five years of formal schooling (1989: 16). A recent report, "Measuring Up 2000," by the National Center for Public Policy and Higher Education confirms that these glaring disparities persist. Hispanic students are more likely than Anglos to attend segregated, poorly funded schools where bilingualism often is regarded as a liability rather than an asset.

In his keynote address for the 2000 Texas A&M University symposium "Literacy and Literary Representations," Jaime Armin Mejía called for a pedagogical approach in composition that "takes a Texas Mexican student's ethnicity into account." However, as Mejía argues, there are no pedagogies yet available that link Chicano studies and composition studies.

The experimental syllabus discussed in this essay suggests one approach bridging these two disciplines to facilitate Mexican American students' success and retention in English studies classrooms. Findings from previous research support Mejía's argument that composition pedagogies that fail to incorporate students' ethnicities "can and will have adverse effects on our students' academic success." My 1996-97 longitudinal study on ethnolinguistic identity and language attitudes of college writers suggests that students and their teachers tend to devalue the language practices of Mexican-origin bilingual speakers in the context of the college composition classroom (Kells 2002). The durability of language and literacy myths is likewise indicated. In this essay, I discuss an experimental approach I used with Mexican American college writers that encouraged them to name and reframe disabling fictions from a historical point of view (Kells 1999).

From the perspective of a teacher of rhetoric and composition, I contend that racism operates most insidiously as implicit language ideologies and prejudice that shape and permeate the college classroom. But it is not merely enough to make linguistic prejudice visible. It is necessary to make the construction of history and ideology, a process and product mediated by language, palpable as well as malleable. We can invite students to articulate and rewrite their histories and to imagine different outcomes of their individual and collective pasts. The aim of this experimental syllabus, therefore, is to engage writers in reflection about how language shapes social relationships. This experimental syllabus takes into account the cultural and historical dimensions of my students' identities as a way into the process of writing development. I call attention to patterns of institutional discrimination that directly bear on their academic experiences, patterns that remain underexamined by administrators and legislators in favor of formulaic models of higher education (Kells 2002).

Part of the experimental syllabus included viewing, discussing, and writing about the film *Chicano* ("Taking Back the Schools"). In general, students' texts in reaction to this film reflect a pattern of anger and shock. The majority indicate that they had been unaware of the issues and events surrounding the Chicano civil rights movement until our course. I examined more than 140 sample texts to question how students consider history in relation to their own experience as college students. I am especially interested in how writers represent their perceptions of social relations and reconfigure the dominant ideology through dialogue and written discourse.

History and Discourses of Identification

Critical theorists Louis Althusser and Norma Fairclough provide the theoretical framework for this study. In "Ideology and the Ideological State Apparatuses," Althusser (1971) argues that the reproduction of labor power requires not only the replication of skills but also the reiteration of attitudes — "a reproduction of its submission to the rules of the established order, the ruling ideology" (133). Recognizing the centrality of the educational system in social formation, Althusser asserts that along with skills and knowledge students acquire "the 'rules' of good behavior, i.e., the attitudes that should be observed by every agent in the division of labour, according to the job he is 'destined' for" (132).

In terms of historical labor market segmentation in South Texas, the educational system has played a key role in the containment of the Mexican American labor force through tracking and other discriminatory practices. Labor market segmentation, class fractions, and educational tracking have served to maintain Mexican Americans in a marginalized sociopolitical and economic condition. Mexican-origin populations have served as both a reserve and a captive (low-mobility) labor force throughout the Southwest for over a hundred years (Acuña 1988).

In Althusser's conception of the state ideological "apparatus," the school replicates the social structure by maintaining the dominant ideology, perpetuating students' "imaginary relationship to their real conditions of existence" (1971: 162). This experimental syllabus attempts to expose the gap between students' perceived relationship within the system and the historical conditions of their existence. The majority in this study represent first-generation college students. Their entry into academe marks a significant shift from an economic condition that only 30 years ago was limited to a tertiary, migrant labor force. Students' attitudes, as expressed through textualized discourse, offer useful indexes of ideological formation and provide insight into historical and current social trends.

Extending Althusser's notion of social formation, Fairclough (1992b) asserts that discourse not only is shaped and constrained by social structures but also can play a powerful role in shaping social change (64). Fairclough allows for a measure of agency and transformative power by subjects that Althusser's model alone does not afford. For Fairclough, discourse operates both as ideological and political practice. As political practice, discourse "establishes, sustains, and changes power relations" (67). As ideological practice, discourse "constitutes, naturalizes, sustains, and changes significations of the world" (67). Fairclough contends that political and ideological practice do not operate independent of each other but work together to naturalize particular power relations. Ideologies embedded in discursive practices prove most effective when they become naturalized and weave themselves into a "commonsense" perception of the way things are (87).

The experimental syllabus attempts to open up the cracks in the "commonsense" perception. As "an accumulated and naturalized orientation," ideology frames our constructions of history and our representations of the present (Fairclough 1992b: 89). The classroom, in particular, is a site where language orders reality into a totalizing worldview that is in accord with the dominant order. As teachers, we can restructure and reorder the priorities and the models by which students acquire academic discourse. I am interested in how students respond to these ruptures and how they represent and resolve these ideological splits. The little cracks in the naturalized worldview present valuable opportunities for critical exploration. I believe that the act of naming as it becomes embedded in text functions as both political and ideological practice. Writing can facilitate critical reflection by bringing ideologies to the surface or, as Fairclough (1992a) argues, "highlight critical awareness of nontransparent aspects of the social functioning of language" (13).

The Experimental Syllabus

To eight sections of first-year composition, I introduced three units of course content centering on issues of ethnolinguistic identity and language attitudes. I divided the syllabus into three 75-minute sessions that included film viewing (45 minutes) followed by cooperative learning group work (30 minutes) and take-home journal writing exercises (20 minutes). I selected three films for their accessible illustration of the linguistic, social, political, and rhetorical value of language. *The Story of English: An English Speaking World* provides a historical examination of English. *The Story of English: Black on White* focuses on the development of African American vernacular English as a linguistic code. The segment "Taking Back the Schools," part of the series *Chicano: The History of the Mexican-American Civil Rights Movement*, documents the historical discrimination of Mexican Americans in the American educational system and the political possibilities of empowered speech.

Using standardized prompts, the three journal writing exercises focused on issues concerning language practice and social power. Every three weeks for the first nine weeks of the spring semester of 1997, the students viewed a documentary, engaged in focused group discussion (with standardized discussion questions), and wrote response journals. At the close of the study, I visited each of the classes that participated in the experimental syllabus to discuss the reasons for my research.

Surprisingly, no more than four writers indicated any prior knowledge of the Chicano movement or the events documented in *Chicano*. Remarkably, it is this absence of knowledge that emerges as the major unifying theme of the entire data sample. Five of the samples are records of group responses as dictated to a representative member. The other six samples are individual journal entries. Together these texts reflect discursive practice (verbal acts of observation, reaction, summary, and analysis) as well as social practice (verbal and nonverbal rituals of the classroom).

> 1. Not much was known about the Chicano Movement. We learned about the level of injustice that was perpetuated on the Mexican people. It was disturbing how they were robbing the Mexicans from attaining an education and opportunities for a better life. History is made by those who write it. (Marco with Lizeth, Marissa, and Juan)

> 2. I knew a little about the Chicano Movement. I think we don't study this movement in our history books because actually Chicanos still have the same problems especially young people who want to continue their education. Day by day they have to confront new rules that gives Chicanos less opportunities to finish their education. I don't believe that things changed. Still the same conditions for every race — blacks, Mexican Americans, and others. But Americans don't want to recognize this discrimination. (Patricia)

> 3. I really didn't know much about the Chicano Movement. I didn't know that schools failed miserably in teaching the Chicano kids. What disturbs me is that these kids were charged for trying to make their schools better in order for them to get well educated. I guess we don't study this movement because they are afraid that students might feel offended in some way and start another Chicano Movement. (Lorena)

> 4. Three out of the four members of our group had little clue of the Chicano Movement. Our group did not realize that Chicanos had a group called the "Brown Berets." We also did not realize that the Chicano Movement helped lead to the *Brown v. the Board of Education* case. What disturbs us about this period is that this video was the first piece of material which taught us of this movement. We believe that this movement wasn't in our history books because our government does not want to start up a controversy. (Connie with André and Denise)

5. As a group, none of us knew anything about the Chicano Movement before viewing this film. Everything we learned from the film was new to us. The lack of education on the part of teachers puzzled us. We don't see this in history books because the movement shows faults in the system. It also shows the inflexibility of the system. There is still a great need for cheap labor in America so the Mexicans are almost forced to go into the job market before they finish school. (Andy with Tony, Lindsay, and Eric)

6. We didn't know about the movement. We learned about the way the Mexicans were treated. It puzzled us because they hid this from us. Also it disturbs us because it shouldn't happen. We don't learn about it because to others it wasn't a big deal or they are embarrassed. (Candy with Saul, Levi, and Andy)

7. No, I did not know much of the Chicano Movement. Everything I saw I had not known. Mexican Americans and other minorities are still seen the same way as in the past. Because I think we are still being discriminated and they may not want for riots to start again. (Sergio)

8. No one in the group knew anything about the Chicano Movement. We learned that there was even such a movement. It bothers us that we are taught in school about the history of black movements and nothing about Chicano movements. It's always been pushed aside, so it doesn't get recorded in history books. (Desiree with Gustavo, Ambry, and Melissa)

9. Before I watched this film, I knew very little about the Chicano Movement. I learned that Mexican American students were traditionally put into Home Ec or shop classes. I find this particularly pathetic because the 1960s were an era of social revolution, but Mexican Americans [seem] to have been largely ignored. This movement is probably ignored in history books because it never achieved as much social prominence as other movements. (Javier)

10. What puzzles me about this period is that even though this was a while back some of the same treatment toward Mexicans is going on. I feel the reason we do not study this movement in our history books is because they are embarrassed by the action that was taken and also because they don't have to answer to some of our questions to why Mexicans were and still are treated the way they are treated. (Yolanda)

11. The film on the Chicano movement reminded me a lot of the black civil rights movement that happened about 20 years ago. The African Americans demanded that they be looked at as equals, not judged on their ethnic background or financial power. The Chicanos demanded the same thing. They were exhausted by the constant suppression and the "routing" into manual labor careers as stated in the film.

> The main reason for their suppression probably was because
> of the difference in culture and dialect. The Chicanos, the most of
> them not knowing English as their first language, usually mixed
> English with their native language thus making them appear less
> intelligent. Judging intelligence amongst unfamiliar peers is com-
> pletely based on oral skills and vocabulary. Only if two individuals
> are known personally is intelligence based on other properties
> such as ability, talent, and wit. The only sensible reaction for the
> Chicanos to overcome this suppression would be an education. To
> learn English like the white man and to sound like the white man.
> But this didn't work because the schools were not convinced that
> they could learn.
>
> The financial situation in all this is reason enough for nonmi-
> norities to discriminate against the economically challenged. Mexi-
> can Americans not being able to speak correct English or English
> at all were unable to acquire good paying jobs. This being the
> case, Chicanos were retained at the bottom of the monetary pyra-
> mid. The movement against the schools in L.A. was imminent and
> could not be avoided. There is no way one group of people
> whether it be Mexicans, Asians, or African Americans can absorb
> so much suppression and disrespect. Fortunately, the movement
> was successful, but discrimination and prejudice will always exist
> as long as we are human. (Mario)

The first group astutely observes, "History is made by those who write it." These writers, like many from the sample, demonstrate an awareness that history is malleable and linguistically constructed. They also recognize that there is a rhetoric to history making. The actions and the omissions that define and reinforce power relationships are contingent on the writers' point of view. These writers link current conditions to the past, realizing the durability of the very issues that motivated the modern American civil rights movements more than 50 years ago.

Most of the writers invoke affective qualifiers to describe this effect, employing states of emotion to depict their orientations toward the subjects of the film narrative. All center their responses on what we might call a *continuum of identification*. As featured at the beginning of this essay, Julissa describes a feeling of anger in the first person plural, assuming a stance of collective identification, while Rosa conveys individual anger and strong personal identification. Rosa's claim "to know this hurts me and really makes me angry" represents a risky act of personal disclosure.

These emotional dimensions can invite response as well as represent an opportunity to confront disabling fictions. Rosa's anger opens into a bold assertion confronting the dominant view of history: "We don't study this movement because discrimination still exists. Many white people don't think our history is important so that's why we go throughout our education learning about George Washington and other whites only." She risks naming what she never had occasion to articulate before. Racism not only colors the past; it colors the present.

Most writers resist nominalizing the agents of oppression in their summaries. Instead, writers rely on the ambiguous third person plural pronoun *they* as exemplified by Marco and his group — "It was disturbing how they were robbing the Mexicans" — and by Lorena, who observes that "they are afraid that students might feel offended." A few respondents, however, do nominalize the agents of oppression; Rosa writes, "White people don't think our history is important," and Connie's group suggests, "Our government does not want to start a controversy." Interestingly, two writers attribute the emotion of embarrassment to the pronominal third person *they*. Yolanda speculates that "they are embarrassed by the action that was taken." Similarly, Candy and her group attribute embarrassment to the pronominalized agents of the narrative.

Finally, Mario's piece is particularly remarkable, linked to the others by its thematic coherence but distinguished by theoretical underpinnings, sophisticated diction, and essay structure. This piece was the only one of more than 140 writing samples that came to me in this highly formalized academic genre. It is also noteworthy that this text was carefully word-processed, an act of document preparation that signifies the heightened rhetorical concern of the writer and an acute awareness of audience.

Mario articulates the interrelationships of labor power, education, race, and ethnolinguistic identity. He, however, does not name the agents of oppression directly but rather implicates the identity of hegemonic forces in the statement, "The only sensible reaction for the Chicanos to overcome this suppression would be an education. To learn English like the white man and to sound like the white man." Although this writer only indirectly identifies with the subject, he does personalize the subjects by attributing affective qualities as reflected in the statement, "They were exhausted by the constant suppression and the 'routing' into manual labor." His defense of the subjects' actions suggests his own political stance of alliance as well as reflects a rhetorical posturing that anticipates critique from a nonsympathetic audience. Mario effectively encapsulates the film's major theme of resistance, even echoing the same sense of closure and resolution as exemplified in the film's narrative.

These texts represent an initial but incomplete process. Where do we go from here? These texts point to the possibilities of students' critical engagement and suggest an initial step toward what Fairclough (1992a) calls "emancipatory discourse" (305). Writing practice has the potential to empower students when it allows them to "successfully contest the practices [that] disempower them" (305). These Mexican American college students recognize that the social conditions that precipitated the Chicano civil rights movement more than 30 years ago still exist today. Naming enduring social inequities of the past and the present can help students realize that civil rights reform is not a once-done-always-done process. It is the burden of each generation, the incomplete project of American civic inclusion. From the point of view of these writers, not only issues of race but also issues of language and literacy factor into this social equation. Linguistic variation acts as a social marker perpetuating prejudice and discrimination. Extending these findings into a classroom praxis will demand implementing approaches that help students turn awareness into productive rhetorical action. To ignore the historical ascriptive inequality our students face is to be complicit in its replication.

References

Acuña, R. (1988). *Occupied America: A History of Chicanos.* 3rd ed. New York: Harper & Row.

Althusser, L. (1971). "Ideology and Ideological State Apparatuses." In *Lenin and Philosophy and Other Essays*, translated by B. Brewster, pp. 127-186. New York: Monthly Review Press.

Fairclough, N. (1992a). *Critical Language Awareness.* New York: Longman Press.

———. (1992b). "A Social Theory of Discourse." In *Discourse and Social Change*, edited by N. Fairclough, pp. 62-100. Cambridge, Eng.: Polity Press.

Kells, M.H. (1999). "Leveling the Linguistic Playing Field in First Year Composition." In *Attending to the Margins: Writing, Researching, and Teaching on the Front Lines*, edited by M.H. Kells and V. Balester, pp. 131-149. Portsmouth, NH: Heinemann.

———. (2002). "Linguistic Contact Zones in the College Writing Classroom: An Examination of Ethnolinguistic Identity and Language Attitudes." *Written Communication* 19(1): 5-43.

Maril, R.L. (1989). *Poorest of Americans: The Mexican-Americans of the Lower Rio Grande Valley of Texas.* Notre Dame, IN: University of Notre Dame Press.

Mejía, J.A. (2000). "Bridging Rhetoric and Composition Studies With Chicano and Chicana Studies: A Turn to Critical Pedagogy." Paper presented at the Literacy and Literary Representations: Posing Questions, Framing Conversations About Language and Hispanic Identities symposium, Texas A&M University, College Station, Texas.

National Center for Public Policy and Higher Education. (2000). "Measuring Up 2000." [Online at http://www.highereducation.org]

Community Archaeology
A Historically Black College Deconstructs Basic Writing

Rhonda C. Grego

Extending "Community" for Composition

Whether Mina Shaughnessy's *Errors and Expectations* (1977) is regarded as a reconfiguration of or a break from traditional approaches to basic writing (see Horner and Lu 1999; Shor 1986), her work undeniably called composition's attention to the agency that teachers have in seeking alternative understandings of student writing processes and products. Though Shaughnessy's actual writing curriculum focused attention on internal sentence structures and accompanying understandings of error, prominent pedagogies since have turned our attention to broader scenes within which student writing occurs, focusing on writing processes (see Elbow 1973, 1981; Elbow and Belanoff 1989; Murray 1982), liberatory critique (see Freire 1990; Shor 1980, 1987), and academic discourse practices (see Bartholomae and Petrosky 1986).

Though they have been seen as very different approaches, each of these alternative scenes for writing instruction invokes the concept of *community* to redefine and unify the external scene within which students' writing development occurs. Process pedagogies and scholarship from the late 1980s focus on writing groups (Gere 1987) or classroom peer review groups (Elbow and Belanoff 1989) as a "community of writers" within which and for which students write. Liberatory pedagogy focuses composition's attention on the parallel communities of the classroom and the larger society, a society whose problems and inequities are revealed by critical literacy assignments and projects that grow from within the experience and perspectives of students in any given classroom population. Bartholomae and Petrosky (1986) focus on the academic world as comprising disciplinary communities themselves constructed by dialogue with/in texts. Our writing classrooms are thus miniature versions of the larger academic communities to which student writers seek entrance by engaging in reading and writing about constitutive texts.

Bringing attention to the relational, social, or academic discourse communities within which writing can be examined has certainly broadened the scope of our analysis of student writing beyond the sentence scene. But the concept of community itself includes more than composition's pedagogical invocations seem to suggest. Are we as compositionists assuming a unity of approach across and despite differing campus and departmental communities? Do we assume that the dynamics of different types of academic institutional histories and communities, as well as the material conditions of work within such communities, do not impact learning as long as students and teachers adhere to one of these dominant pedagogical scenes (and/or accompanying textbook) to guide the work of any particular course? Our own professionalization as a discipline might seem to demand this assumption, even while doing so runs counter to composition's own agreement that "literacy . . . is highly culture-dependent," that "the use of literacy grows directly out of the immediate social environment" (Gere 1987: 117).

Actually, I believe that those of us who teach and work with student writing do attend to the immediate social environment. But because the theories or frameworks that are used to talk about our work do not acknowledge or account for the influence of sociopolitical and institutional realities in which the full past, present, and future lives of program participants are embedded, it is difficult for those of us working within such frameworks to articulate (within the terms offered by that system) the ways in which our "immediate social environment" influences academic literacy development in ways that can be heard by the system, program, discipline, or institution. This difficulty has several important consequences for composition program participants (including instructors, students, and administrators). First, it becomes difficult to defend the system itself from influences that lie outside the program framework or system, a lesson well taught, to name just one example, by the recent history of basic writing in American colleges and universities. The 1990s in American higher education saw renewed debate over the place of "remedial," "developmental," or "basic" courses in four-year institutions — most visibly in the state systems of New York and California. In the early 1990s, the South Carolina Commission on Higher Education decided that basic writing courses would not receive graduation credit at four-year state-supported institutions because it was inappropriate for such institutions to support remedial education. Knowing that in the past similarly identified students had been either encouraged or rebuffed by the university, depending on the social climate and student population of the moment, my colleague at the time, Dr. Nancy Thompson, and myself had our eyes opened to just how politically — not disciplinarily — based our basic writing program was at the University of South Carolina.

That political push, however resented at the time, also gave more weight to other questions we had raised in a recent basic writing practicum about the extent to which traditional formulations and explanations for "deficient" student writing at our campus did not seem to take into account local dynamics of time, place, personality, previous educational experiences, and current socioeconomic positioning of those students tested at the University of South Carolina as "remedial" writers. If we could no longer look at our student writers through lenses provided by our state's and discipline's characterizations, how then would we regard them? Our teacher-researcher impulse to look with students at writing (rather than at them) led us to construct, argue for, pilot, and eventually institutionalize the Writing

Studio program (in operation since 1992). The Studio model creates an outside-but-alongside structure for small-group supplemental help and simultaneous interactional inquiry into first-year student writing, with experienced teachers acting as group leaders and former remedial or basic writing students attending weekly small-group meetings while enrolled in regular first-year composition courses (Grego and Thompson 1995, 1996).[1]

One of the consequences directly affecting students and teachers in first-year composition programs, who may know little about the professional discipline or program-design aspects of composition, is that a rhetorical distance is created between participants by the "absent presence" of the very "unsayable" dynamics and experiences that construct their everyday experiences with writing. Rhetorical distance is created when a set of factors and influences that affects participants is ignored, or when attention is diverted to some more abstract or idealized version of that scene, or when that abstract/idealized perspective or position is insisted upon as "correct" or "standard" — perhaps because a certain position is "traditional" or "familiar" (or not) or easier (or not) for the controlling institution to deal with. Such a system can maintain power by compelling participants to act within these abstracted "shadow scenes" that fit a preferred "master narrative" of student writing development (or "error"). Realities and complexities that do not fit remain unacknowledged and are left to frustrate participants, who will, after all, leave the system.

Though it took me some time to realize it, it was the oppressive influence of this "absent presence" that I felt when I arrived at Benedict College, a historically black college just one mile down the road from the University of South Carolina. In 1995, under the direction of its new president, Dr. David Swinton, Benedict College (a small, four-year, private institution with an open-admissions policy) decided to explore alternatives to remedial courses in both math and English. Unlike South Carolina's Commission on Higher Education, however, Dr. Swinton's concerns were based on his awareness as a Harvard-trained economist of problems faced by his campus's predominantly African American student population; he noted the ways in which semesters and sometimes years of remedial coursework hampered the education of already disadvantaged students by adding to the rising time and costs of a college education for a segment of the American population who could ill afford either.

In the 1995-96 academic year, a pilot study was conducted at Benedict College in which one course section of students who scored below standard on the college's holistically scored writing placement test were put in a regular first-year composition course with the addition of weekly lab work under the direction of an English learning specialist. On this small and very tightly controlled scale, the experiment seemed successful: Students did well and passed the course. Thus, beginning in the 1996-97 academic year, Benedict College registered all students whose placement test scores indicated that they needed remedial writing courses in regular first-year composition courses with attendant writing lab sections. All this was done with little to no awareness of debates over basic writing at the national level and with an equal lack of awareness of anything but the rudiments of process pedagogies from the early 1970s.

Problems arose when the original plan was expanded to the entire first-year student population; burgeoning enrollments overall and larger student numbers in both the courses and the lab sections made the pilot's close cooperation between course instructor and learning specialist impossible within traditional class and lab section structures. With preliminary evidence that another structure for organizing both lab sections and the joint efforts of faculty members and learning specialists was needed if students were to be successful without basic writing courses at Benedict College, Dr. Christopher Chalokwu (then dean of the School of Arts and Sciences) and myself (then a new faculty member at Benedict College) applied for and received a FIPSE grant to assess the adaptation of the University of South Carolina's Studio model to Benedict College's historically black, open-admissions environment.[2]

The Bridges Writing Program at Benedict College

Benedict College is an open-admissions college whose student enrollment has grown from just over 1,000 in Fall 1996 to just under 3,000 in Fall 2001. The college was founded in 1870 in Columbia, South Carolina, on the grounds of a former plantation, to provide education to recently emancipated African American slaves. Today, Benedict College is a unique campus community in its level of commitment and dedication to surrounding historically black communities and neighborhoods in the heart of the city. In an important sense, African American students have never had to "storm its gates," but even a historically black college such as Benedict can be subject to the ways that institutions of higher education generalize programs and approaches across very different institutions. Thus, though the course descriptions for English 135 and 137 (Freshman Composition I and II) had been revised in the 1980s to reflect a process approach to writing assignments, only a handbook was used as a course text in Fall 1996, with chapters on commas, spelling, etc., making up the backbone of the official course outline and a modes approach as the basis for paragraph and essay assignments.

Despite the seemingly confined nature of writing instruction as it appeared "on the page" and the gulf between the official course outline and what I, as a rhetoric-trained compositionist, knew to be current directions in writing pedagogy and research, I soon found that there was more to the Benedict College faculty than what this gulf and the current state of official first-year writing curriculum suggested. My Benedict College colleagues were very committed to the HBCU mission, and there were (and are) tensions between the appearance of a narrowly current traditional approach and faculty members' actual, everyday work to enact that mission. What I have continued to see in my work with my Benedict College colleagues and our African American open-admissions students are the ways that my colleagues (several graduates of HBCUs if not Benedict College itself) negotiate the rhetorical distances described above. Their own sociopolitical positioning in white, mainstream American society (not to mention conservative Southern history and politics in South Carolina) combined with their experience as teachers of primarily African American students has given them much valuable experience in ways to acknowledge and work with the "present absence" of those "unsayable" dynamics of their everyday experiences with student writers. I came to see that perhaps the knowledge and approaches developed by Benedict College's core faculty and learning specialists (who became the group leaders in our program) could not be written (or clearly articulated) within current pedagogical paradigms for or conservative institutional perspectives on first-year composition. What I came to hope was that the Bridges Writing Program (Studio) model brought by our FIPSE grant to Benedict College would work to better support and make more widely available across our larger campus community an appreciation for, and articulation of, this experiential knowledge.

In Fall 1997, the Bridges Writing Program (BWP) began its work at Benedict College. Our primary objective was to adapt and assess an alternative structure for providing supplemental instruction to students who previously at Benedict College would have been placed in separate basic writing courses according to the results of our freshman placement testing.[3] Instead, the BWP placed these students (approximately 300 out of 600 freshmen each fall semester, with an additional 50 to 75 new admissions testing into the program each spring) in regular first-year composition courses with the addition of a small-group writing workshop meeting once each week in the English lab room outside-but-alongside regular first-year composition course class meetings.

At the time of the initial program, we drew on those aspects of previously existing programs (both at Benedict College and elsewhere) that would allow for the most input from both students and staff in the program. Rather than dictating approach, we wanted each aspect of our program structure to open up for examination the external scenes that influenced students' writing and to discuss ways in which we could thereby broaden the scope of our analysis of the internal scenes, agents, actions, etc., that influenced the writing our students produced. Each small group was led by BWP-trained English faculty or a learning specialist. BWP staff group leaders worked with each of their five groups of students (five to seven students per group) each week on writing assignments in progress; assignment drafts came from their English composition classes or from other general-education courses, including Freshman Seminar, Biology, Introduction to Religion (now Comparative Religion), World Civilization, and so on. Students brought their course materials, notes, texts, and drafts of any writing assignments, as well as graded and marked papers, for examination and discussion with group members.

Thus, the BWP did not make or set its own assignments; we facilitated and documented students' weekly work and engaged students in reflecting on their progress through the semester or year in midterm, progress, and final reports, and in weekly learning logs. Because these small groups are very different in dynamics from the traditional one-on-one writing center tutorial, group leaders had to work hard to get other student group members involved in this cooperative learning process by drawing students out so that they would share knowledge and help one another with feedback and response to writing. English faculty members serving as group leaders had to resist the temptation to lecture or revert to tactics more appropriate for classroom settings. English learning specialists had to resist the pull of their experience working with students in a primarily one-on-one dynamic.

Together we discussed how many African American students who underperform typically have trouble articulating their work processes, assignments given, and the meaning of classroom activities and assignments. In addition, weekly discussions with student and staff groups as well as periodic conversations with course instructors made us realize the extent to which many of our program's ancillary instructors, like graduate teaching assistants at large universities, were not always aware of all the assumptions and history behind the assignments and approaches employed in their courses and/or guiding the rhetorics/readers that the BWP staff group began to choose. (This lack of awareness is particularly true in small local colleges, which often hire instructors or adjunct faculty to cover courses without being too concerned about the specific kinds of training brought by those who will teach first-year writing courses.) Thus, it was important for BWP group leaders to:

1. push students to articulate details, to describe more fully the activities in their college classes, to explain what they had done or tried to do with an assignment, and to project what they yet needed to do;

2. supply more in-depth understandings of the motivations behind the course, assignments, and evaluations of their writing when students were unable to do so;

3. discuss and model ways that students could ask questions to draw their instructors out so that students could better understand or glimpse hidden scenes and motivations that informed assignments and readings, as well as raise their instructors' consciousness about those very matters; and

4. help students pull the pieces together, to use knowledge about the course, its relationship to institutional or disciplinary history and to other courses, about the instructor and his or her background, about the assignments and their intended relationship to real-world or academic expectations or assumptions, about the patterns of strengths and weaknesses in a particular student's or group's work, and to see all

this knowledge as part of the "story" of writing, as part of everyone's journey toward heightened awareness of the complex mix of rhetorical scenes in which academic writing occurs.

The BWP initiated increased communication between lab staff and course instructors through a departmental newsletter, and through midterm, progress, and final reports; it increased communication college-wide about writing through faculty institutes and summer workshops designed to extend our exploration of scenes across campus faculty and programs.

Just having a named and visible program, along with provision of yearly institutional progress reports, made the institution and our campus/composition community more visible to itself and made faculty members aware of differences among themselves. It also got us talking about specific cases and instances of student writing instead of just focusing on idealized forms or decontextualized deficiencies. Those English faculty members and learning specialists who worked as primary staff in the BWP project from 1997 to 2000 — Ruby Blair, Stephen Criswell, Ethel Taylor, Anne Colgate, Doris Greene, and Vareva Harris — brought their experiences as African American students and/or their experiences working with African American students in learning environments outside traditional classroom settings. Despite our often conflicting philosophical or pedagogical allegiances, all of our experiences predisposed us to understand that our students' struggles with college writing were struggles with the shifting and often tacit scenes (and hidden or masked acts and agents) found in college writing assignments, textbooks, instructors, and classroom interactions. We recognized that our students' struggles were with academic discourse(s) as filtered through the general-education curriculum and the range of approaches used by those who are hired to teach lower-level courses at our institution. Our students also struggle to deal with heavily competing economic and emotional demands of family and home and the assignments and deadlines of the academic world. Although we initially shared general fears for our students and their writing development without separate basic writing courses, once we became comfortable with one another, we were also very willing to concede that many of these student issues were not being addressed by traditional programs, curriculum, and textbooks.

Group leaders, myself as program director, and Dr. Nancy Thompson (acting as our local assessment consultant) were each required to bring a one-page informal write-up of concerns, observations, stories, queries, etc., to our weekly staff meetings. We began each meeting by spending a few moments to read each one-pager silently. Our staff meeting agenda then arose organically from grouping similar concerns found in and among the one-page write-ups each week. Thus, an important feature of our work was the way in which we used weekly reporting and reflection mechanisms to "theorize the cross-section" (Crawford et al. 1992) of the everyday details and insights into the world of our student writers.[4]

A basic goal of our weekly staff meetings was to confront observations about student behaviors, attitudes, past experiences, and ideas about writing that did not fit the typical idea that student writing is poor simply because students are ignorant of basic writing rules. We looked at how the local institutional environment and the mix of writing program history, personnel, curriculum, types of assignments, etc., affected students' performance and progress. Our weekly write-ups served to bring different aspects of this mix to the table for our collaborative reflection about the influence of different factors on our population of African American college student writers. Different group leaders could see the influence of different factors; pooling our experience, insights, observations, and information helped us move as a group past incomplete or "complicit" misunderstandings of student writing problems (Bourdieu, Passeron, and Martin 1994).

Mapping Rhetorical Distances

Instead of assuming linguistic or grammatical ignorance as the cause of student writing problems, our BWP small-group action inquiry allowed — even pushed — us to contextualize student writing development as part of an overall set of relationships within the higher education institution: relationships among students, teachers, curriculum, classroom environments, institutional structures, assignments, and both students' and teachers' past experiences.

What did we find when we did so? In general, we saw that our African American students who struggle with standard academic writing are often confused about the people, places, and events that are part of whatever subject they choose to, or are required to, write about or the situation that they are required to write within. People and systems (subjects), actions and methods (verbs), time frames (tense), and motivations (causality, etc.) provide the contexts (and sentence grammar) that are key to comprehension and critical consciousness in first-year college writing programs. But for many of our students, confusion about such contexts and the resulting lack of connections lead to writing struggles and/or the avoidance of such details altogether. Their confusion is compounded by difficulty discerning the discourse cues that signal an instructor's turn from academic texts to the subtexts of classroom discussion, instruction, and even different kinds of commentary on their own written texts. In addition, the fragmentary nature of many students' past educational experiences reverberates with similarly fragmented experiences in first-year writing programs; first-year college student writers may have teachers from any one of the many different disciplinary orientations that live within the graduate programs in English from which their instructors matriculate, and each one of these instructors may be operating out of very different assumptions about writing, student writers, and levels of experience with writing itself. When these underlying contexts were not well understood or examined by students and their teachers, the resulting rhetorical distancing and alienation manifested itself in our students' writing in a variety of ways.

Student writers may shift from among different formulas that they were taught about "school" writing, whether they are appropriate for their current writing assignment or not. For example, a past teacher's instructions never to use *I* in formal writing or never to shift verb tenses may result in stilted and convoluted sentence patterns in narratives or narrative sections where the use of first person is common and verb tenses must shift with the chronology of the story being told. (BWP staff spent two hours in just one staff meeting in Spring 1999 working through a confusing pastiche of problems created, domino-fashion, by a student trying to follow such dictums to complete an essay assignment.) Everyday speech patterns may also manifest themselves in writing in ways that the academic world identifies as nonstandard, but this shift serves a very rhetorical purpose from the student writer's standpoint: The student is working in a comfortable home language to make sense of a given writing situation as best she or he can. Although we have noted in working with BWP students that not every sentence has African American vernacular English (AAVE) errors (such as the dropped *ed* verb ending), the unconscious transference of oral speech patterns to writing may occur in places where students feel confused about something in the scenes embedded in the topic being written about (its history or place in larger events or relationship to other subjects) or in the scholastic scene and accompanying subtexts constructed by assignment parameters and a specific teacher's preferences.

Other shifts in tense, number, or verb form and coherence problems seem more akin to reference problems. Students' sentences that jump around actually refer to scenes or situations that lie "behind," or are embedded in, readings and research references and thus manifest students' struggles to sort out which scene they are supposed to be referring to. Undoubtedly, some such reference problems are created because of cultural conflicts, as well. The extent to which AAVE favors verb forms that express nuances of meaning, situation, and/or action within a continuous present (Baugh 1999; Smitherman 1986) suggests a possible conflict with academic culture's general preference for separating the "researched knowledge" of the past from the less differentiated knowledge of the present "research-in-progress" moment.

In BWP staff discussions, we also noted the way in which general-education courses and texts tend to focus on content and to pay much less (if any) attention to the rhetorical construction of knowledge by people and processes or methods. Higher education in general tends to save the examination of such methods and scholarly bodies of work until upper-undergraduate or graduate-level courses of study, focusing in lower-level courses on dialogue between texts in a more classical tradition. Yet this hurts nonmainstream students, who need to understand these methodological and pragmatic scenes of academic culture and how the construction of knowledge within disciplinary worlds works if they are to become academic writers who can, like Geneva Smitherman, use their sense of need for an explanation of underlying, unnamed, or assumed scenes as a signal to *code-switch*. This ability to code-switch both supplies understandings from their perspectives to an academic world that needs to hear from historically excluded perspectives and includes those listeners and readers in the academic world who would otherwise have been excluded.

As we worked in staff meetings to analyze and understand the dynamics of our program through formative and summative assessments with outside consultants (Dr. Nancy Thompson, and later Dr. Marie Wilson-Nelson), we came to better appreciate how conservative and deeply etched societal assumptions about linguistic inability and ignorance actually are within our campus and composition community. These conservative societal assumptions kept community members from communicating with one another about what they know about the complex dynamics that give rise to and sustain students' confusion and to instructors' faulty assumptions about the sources of students' writing problems. Handbooks, textbooks, and stepwise skill-focused assignments force self-fulfilling prophecies of deficiency on to student writers who are then supplied with grammatical explanations that assign the label "error." Such inadequate explanations help to deal with large numbers of students in a particular class or program, but they ignore what are often, we came to see, inexperienced responses to the rhetorically complex situations our African American students encountered within academic culture. These situations required sophisticated interpretation of relationships at the institutional and organizational levels between people, their roles, and the academic system itself. The hiding or masking of scenes (along with the actors, agents, and their accompanying motives) is often amplified by the way that content knowledge is presented in general-education courses, a presentation of knowledge that abstracts and further distances content from the people and processes by which that knowledge was constructed and is always being revised.

Often it is the scenes and not the sentences that need parsing. In one illustrative case, a BWP student's paper was marked with the teacher's comment that she had "severe problems with fragments." Examination and discussion of the paper with her lab group found that these fragments appeared only in the first page of the paper and not significantly thereafter. In the course of probing and discussion among student group members, it became clear that the student had had trouble knowing how to begin and how to frame the narrative essay about herself (Who was her audience? What was her purpose?), and so she imitated the fragmented style typical of voice-over narration often heard on TV and in movies as she played the visual story of her life in her own mind and transferred that to the page. Being assigned a handbook exercise on fragments per the course outline would not give this student the awareness of other strategies that she might use to begin her paper, strategies that would "fix" her fragment problem. Handbook exercises using sentences removed from the rhetorical contexts that shape meaning during the writing process had not provided her with the awareness of different communicative relationships and contexts within which writers work and within which some strategies are deemed appropriate and others not. Unearthing and developing such understandings was, we saw, crucial to developing students' abilities to revise their writing. Experienced instructors at Benedict College engaged students to discover such lack of larger understandings, though we also saw how less experienced or invested instructors were less likely to do so and were more likely to assign handbook chapters as topics for class meeting periods.

When students are assigned only handbook exercises on problems with mechanics and are not given the broader rhetorical awareness and understanding of the issues and relationships implied by sentence mechanics and style, they are likely to become further distanced or alienated from what they perceive to be arhetorical and arcane academic "rules" for writing. In BWP groups, for example, we saw how students consistently given those kinds of assignments were more likely to believe that their teacher (or "the system") does not care about what they were trying to say or write or why. BWP inquiry also suggests that it may be African American students' perception of this lack of caring — this distance from their everyday experiences of what they are asked to do and how they might actually accomplish the task set — that they associate with "school" writing. Seen in this light, "talkin' white" may well refer not just to syntax and diction but also to an attitude they perceive in the mainstream language of mastery. From some African American students' perspectives, standard-edited English seems disembodied from the rhetorical contexts of communication that are real and meaningful to them. The people, processes, and histories that underlie various disciplinary knowledges and the accompanying standards by which their writing is being evaluated (and found deficient) have not been unmasked for them and seem removed from their experiences as writers.

BWP staff also saw many times how our African American students' lives and home culture presented them with personal situations and dilemmas that the academic world does not address and clearly prefers that students forget or transcend to succeed. Those students (and faculty) whose lives allow more of this transcendence (and have in the past) are those who are more "prepared" for college; less transcendence of the everyday problems (food, shelter, clothing, transportation, money for books, etc.) often means being "disadvantaged" and even "underprepared." And, of course, money most often buys transcendence; the ability to live in an academic economy of texts and to be comfortable in the accompanying scenes presupposes having other economic means available so that you can spend less time and energy in those "other," more everyday worlds. But the ability to transcend everyday distractions and problems does not rely only on money, food, and shelter — on issues of socioeconomic class status. Where the master narrative of higher education has systemically embedded a white, middle-class perspective through years of control over so many disciplinary depictions of the world around us (including history, sociology, science, technology), achieving this transcendence also seems to require learner-researchers of nonwhite ethnicity and race to deal at conceptual, emotional, and rhetorical levels with many intervening scenes and motives to "identify" academically (see Gilyard 1991; Villanueva 1993).

It is in academic culture's preference for the ideal over the real that African American students feel the racism of higher education, despite the ways higher education has distanced itself from its most obvious and originating racisms. To the extent that HBCUs provide an overall environment of organized resistance and insistence on black presence, those of us working in HBCUs may have more immediate community support for seeing the larger coherence in the work of our African American student writers. Though a full understanding of the specific influence of differing campus communities and social environments on writing instruction and student writing development requires much more study, I can say that it is an ability to bring the *real* into class discussions and group meetings that I noted as characteristic of Benedict College's most experienced and dedicated African American teachers and group leaders. BWP student group discussions, ranging far afield from traditional academic texts into the territory of family, friends, hairstyles, dating, etc., were in reality a necessary reconstitution of the canonical textual "fields" available for interpretation as students constructed their own academic identities and motivations.

Likewise, BWP students and staff benefited from staff small-group discussions about the ineffectual institutional policies, practices, paperwork, lack of administrative respect for or awareness of past program history, and disciplinary formulations for writing instruction that assume both mainstream students are being served and that certain levels of infrastructure and resources are available. Such discussions opened up all our understandings of current programmatic practices and realities — and helped us reconstitute our own academic identities and motivations, as well. Certainly we came to see that disembodying our students' writing and our own writing instruction from the dynamic that makes both our tasks complex (real and less than ideal) only continues to deny all of us within educational institutions — as well as the institutions themselves — vital avenues for greater self-awareness and growth.

Program Assessment

After three years (1997 to 2000), what results did our program produce? Analysis of student course grades over this period shows conclusively that "remedial" students previously placed in either separate courses or large writing lab sections at Benedict College (some 250 out of an entering freshman class of roughly 700 each fall) can and do succeed in regular first-year composition courses when supplemental instruction is provided using BWP's small-group inquiry-based approach. In fact, these writing students can — and did — outperform students who scored higher on the writing placement test. As shown in the table opposite, BWP-par-

Course Grades Comparison Across All Semesters of FIPSE Grant Funding: Fall 1997, Spring 1998, Fall 1998, Spring 1999, Fall 1999, Spring 2000

Semester/English Course	BWP Participants Earning A, B, or C in First-Year Composition Courses	General Population Students Earning A, B, or C in First-Year Composition Courses
Fall 1997/135*	79%	73%
Spring 1998/135	86%	48%
Spring 1998/137	84%	69%
Fall 1998/135	89%	76%
Spring 1999/135**	100%	63%
Spring 1999/137	79%	73.5%
Fall 1999/135	88%	60%
Spring 2000/137***	87%	58.5%

*In Fall 1997, BWP was experimenting with two different structures and not all students were working in the small-group structure that was completely operationalized by Spring 1998.

**Spring 1999 saw a much smaller number of Eng 135 students participating in BWP, which we believe contributed to this unusually high success rate.

***In Spring 2000 there were no Eng 135 students in BWP due to another experimental program initiated by a new dean with newly registered students.

ticipating students earned A's, B's, and C's consistently at rates above those of general population students in the same courses who had not been required to participate in the lab.

BWP-participating students not only did as well as but outperformed our general population, first-year composition students in the cumulative percentages of A's, B's, and C's earned in English 135 and 137 each fall and spring semester. The following trends also suggest that the BWP approach is successful at retaining students in Benedict College's first-year composition courses:

- BWP students registered far fewer WA (Withdrawn Administratively for failure to adhere to the college's attendance policy) grades, which may well account for their overall better performance as a group. The no lab, general population students recorded WA percentages four to six times higher than those of BWP students.

- The poorest performing group were those students who, according to placement test scores, should have participated in the BWP small-group lab program for English 135 each fall semester but who did not attend. Their poor performance indicates what can happen when these students are mainstreamed into first-year composition courses without supplemental instruction or attention such as that provided by the BWP.

- WA rates in English 137 among students who had participated in the lab in the fall but not in the spring were much higher than were WA rates among students who continued participating in BWP each spring but still consistently lower than WA rates for the general population students in English 137. That students who participated in the lab in the fall but not in the spring still performed better than did students who didn't participate at all is perhaps indicative of a carryover effect of the lab.

Overall, our project results made it clear that the BWP helped its participants make and maintain vital connections to their courses and their learning — and to better deal with the inevitable frustrations faced by many of our students whose own view of their writing was shaped by previous academic experiences and programs that relied on arhetorical concepts of "writing deficiencies."

In Conclusion: Bridging Rhetorical Distances

Our work in the Bridges Writing Program has shown us the importance of finding ways to open up, bring forward, bring out, articulate, and explore the social contexts and politics of knowledge construction in our specific higher education learning environment. Our work has also helped us recognize the intellectual-affective processes involved in untangling these layers of built-up scenes and the attendant confusion created by academic blindness and organizational amnesia.

The ways in which academic knowledge is constructed — and the learning and engagement processes whereby students are helped to understand and construct their place in this work — remain far less *systematically* and *systemically* engaged and analyzed in college-level academic programs and course curricula than they need to be to combat the fragmentation and distancing experienced by currently under-served student populations.

BWP group leaders and course instructors were helped to place student difficulties in the context of individual and institutional life and to devise learning and assignment strategies that address these more specific, yet more fully contextualized, understandings of student writing development and our own writing instruction. As BWP group leaders saw inconsistencies, confusions, misdirections, and misunderstandings created by educational settings (past and present), we realized how fragmented our students' writing experiences had been, and to some extent still were. Even with uniform course outlines, texts, and a common final exam in our college composition program at Benedict College, differences in faculty backgrounds and assumptions (as well as students) made for (and will always contribute to) miscommunication and misunderstandings that lead to the motivation and attitude problems affecting African American student writing development and performance. To the extent that BWP weekly student group meetings, staff meetings, department reports, newsletters, and workshops could make visible and bridge these rhetorical distances, students were able to be successful in their college writing and coursework, as evidenced by their final course grades, teacher responses, and student self-reflections in program reports, meeting narratives, and learning logs.

Rather than live with a *shadow scene* of an abstracted "community" for writing, BWP groups worked from within the conflicts, tensions, and complexities of the local campus community in which all program participants found themselves. The development of deeper rhetorical understandings (for both teachers and students) of what our students are doing in their writing and why helped boost overall program coherence as BWP staff worked with composition course instructors to examine and articulate assumptions. The BWP groups recognized that confusions caused by unvoiced assumptions could be rearticulated in ways that were cooperative, not threatening, in ways that were conducive to greater self-awareness on the part of individuals, and in ways that fostered grass-roots change(s) for program participants.

Thus, in BWP student groups and staff discussions, we helped one another see, and celebrate, ways that attending to and respecting our immediate social environments worked to reconstitute the academic environment of our classrooms and lab groups. We focused on capitalizing on the richness of all our lives, creating ever more openings for the kind of deeply structured playfulness that will extend, I hope, beyond the life of the program itself.

Notes

1. During the 1990s, similar programs arose in other states and at other colleges and universities, as well — simultaneously at the University of Washington, later at the University of Arizona with its Stretch Program and Florida International's Writing Circles program (Lalicker 1999). To date, we are aware of specific offshoots of the Writing Studio program in the Opportunity Scholars program at the University of South Carolina, Benedict College (where I am now located), the University of Miami at Middletown, Nyack College in New York, and Grand Valley State University in Michigan.

2. For reports on other projects working through alternative approaches to mainstream basic writers, see Soliday 1996 and Gleason 2000. Though we were aware of these and other programs, they were all, including the Writing Studio program at the University of South Carolina, situated in large state universities. Benedict College faculty were skeptical about the extent to which such programs could be regarded as suitable models, given the differences in institutional size, history, student populations, and resources.

3. Benedict College's freshman placement test in English consists of two parts: a holistically scored, timed, essay component and a multiple-choice editing test.

4. For complete background sources for what Thompson and Grego (1995, 1996) have termed an "interactional inquiry" approach to program research and participatory inquiry, see Reason and Rowan 1981, Haug 1987, Reason 1988, and Crawford et al. 1992.

References

Bartholomae, D., and A. Petrosky. (1986). *Facts, Artifacts and Counterfacts: Theory and Method for a Reading and Writing Course*. Portsmouth, NH: Heinemann Boynton/Cook.

Baugh, J. (1999). *Out of the Mouths of Slaves: African-American Language and Educational Malpractice*. Austin: University of Texas Press.

Bourdieu, P., J.-C. Passeron, and M. De Saint Martin. (1994). *Academic Discourse: Linguistic Misunderstanding and Professorial Power*, translated by R. Teese. Stanford, CA: Stanford University Press.

Crawford, J., S. Kippax, J. Onyx, U. Gault, and P. Benton. (1992). *Emotion and Gender: Constructing Meaning From Memory*. The SPUJJ Collective. London: Sage.

Elbow, P. (1973). *Writing With Power*. New York: Oxford University Press.

———. (1981). *Writing Without Teachers*. New York: Oxford University Press.

Elbow, P., and P. Belanoff. (1989). *A Community of Writers: A Workshop Course in Writing*. New York: Random House.

Freire, P. (1990). *Pedagogy of the Oppressed*, translated by M.B. Ramos. New York: Continuum.

Gere, A.R. (1987). *Writing Groups: History, Theory, and Implications*. Carbondale and Edwardsville: Southern Illinois University Press.

Gilyard, K. (1991). *Voices of the Self: A Study of Language Competence*. Detroit, MI: Wayne State University Press.

Gleason, B. (2000). "Evaluating Writing Programs in Real Time: The Politics of Remediation." *College Composition and Communication* 51(4): 560-588.

Grego, R., and N. Thompson. (1995). "The Writing Studio Program: Reconfiguring Basic Writing/Freshman Composition." *Writing Program Administration* 19(1-2): 66-79.

————. (1996). "Repositioning Remediation: Renegotiating Composition's Work in the Academy." *College Composition and Communication* 47(1): 62-84.

Haug, F., et al. (1987). *Female Sexualisation: A Collective Work of Memory*, translated by E. Carter. London: Verso.

Horner, B., and M.-Z. Lu. (1999). *Representing the "Other": Basic Writers and the Teaching of Basic Writing*. Urbana, IL: NCTE.

Lalicker, W.B. (1999). "A Basic Introduction to Basic Writing Program Structures: A Baseline and Five Alternatives." *Basic Writing e-Journal* 1(2). [Online at http://www.asu.edu/clas/english/composition/cbs/bwe_fall_1999.html]

Murray, D. (1982). *Learning by Teaching: Selected Articles on Writing and Teaching*. Montclair, NJ: Boynton/Cook.

Reason, P., ed. (1988). *Human Inquiry in Action: Developments in New Paradigm Research*. London: Sage.

Reason, P., and J. Rowan, eds. (1981). *Human Inquiry: A Sourcebook of New Paradigm Research*. Chichester, Eng.: Wiley.

Shaughnessy, M.P. (1977). *Errors and Expectations: A Guide for the Teacher of Basic Writing*. New York: Oxford University Press.

Shor, I. (1980). *Critical Teaching and Everyday Life*. Boston: South End.

————. (1986). *Culture Wars: School and Society in the Conservative Restoration*. Chicago: University of Chicago Press.

————. (1987). "Educating the Educators: A Freirean Approach to the Crisis in Teacher Education." In *Freire for the Classroom: A Sourcebook for Liberatory Teaching*, edited by I. Shor, pp. 7-32. Portsmouth, NH: Heinemann Boynton/Cook.

Smitherman, G. (1986). *Talkin' and Testifyin': The Language of Black America*. Detroit, MI: Wayne State University Press.

Soliday, M. (1996). "From the Margins to the Mainstream: Reconceiving Remediation." *College Composition and Communication* 47(1): 85-100.

Villanueva, V., Jr. (1993). *Bootstraps: From an American Academic of Color*. Urbana, IL: National Council of Teachers of English.

Pluralism in Practice

An Approach to Language Variety

Dan Melzer

In *Voices of the Self: A Study of Language Competence*, Keith Gilyard (1991) describes three approaches to language instruction taken by institutions and individual teachers in response to African American students who speak and write in features of African American vernacular English (AAVE): eradicationism, bidialectalism, and pluralism. Eradicationists associate AAVE with cognitive deficiency; they believe standardized English is the only language variety that has a legitimate function in schools. Most bidialectalists oppose this deficiency model; they argue for the value of *code-switching* between AAVE and standardized English. But Gilyard feels that those who argue for this position, like the eradicationists, often fail to consider that the setbacks African Americans face in society have more to do with racial prejudice than "linguistic output" (1991: 72). Gilyard argues instead for pluralism, a way of teaching writing that considers all dialects as valid without denying the imbalance of power between standardized English and other language varieties.

Although Gilyard has done much to further its cause, pluralism is by no means a new idea. The Conference on College Composition and Communication's (CCCC's) 1974 resolution "The Students' Right to Their Own Language" argues a pluralist position, insisting on "students' right to their own patterns and varieties of language — the dialects of their nurture or whatever dialects in which they find their own identity and style." This position is reinforced in CCCC's recent statement on ebonics. The statement asserts that AAVE is not an obstacle to learning. Rather, "the obstacle lies in negative attitudes towards the language, lack of information about the language, inefficient techniques for teaching language and literacy skills, and an unwillingness to adapt teaching styles to the needs of [e]bonics speakers" (1999: 524). Geneva Smitherman, a leading force behind both resolutions, has been making the case for pluralism since the 1960s, in a writing style that is itself pluralist, combining features of standardized English and black English in books such as *Talkin' and Testifyin'* (1986).

Despite this call for pluralism that began as early as the 1960s and despite all of the talk of pluralism "in theory" in books and journal articles, pluralist *practice* in the teaching of composition is still a new — and often controversial — idea at many institutions. This is especially true of the institutions where it is needed most, such as open-admissions community colleges. As Tom Fox points out in *Defending Access*, the curriculum in basic writing has lagged behind changes in writing instruction. Fox laments that even open-admissions institutions take a *gatekeeping* rather than a *gateway* approach in freshman English (1999: 55). I believe that a pluralist pedagogy is one of the most effective ways to teach students who speak and write in a home language different from standardized English: students who are often labeled as "basic" writers. To make my case for pluralism, I present a narrative of my successes and failures as I moved toward a pluralist model in my freshman writing course at an open-admissions community college in Tallahassee, Florida. In the spirit of my emphasis on pedagogy, I present specific suggestions for teaching practices that emulate Smitherman's and Gilyard's pluralist pedagogy. My hope is that my story and my suggestions for teaching practice will give teachers solid strategies for teaching a diverse student population.

Just Another White English Teacher

In Fall 2000, I took an adjunct job teaching ENC 1102, an argumentative writing course, at a local open-admissions community college. The community college has a diverse student body, and the majority of my students were African American and the first in their family to attend college. To get a sense of their writing history, during the first week of classes I asked students to write about their previous experiences in English courses, both positive and negative. I asked them to be honest, and what I found out surprised me.

One student wrote that her ENC 1101 instructor, in a one-on-one conference, told her that she wrote "too black." "I'm always getting into trouble with English because I write like I speak," this student said, "and I need to learn how to write correctly." Another talked about the 50-minute timed writing essay exams he took in ENC 1101, exams designed to prepare students for the CLAST, a state-mandated academic skills test. This student said that the only response he received from the instructor was the phrase "Bad grammar!" and the letter grade D written at the end of the essay. Another student felt that ENC 0020, the college prep English course, did not do enough to prepare her for college writing. She said that in prep they never wrote anything longer than a paragraph, and she struggled when she was faced with a 10-page research paper in her history class the next semester.

Not all the African American students had had bad prior experiences with English courses, and not all of them exhibited features of AAVE in their writing. But the ones who did write and speak using features of AAVE had experienced teachers who often equated their home language with bad thinking. David Wallace and Arnetha Ball argue that "minority students' cultural differences are often seen as deficiencies that must be corrected, or at best disregarded" (1999: 314). This was certainly the situation many of my students had faced. With this knowledge of my students' prior experiences and my own concern about being just another white teacher acting as monocultural gatekeeper, I searched the course textbook, *Elements of Argument* (Rottenberg 1997), for essays by African American writers.

Multicultural Mistakes

I was happy to find what I thought would be a good essay for my purposes, Martin Luther King's "Letter From a Birmingham Jail," which makes a persuasive argument and uses features of African American oral traditions. I thought that by assigning King's essay I would at least be making a move toward multiculturalism. But my class, normally full of spunk and opinions, was silent and bored on the day we discussed "Letter." When I asked them why they were not interested, one student said, "We always read this essay. Since high school I've been reading this essay. Every textbook you read has one essay by MLK. It's like they won't put a black man in a textbook unless he's been shot." As you can see from this quote, my students are adept at making persuasive arguments. So I looked for a way to change my pedagogy, and I went back to *Elements of Argument.*

I thought I was in luck again when I found an essay by Barbara Ehrenreich that defended rapper Ice T's song "Cop Killer" as a symptom of social problems created by racism. I knew from class conversation that most of the students were hip hop fans, and I wanted to be student-centered. Gilyard argues that "you can't effectively help those you don't respect" (1991: 72), and I thought an essay that presented a thoughtful analysis of rap music might be a show of respect to the students' home culture. In one sense I was right, because the essay sparked a class discussion about the media-coined term *gangsta rap* and the ways members of the media and politicians equate all hip hop with gangsta rap. A few students, however, saw the article as dated. "Ice T is old school," one student said, and I realized that despite my attempt to be student-centered, I had a long way to go. And despite my liberal, multicultural claims, every essay I had assigned, including the essay on hip hop music, had been written in standardized English. My writing assignments, which I also thought of as multicultural, required standardized English at all stages of the writing process. As my students might say, it was time to "come correct."

How I Flipped the Script

In *Let's Flip the Script: An African American Discourse on Language, Literature and Learning,* Keith Gilyard (1996) argues that despite all our multicultural talk about honoring African American culture and history, educators often treat AAVE as something outside of that culture and history, not fit for the kind of writing required in freshman English. My goal, then, was to move from a watered-down multiculturalism to a kind of pluralism that would include more varieties of African American discourse. I felt that the only way to accomplish this was by truly enacting the student-centered philosophy I gave so much lip service to.

I began by asking students to bring in CDs they listened to and books and magazines they read. We put *Elements of Argument* down for a while and instead talked about the lyrics and poetry of Tupac Shakur. We compared the news coverage delivered in the local NAACP newspaper with the coverage in the *Tallahassee Democrat*. We analyzed scenes from Spike Lee and John Singleton movies and listened to and discussed the social commentary of comedian Chris Rock. I brought in speeches by Malcolm X, and we analyzed differences in his tone, style, and word choice when he addressed working-class Harlem residents versus the white media and white politicians. We worked under the assumption that AAVE was a language variety every bit as eloquent and powerful as standardized English.

A Right to Their Own Language

Bringing this variety of voices from my students' cultural background was only one part of my shift to pluralism. After reading Gilyard, Smitherman, Fox, and the CCCC position statements, I began to see that to come closer to achieving pluralism, I would also need to include student writing using features of AAVE as part of the course. Instead of just asking students to change for the academy, I wanted to have the academy change to fit the needs of the students: to convince them that the academic community can also be their community.

Like my original attempt to be multicultural, my first step toward pluralism in my writing assignments was a hesitant one. I told students that they would be keeping a journal of their responses to the essays, songs, and movies we discussed in class. This journal was "informal," meaning they could write in AAVE. The formal essay assignments, however, were still written in standardized English. When I found that a number of the students whose writing seemed stilted and underdeveloped in standardized English had written in a more interesting style with a deeper exploration of their ideas when they wrote in AAVE, I began encouraging students to write rough drafts of their formal essays in AAVE if they were more comfortable working in that language variety. Despite these changes, however, I was still treating AAVE mostly as a bridge to standardized English.

So I went a step further. I began offering my students more choices. Instead of writing their essays to the monocultural audience of me, the white teacher, I asked them to exhibit a wider variety of rhetorical skills. I gave them the choice of writing in a variety of genres for a variety of audiences: opinion essays aimed at the readers of *Vibe* magazine, rap songs, editorials for local African American newspapers, and an online dictionary of hip hop expressions. Many of these pieces not only encouraged but required students to write using features of AAVE, as using AAVE would help the writer's credibility with the target audience. Students who felt more comfortable writing in standardized English also chose a variety of audiences and purposes: academic essays in response to articles in *Elements of Argu-*

ment, reactions to editorials in the student newspaper, and argumentative pieces aimed at magazines like *The Atlantic Monthly* and *Time*.

Encouraging this kind of variety paid dividends for the final assignment, a research project of the students' own choosing. Yes, I did receive a few of the old standards: an argument against the death penalty, a case for legalizing marijuana. But I also received some strikingly original research projects that combined features of AAVE and standardized English. One student wrote a multigenre essay on the Harlem Renaissance that included folklore and poetry in AAVE, critical commentary about the Harlem Renaissance from scholars writing in standardized English, and the student's own analysis in a style that used both AAVE and standardized English. Another student who used both AAVE and standardized English in her final project was a young woman who investigated police harassment in Tallahassee. She compared interviews with her family, friends, and peers in the class with quotes from Tallahassee police officers. Many of the interviewees spoke in AAVE, while most of the police officers used standardized English, a fact that further highlighted the politics of language use. Another student analyzed misogyny in the lyrics of rap music. This student was able to take a critical stance toward his own language use, exposing the gender bias behind many of the slang terms in the music he listens to. Because of their complex rhetorical purposes, all these assignments called on students to be proficient in a wide variety of dialects, from AAVE to standardized English.

Despite their arguments in favor of pluralism, both Gilyard and Smitherman believe that because standardized English is the language of wider communication, we should not abandon its use in freshman writing courses. My students and I are not naive about language use: We acknowledged that standardized English is the language of wider communication in America. As pluralists such as Gilyard and Smitherman have argued, denying students access to standardized English is denying them access to power. But we also investigated the politics behind the ways that standardization occurred and continues to occur. Any debate about language is shot through with issues of power and politics. Even as I encouraged students to write in both AAVE and standardized English, I acknowledged an important point from the "Students' Right" statement: "The claim that any one dialect is unacceptable amounts to an attempt of one social group to exert its dominance over another."

Although many composition courses teach standardized English without acknowledging the current debates in composition studies and linguistics concerning the politics of its use, I decided to help make my students more aware of these debates by using Gerald Graff's "teaching the conflicts" model (1992). Graff argues that instead of hiding from students the conflicts that occur in our particular academic discipline, we should teach these conflicts as the subject of the course. To explore conflicts over language acquisition and use, I had students read and discuss chapters from Richard Rodriguez's *Hunger of Memory* (1981) and bell hooks's *Talking Back* (1989), whose authors present examples of both the rewards and the costs of moving between home and school language communities. We also investigated the arguments presented by conflicting voices in the debate over the use of AAVE in college writing courses. We discussed passages from Gilyard's *Voices of the Self* and Smitherman's *Talkin' and Testifyin'* and contrasted their views of language use with those of conservative commentators such as Dinesh D'Souza, author of *Illiberal Education* (1991). Rather than simply presenting standardized English as a given, I helped make students aware of the politics behind the history of its standardization as well as the current debates over its use in college writing courses.

I Heard It Through the Grapevine

My students were not the only ones struggling with the rewards and the costs of academia. One Monday morning in November, a full-time professor approached me and asked whether it was true that I was teaching students black English. I assured him that I was not qualified to teach black English. Later I found out that he had heard from tutors in the writing center that some of my students had claimed I was accepting papers written in street slang. Apparently the tutors had tried to correct the students' grammar, and the students had a hard time explaining to the tutors that they did not need to write in standardized English for those particular pieces. "You mean standard English?" the tutor had asked.

Despite the fact that my pluralist pedagogy was not always accepted with open arms, it was the strategy that worked best for my students, and it is the strategy recommended by leading African American linguists and compositionists. I accompany this essay, then, with a description of some of the activities I created as I moved to a pluralist pedagogy in the hope that more teachers will adopt a pluralist stance. The activities and assignments are tailored to classes of students who speak and write in more than just a single, "standard" language, and for teachers who see this not as a problem but as an opportunity.

References

CCCC Executive Committee. (1974). "The Students' Right to Their Own Language." [Online at http://www.ncte.org/ccc/12/sub/state1.html]

———. (1999). "CCCC Statement on Ebonics." *College Composition and Communication* 50(3): 524.

D'Souza, D. (1991). *Illiberal Education: The Politics of Race and Sex on Campus.* New York: Macmillan International.

Ehrenreich, B. (1997). "Ice-T: The Issue Is Creative Freedom." In *Elements of Argument*, edited by A.T. Rottenberg, pp. 504-506. Boston: Bedford Books.

Activities for Getting to Know Students

Previous Experiences With Writing: Have students write about their previous experiences with writing, both good and bad. Students can write about school experiences or writing that was done outside school: for example, letters, email, creative writing. To spark a class discussion about prior writing experiences, share some of these responses on an overhead or handout.

Small-Group Interviews: During the first few weeks of classes, have students meet with you in small groups. Discuss the students' goals, interests, and what they would like to write about if given the choice. Ask the students about what they read for pleasure, the kind of music they listen to, and what their favorite movies and television shows are. Keeping a list of some of this information can help you design student-centered in-class activities and essay assignments.

Activities for Teaching Invention and Drafting

Tape and Transcribe: Have students "freewrite" aloud on tape. They can pretend they have a specific audience they are telling a story to or trying to persuade in an argument. Students can then transcribe the taped argument to create a typed draft. This activity works especially well for students who have difficulty with writing because they are so focused on getting every sentence correct in standardized English that they lose the fluency they exhibit in speech.

Authority List: To generate essay or research project topics, have students create a list of things that they are an authority on and another list of things they want to know more about. Then have them use these lists to brainstorm topics to write about. Have all the students share these topics aloud to generate a list for the entire class.

Activities for Teaching Revision

Revision in Music: Have students bring in recent songs that revise earlier songs and discuss the revisions in light of revising essays. Revision is especially common in hip hop and jazz music. For example, the rap group Public Enemy's song "911 Is a Joke" uses an ironic revision of Bobby McFerrin's song "Don't Worry, Be Happy." An example from jazz is John Coltrane's revision of the Julie Andrews song "My Favorite Things," which is an excellent illustration of significant *reenvisioning*.

Revision for Audience: Have students write a letter to a friend about a funny or embarrassing incident that happened to them recently. Then have them revise the letter so that it is written to their mother, father, or a grandparent. Discuss the ways audience affects the revision of the letter.

Activities for Teaching Style

Sentence Rhythm: Have students bring in music to discuss the parallels between rhythm in music composition and rhythm in written composition.

Compare, for example, the effect on the audience of the steady repetition of a simple rap or blues beat with the more varied structure of jazz rhythms. To make the comparison to writing concrete, you can bring in essays whose sentences achieve rhythms similar to the rhythms in the songs.

AAVE and Style: Use essays, songs, stories, and poems from a variety of African American writers and singers to discuss style and AAVE varieties. I have had success using essays by Geneva Smitherman, songs from CDs my students brought in, stories from writers such as Zora Neale Hurston and Alice Walker, and poems from Langston Hughes and Ishmael Reed. This exercise can lead into a discussion about handbook rules and language. Just as there is no single "black English," there is no single "standard English."

Activities for Teaching the Rhetorical Situation

Speech Analysis: Give students speeches from African American leaders in a variety of rhetorical situations, such as Malcolm X arguing to a working-class audience in Harlem as opposed to an audience of white academics. Discuss the audience and purpose for each speech and reasons why the speech was or was not effective. This is also a good activity for teaching ethos, pathos, and logos.

Magazine Ad Analysis: Bring in magazines written to a broad spectrum of audiences, for example, *Vibe, Newsweek, Vogue, Ebony, Sports Illustrated.* Then have students choose advertisements and discuss them in terms of audience and purpose, answering questions such as Who is the target audience? What is the purpose of the ad? Is the ad persuasive? Why or why not?

Activities for Generating Discussion

Role Playing: In the format of a talk show or a panel, have students role-play representatives of different positions, with the remaining students acting as the studio audience and asking questions and joining the debate. For example, a talk show about the image of hip hop could involve students role-playing rappers, African American political leaders, and writers from various magazines.

Journals: Have students write brief, informal journal responses to class readings and share them with the class by reading them aloud to spark discussion. Another option is to have students form groups and choose one group member's journal to read aloud.

Research Projects

Ethnography: Have students observe a subculture or other close-knit group and interview members from the group. Students might discuss oral and written language use, rituals, dress, etc. Some of my students wrote about the church they attend, a local barbershop, and the black student union.

<u>Family History:</u> Have students research their family history, including interviews with family members and archival research.

<u>Investigative Journalism:</u> Have students write an investigative journalism piece about a local issue, using examples from local newspapers as models. In the past, my students have written about Jeb Bush's dismantling of affirmative action in Florida, a cut in funding for the black student union, and the handling of election balloting in predominantly African American precincts in Tallahassee.

<u>Service-Learning Projects:</u> Contact local nonprofit agencies and campus groups and inquire about writing and research projects that students can assist in. In the past, my students have created a website for a black fraternity and a resource booklet for first-generation college students.

<u>Zines:</u> Zines are student-produced magazines on popular culture topics of interest to the students. In the past, my students have created zines about underground rap music and a review of Spike Lee's movies.

<u>Multigenre Projects:</u> Multigenre projects use a variety of voices, styles, and media: black English and standardized English; poetry and fiction; expository and argumentative writing; and printed text, hypertext, video, art, and music.

Resources for Class Activities

<u>Poets, Novelists, and Playwrights:</u> Charles Chesnutt, Zora Neale Hurston, Langston Hughes, Ralph Ellison, Richard Wright, James Baldwin, Gwendolyn Brooks, Rita Dove, August Wilson, Maya Angelou, Amiri Baraka, Nikki Giovanni, Gloria Naylor, Reginald McKnight, John Edgar Wideman, Sonia Sanchez, Toni Cade Bambara, Ntozake Shange, Toni Morrison, Ishmeal Reed, Ernest Gaines, Jamaica Kincaid, Alice Walker

<u>Essayists:</u> Frederick Douglass, W.E.B. Du Bois, Eldridge Cleaver, James Baldwin, Ralph Ellison, Geneva Smitherman, Cornell West, Henry Louis Gates, bell hooks, Keith Gilyard, William Raspberry, Shelby Steele, Jacqueline Jones Royster, Arnetha Ball, Tricia Rose, Michael Eric Dyson

<u>Orators:</u> Frederick Douglass, Sojourner Truth, Marcus Garvey, Ida B. Wells-Barnett, Martin Luther King, Jr., Malcolm X, Thurgood Marshall, H. Rap Brown, Eldridge Cleaver, The Last Poets, Jesse Jackson, Carol Moseley-Braun

<u>Hip Hop Artists:</u> A Tribe Called Quest, Ice Cube, Sister Souljah, KRS ONE, Public Enemy, Queen Latifah, Dr. Dre, Cypress Hill, Tupac Shakur, Fugees, Nas, Disposable Heroes of Hiphopcrisy, De La Soul, The Roots, Busta Rhymes, Outkast, Dead Prez, Black Eyed Peas, Snoop Doggy Dogg, Nelly, DMX, Mos Def

Fox, T. (1999). *Defending Access: A Critique of Standards in Higher Education.* Portsmouth, NH: Boynton/Cook.

Gilyard, K. (1991). *Voices of the Self: A Study of Language Competence.* Detroit: Wayne State University Press.

———. (1996). *Let's Flip the Script: An African American Discourse on Language, Literature and Learning.* Detroit: Wayne State University Press.

Graff, G. (1992). *Beyond the Culture Wars: How Teaching the Conflicts Can Revitalize American Education.* New York: W.W. Norton & Co.

hooks, b. (1989). *Talking Back: Thinking Feminist, Thinking Black.* Boston: South End Press.

Rodriguez, R. (1981). *Hunger of Memory: The Education of Richard Rodriguez.* Boston: Godine.

Rottenberg, A.T., ed. (1997). *Elements of Argument.* Boston: Bedford Books.

Smitherman, G. (1986). *Talkin' and Testifyin': The Language of Black America.* Detroit: Wayne State University Press.

Wallace, D., and A. Ball. (1999). "Being Black at a Predominantly White University." *College English* 61(3): 307-327.

Community and Mexican American Students of Composition
Papeles de Honor

Jaime Armin Mejía

> If we agree to aim for a radical, transcultural democracy as [Martin
> Luther] King did, then we need pedagogies to foster the develop-
> ment of the critical and astute citizenry that would pursue the task.
> In this regard, the best strategies involve maximizing various epis-
> temologies, searching for transcultural understandings, opening up
> spaces for imaginative wanderings, for scholarly recreation. These
> are our best chances of obtaining and maintaining the widespread
> student-citizen involvement we seek. (Gilyard 2000: 262)

Mexican intellectual Gustavo Esteva has recently been advancing ideas that in some ways correlate with Gilyard's notions about developing a critical and astute citizenry to advance a transcultural democracy. For Esteva, though, a transcultural democracy has to be carefully negotiated from an almost uncompromising local position because of external threats to the autonomy and cohesion of local communities. His ideas over the autonomy of local communities revolve around a particular kind of localism whose means for maintaining autonomy have to be used today to thwart the disruptive effects globalization has had and is having in many communities in regions of southern Mexico such as Chiapas and Oaxaca.[1] His ideas are compelling to me because, in some ways, they fit quite well with how many Mexican Americans group themselves in what Chicano anthropologist Carlos Vélez-Ibáñez calls *clustered extended families*. In *Border Visions: Mexican Cultures of the Southwest United States* (1996), he shows us these types of families in an ethnographic study he conducted in Tucson, Arizona, in the 1980s.

Common to both Esteva and Vélez-Ibáñez are notions of community that are significant to us as compositionists because of how many Mexican American students compose essays in college composition classes. That is, through the relationships that members of clustered extended families form, certain types of collaborative behavior become engendered in them. I have observed these behaviors in classes I have taught for community college students during the past few summers at my university. In these classes, mainly made up of Mexican Americans

---

I presented a version of this essay as the 9th Annual Kenneth Burke Lecture, April 10, 2001, for the English Department's rhetoric program at Penn State. I thank Michael Hennessy and Cheryl Glenn for their invaluable feedback when preparing that version.

from South Texas, the students came to form a sense of community among themselves, which grew out of a common set of beliefs about how their identities are constructed from comparable funds of cultural knowledge. As they began seeing drafts of what their classmates were writing about their families' festive occasions, a sense of urgency, or what Kenneth Burke (1950) calls *earnestness*, became apparent among them because they found they had an audience sharing their unique but common family backgrounds.

In his noteworthy study of clustered families, Vélez-Ibáñez found that many Mexican American families cluster themselves around a core family of elders who guide and organize the various activities that serve to keep these families clustered together.[2] And given what are often adverse economic and political circumstances that many Mexican Americans have historically endured in the Southwest, the economic and cultural well-being of these families highly depends on this organizational structure. Simply put, there is strength in numbers, but the glue keeping these families together is specifically found in ethnically based funds of cultural knowledge. These funds of knowledge are disseminated among all the members of these clustered families, with women playing key roles in the dissemination of these funds of cultural knowledge as well as in the structure and organization of these families' activities, such as during their festive occasions.

The structure of these clustered families cultivates particular types of behavior among the younger members of these families, behaviors engendering collaboration among them all. Vélez-Ibáñez further suggests that these types of behaviors are threatened by educational strategies, which can be divisive and deleterious to students from these families because of the competitive drive ingrained in them that is often used for determining how students must behave in schools. The consumerism advanced outside schools in American society also has an adverse effect that threatens to pull these clustered families apart. But through all these adverse influences, at times pulling these families apart, a distinct kind of community is nevertheless maintained through the resilient efforts of members in these clustered families. Esteva's ideas of localism also advance similar types of notions about community formation, which are used to fight off outside influences stemming from globalization that can and often do enter and threaten to disrupt small Mexican communities.

In *Grassroots Post-Modernism: Remaking the Soil of Cultures*, Esteva and Prakash also advance the idea that the global thinking furthered by economic globalization posits the false notion that economic globalization provides everyone the necessary goods and services and raises the standard of living for all of humanity. These goods and services, they suggest, have been classified under the modern moral umbrella of "human rights" (1998: 10). But as Esteva and Prakash state, "To enjoy the shelter offered by this umbrella, people all over the world must abandon their own culturally specific local ways of living and dying, of thinking and working, of suffering or healing, of eating and defecating in order to become part of the global economy" (1998: 3). In fact, these two authors further state that:

> Academic post-modernists engaged in race, class, and gender studies, seeking to liberate multiculturalism from patriarchal [W]estern hegemony, dream of a world in which all those women and children, those classes and races deprived of their human rights in the modern era, will finally be "saved," a salvation supposedly secular and culturally neutral or transcultural. In the morally progressive, egalitarian, and just global economy of the postmodern era, every individual will enjoy exercising his or her human rights. The [W]estern recolonization inherent in the global declaration of these human rights remains as imperceptible to postmodernists as to the modernists they accuse of cultural imperialism. (11)

This type of recolonization is, as Vélez-Ibáñez maintains, precisely what Mexican American clustered families typically resist through the organization of their families and through behaviors cultivated among them in these clustered families.

For many Mexican Americans, then, the type of community in which they are raised often differs from that of other Americans not raised in such clustered, extended families. My teaching experience has shown me that when asking students to compose essays, there are often differences among them in terms of how they collaborate among themselves when composing their essays. That is, not all students readily demonstrate collaborative behavior when composing essays, so determining why these differences exist became something I pursued with my community college students over the past few summers. My assignment asking my students to write about their families' festive occasions was therefore quite fortuitous, as this assignment allowed me to understand their family backgrounds in ways other assignments would not have afforded.

This assignment thus came to work in more than one way, because as they wrote about their family backgrounds, I could observe their behavior as they composed their essays. As they went about writing their essays, I eventually learned which students came from clustered, extended families and which did not. And as they wrote their essays, the collaborative nature Vélez-Ibáñez documents as being cultivated among members of Mexican American clustered families was coincidentally confirmed at the same time. You should also know that these community college students over the past few summers have been coming to my university, Southwest Texas State University, as part of a federally funded grant program in the College of Health Professions.[3] This program seeks to recruit community college students from South Texas into three of our university's health profession fields: Respiratory Care, Clinical Laboratory Science, and Health Information Management. This program's recruitment efforts, though small, attempt to matriculate minority students, particularly Mexican American students, in these health-related fields where they are highly underrepresented.

Although not all the students have been Mexican American, that some have not been Mexican American further allows me to speculate that certain notions of community are at play among many of the Mexican American students as opposed to students not coming from such backgrounds. And though not all the students were Mexican American and even some of the Mexican Americans did not identify ethnically with Mexican culture(s), the majority of them did in significant and important ways. This identification with Mexican culture(s) by many of the Mexican American students was confirmed through the essays they composed, but what was more interesting — and important — was the way many of them composed their essays. Those Mexican American students who could more readily write about the festive occasions held by their families came from exactly the same types of clustered families Vélez-Ibáñez discusses in his study of Mexican American families. And unlike their classmates not originating from such family backgrounds, these Mexican American students unequivocally collaborated more among themselves when composing their essays. This difference in the behavior these students exhibited when composing their essays, unlike their fellow classmates who did not come from this type of family background, certainly caught my attention. That is, I believe when Mexican American students come from clustered families, they are more likely to have learned collaborative behaviors than are students not coming from such families. This observation to me signals the effect family backgrounds can have on how they compose their essays.

Not all the students in my classes, however, readily collaborated, much less engaged, in writing their essays. A few had great difficulty writing their essays about their families' festive occasions because there were indeed serious troubles in their family backgrounds. Vélez-Ibáñez's chapter "The Distribution of Sadness: Poverty, Crime, Drugs, Illness, and War" documents many disruptive troubles against which many Mexican Americans, including those from clustered extended families, must guard themselves. "What I mean by 'the distribution of sadness' is that there is no doubt that Mexicans throughout the Northern Greater Southwest into the next half century (to 2050) will face great sadness because of the effects of miseducation, poverty, physical and mental illness, crime, drugs, and overparticipation in wars" (Vélez-Ibáñez 1996: 182). The effects of these disruptive elements in the lives of many Mexican Americans as well as other minority students can indeed be overwhelming, causing some students to just balk altogether at writing essays about their families. This aspect of this assignment certainly existed for some of my Mexican American students and is therefore one composition teachers must be ready to deal with, if they are to make this type of assignment a positive one for students coming to our classes with these types of troubles.

Key to this type of assignment, though, was the subject — the festive occasions their families organize and hold throughout the year. I anticipated most of the students identifying, at some level, with this particular subject because most

Mexican American families do organize and hold festive occasions. But according to my Mexican American students, this subject was one they had never been invited to write about and analyze in all their previous schooling. Imagine going through 12 years of public schooling and a year or two of community college classes, as these students had, and never being asked to write about what is highly important in the social and cultural formation of one's identity. In some ways, this particular assignment presented all these students with an invitation to communicate what they knew to be a major part of who they are and how their identities are constructed by their families.

With this essay assignment, then, these students ostensibly became engaged with what Kenneth Burke calls "the simplest case of persuasion" (1950: 55). As he says, "You persuade a man [or a woman] only insofar as you can talk his [or her] language by speech, gesture, tonality, order, image, attitude, idea, *identifying* your ways with his [or hers]" (1950: 55). That is, this type of simple persuasive effort grounds itself in identification because, as Burke suggests:

> Identification is affirmed with earnestness precisely because there is division. Identification is compensatory to division. If men [or women] were not apart from one another, there would be no need for the rhetorician to proclaim their unity. If men [or women] were wholly and truly of one substance, absolute communication would be of man's [or woman's] very essence. It would not be an ideal, as it now is, partly embodied in material conditions and partly frustrated by these same conditions; rather, it would be as natural, spontaneous, and total as with those ideal prototypes of communication, the theologian's angels, or "messengers." (1950: 22)

So to compensate for the initial division existing among the students because they came from different community colleges, families, and even cultures, they needed to identify with themselves as a community of writers, and they needed to do so with earnestness. In other words, I had initially anticipated a common enough understanding among the Mexican American students about their family backgrounds that writing essays about and analyzing their families' festive occasions would not present too many difficulties. However, such identification among my students, which confronts the implications of division, was not as easy as I initially thought, and several complications with this assignment and how the students went about composing their essays are worth discussing here in more detail.

We, as compositionists, are now said by some composition theorists to be in a postprocess era of our profession. In Thomas Kent's *Post-Process Theory: Beyond the Writing-Process Paradigm*, for instance, the collected essays therein advance our understanding about functioning in a postprocess time, even though many of us as practitioners fail to acknowledge this about our profession. About this new postprocess paradigm, Kent states, "Most post-process theorists hold three assumptions about the act of writing: (1) writing is public; (2) writing is interpretive; and (3) writing is situated" (1999: 1). About the first assumption, Kent says,

"By 'public,' post-process theorists generally mean that the writing act, as a kind of communicative interaction, automatically includes other language users, as well as the writer" (1999: 1). He adds, "If writing is a public act — if what we write must be accessible to others — then the possibility for a 'private' writing evaporates" (1999: 1). About the second assumption, Kent says, "By 'interpretive act,' post-process theorists in general mean something rather broad, something like 'making sense of' and not just exclusively the ability to move from one code to another. To interpret something means more than only to 'translate' or to 'paraphrase'; to interpret means to enter into a relation of understanding with language users" (1999: 2).

And about the third assumption that holds writing as situated, Kent says, "writers are never nowhere" (1999: 3), because

> a communicative act is possible only because we hold a cohesive set of beliefs about what other language users know and about how our beliefs cohere with theirs. In other words, we all require beliefs that help us start to "guess" about how others will understand, accept, integrate, and react to our utterances. (1999: 3-4)

He calls this set of beliefs a "prior" theory, but says what is really important is how writers use this prior theory in the communicative act, an action he calls a "passing" theory (1999: 4). He adds, "Our prior theories do not need to match the prior theories of other people; that is, we do not need to come from the same communities, nor do we need to believe the same things about the world or even speak the same language in order to communicate" (1999: 4). But he then ironically says,

> Being positioned in relation to other language users . . . means that you always come with baggage, with beliefs, desires, hopes, and fears about the world. What matters is how we employ these beliefs, desires, hopes, and fears to formulate passing theories in our attempts to interpret one another's utterances and to make sense of the world. (1999: 4)

Generating passing theories, however, can never be reduced to a predictable and set process for composing essays, as generally held by compositionists holding to the process approach to teaching composition.

> When we write, we elaborate passing theories during our acts of writing that represent our best guesses about how other people will understand what we are trying to convey, and this best guess, in turn, will be met by our readers' passing theories that may or may not coincide with ours. This give and take, this hermeneutic dance that moves to the music of our situatedness, cannot be fully choreographed in any meaningful way, for in this dance, our ability to improvise, to react on the spot to our partners, matters most. By way of summarizing, then, post-process theorists hold that the writing act is public, thoroughly hermeneutic, and always situated and therefore cannot be reduced to a generalizable process. (Kent 1999: 4-5)

Postprocess theorists thus move beyond the process paradigm because, according to Kent, our ability to improvise with passing theories of communication will matter most, if the communicative act of writing is to have any chance of succeeding.

In "Toward a Post-Process Composition: Abandoning the Rhetoric of Assertion," Gary Olson points out other limitations of the process movement of composition. Key among these limitations is "that the process orientation . . . imagines that the writing process can be described in some way; that is, process theorists assume that we can somehow make statements about the process that would apply to all or most writing situations" (1999: 7). He adds:

> When we conceive writing as a "process" that can be codified and then taught, we are engaging in theory building. The post-modern critique of theory as totalizing, essentialist, and a residue of Enlightenment thinking has made clear that any attempt to construct a generalizable explanation of how something works is misguided in that such narratives inevitably deprivilege *the local,* even though it is precisely *the local* where useful "knowledge" is generated. (1999: 7-8, italics added)

Writing situations are thus contingent, situational, and dependent on "local" exigencies, on the complexities of the rhetorical situations writers often find themselves in when composing their essays.

Olson also states that although

> some compositionists over the years have advocated introducing into the composition class alternative kinds of essays that are less conspicuously thesis driven or argumentative, . . . even those who recommend that students write "exploratory" essays or purely personal narratives typically expect such essays to make a point or points. In short, despite our attempts to introduce alternative genres, to help students become more dialogic and less monologic, more sophistic and less Aristotelian, more exploratory and less argumentative, more personal and less academic, the Western, rationalist tradition of assertion and support is so entrenched in our epistemology and ways of understanding what "good" writing and "thinking" are that this tradition, along with its concomitant assumptions, defies even our most concerted efforts to subvert it. (1999: 9)

What Olson finds problematic with the "Western, rationalist tradition of assertion" is that teaching composition is too often associated with asserting that something is true, when the truth about all too many things is often too slippery for any of us to grasp in any absolute manner. Yet, asserting such truths is often what process-compositionists ask their students to do, when the experience of writing can actually serve other purposes entirely. The rhetoric of assertion is also problematic for Olson because, quoting Lacan, such a stance, especially in academic writing, assumes "the discourse of the master" and should obviously be resisted because it supports "structures of power and domination" (1999: 13-14).

Teaching students to produce academic writing using a process approach is thus fraught with problems many process-compositionists never anticipated. Essay assignments today should therefore resist the kinds of problems postprocess theorists suggest and should allow students to acknowledge the local exigencies from which they must improvise to practice a hermeneutic dance allowing them to search for a common set of beliefs gathered from passing theories. But the problematic nature of the rhetoric of assertion and the discourse of the master will also prove highly distracting to students if they have been previously cultivated to collaborate when seeking what the anthropologist Clifford Geertz (1983) calls "local knowledge." Moreover, essay assignments can and should serve other purposes than just replicating the rhetoric of assertion and the discourse of the master. Such alternative writing assignments, such as exploratory essays, could work to serve other perfectly viable rhetorical purposes, such as allowing students to think and write as subjects working to construct their identities.

However, I do not entirely subscribe to everything postprocess theorists advance, because students should be taught the difference between these types of assignments. By this, I mean that if students have not succeeded in assimilating the rhetoric of assertion as well as the discourse of the master, we should nevertheless show them how to understand and interpret this type of academic writing. We should obviously also make them aware of other kinds of writing that can arise from a variety of circumstances stemming not just from their academically diverse rhetorical situations but also from their cultural backgrounds. For minority students academically at risk, as well as at risk politically and economically, failing to teach these different genres of writing and the differences among them serves no good purpose.

So when I initially asked my most recent community college students to write essays about their families, I gave them Vélez-Ibáñez's chapter on clustered, extended families and the festive occasions they organize and hold. By giving them this chapter, I wanted them to have a common understanding about this topic as they composed their essays. But many students still had difficulties beginning to write because, as I have come to believe, there was an insufficient set of common beliefs among them that they could use for writing about something they had not before been asked to write about.

Vélez-Ibáñez's chapter on clustered households is in some ways an example of academic writing; yet in other ways, Vélez-Ibáñez, like Clifford Geertz, resists falling into the discourse of the master that so often distinguishes academic writing. Eventually, most of the students managed to get past the academic discourse found at the beginning of his chapter, and as they plowed on, they found that Vélez-Ibáñez discusses the festive occasions the families in his ethnographic study practiced and that very much resembled their own families' festive occasions. Included in his discussion of these occasions were the art and, yes, the rhetoric of making tamales, a topic very near and dear to the hearts and appetites of most all my Mexican American students. But what truly amazed them was his accurate and detailed description of these families' festive occasions, a description most all of the students (even the non–Mexican American students) were familiar with at some level. This description is especially amazing because the art and rhetoric of making tamales (and how women play such a large role in organizing the festive occasions that surround the making of tamales) culturally and rhetorically parallel many of the students' own families' festive occasions almost exactly.

As a result, many students identify with the families in the Vélez-Ibáñez chapter. They end up doing what many writers do: They begin *guessing* and *improvising* and generally resist following the set process for composing essays I had attempted to impose on them. The resistance by some of them to this set process, which I had foolishly imposed, was indeed quite notable. But as they began reading one another's slowly formed drafts, some of them discovered a common ground and set of beliefs about how to write their essays and about who they were culturally, as revealed in their essays. And as they did, the common ground in their rough drafts revealed their shared situatedness as writers, which further caused them to expand their drafts at an ever accelerating pace and to produce quite lengthy essays, which also included scanned photographs of their families and of themselves.

In the four classes I have taught for this grant program using the students' family backgrounds and festive occasions as the primary topic, the students eventually prided themselves on the work they did to produce their essays. And this commonly shared pride was especially the case with the last three classes after students learned to insert scanned images into their essays. This element of inserting scanned images of their families with their computers is an added feature to their composing essays, because the digital divide among minority students is unquestionably quite real. There is great value in exposing students to computers and to what these machines can do for advancing their communicative skills; learning to insert images added yet another rhetorical tool, giving them what I then thought to be a growing collective sense of agency.

Students' gaining a sense of agency, however, is not likely to happen in classes using a process approach. In "Paralogic Hermeneutic Theories, Power, and the Possibility for Liberating Pedagogies," Dobrin begins his academic essay with a provocative epigraph by Thomas Kent: "No course can teach the acts of either reading and writing" (1999: 132).[4] He then says,

> Certainly, process pedagogy is convenient; process pedagogy
> makes it easy to define texts and to write texts. We can unprob-
> lematically, clearly present a body of knowledge and evaluate stu-
> dents' abilities to absorb and rehash that body of knowledge, that
> process. So even liberatory pedagogies that promote students'
> becoming critically conscious depend on process paradigms: mul-
> ticultural readers, conflict in the classroom, and contact zones all
> prescribe processes by which students become "better" people

> and "better" writers. But these endeavors do not promote agency. Traditionally process thinking does not allow the opportunity to name the world since prescribed processes take care of the naming. This activity means learning only the processes of a particular dominant discourse and simply reinscribing sets of processes. In many ways, this activity is exactly the sort of oppressive education against which liberatory pedagogies work. (Dobrin 1999: 139-140)

Dobrin's remarks here resonate well with my teaching my students to write essays using the process approach, because they resisted working under the process paradigm.

The resistance for some of them, however, stemmed from the difficulty of how to negotiate the social, economic, and health-related troubles some of their families had to endure and overcome. So following a set process of drafting certainly seemed an insufficient means for them to become engaged in writing their essays, as most of them had other issues to deal with first. They simply had no sense of situatedness from which to negotiate these issues. What finally got them to write was creating a zone of comfort by becoming a community of writers with a common set of beliefs for formulating their "passing theories." They came to desire communicating with one another about the kinds of families they come from and the festive occasions they celebrate. This desire is clearly what compelled them to move forward as they began feeling comfortable and safe among themselves as a community of writers. Leading these efforts, though, were those students who early on collaborated the most among themselves and who coincidentally came from clustered, extended families.

Dobrin's theoretical notions about the process approach and its general failure to promote a sense of agency in students should be troubling to compositionists teaching academic writing skills to students coming from clustered, extended families. Composition classes should indeed offer students opportunities to develop skills that afford them a sense of agency over their written communicative acts. And the actual method of facilitating a writer's agency certainly remains highly problematic, as postprocess theorists suggest. Still, students' development of writing and rhetorical skills that give them a sense of agency is highly contradictory to notions of collaboration, where the sense of agency is shared. Postprocess theorists as well as those working with the process paradigm have both sought to have writers gain this sense of agency, yet they have seldom considered how this agency might play into a process that pulls communal relationships and collaborative behavior apart.

In my view, notions over a writer's sense of agency too often translate into terms supporting the "myth of the individual self." As Esteva and Prakash state,

> Neither modernists nor their post-modern academic critics dare to recognize the transmogrification of the human condition operated through the individualization of "the people." Neither seem capable of even conceiving "the good life" other than that being defined or

> sought by the individual self, more and more suffering within the unbearable straitjacket of loneliness, the dis-ease of homelessness. All that contemporary communitarians seem to be conceiving or offering are devices and techniques for plugging the contemporary individual self into social constructs [that] create the illusion of "interpersonal connectedness." (1998: 11)

Although postprocess theorists suggest that writing is public, interpretive, and situated, they fail to mention the particular publics in which interpretative acts of writing are situated for culturally diverse writers. This is why Kent's notions about "prior theories" of communication seem to me to be so barren of the cultural realities constructing the identities of so many Mexican Americans as well as other ethnic minority students. Kent's prior theories of communication sound much like the global thinking Esteva and Prakash resist with their ideas of localism. Burke's notion of identification ironically seems closer to the mark than many postprocess theorists when he states that persuasion only works when "*identifying* your ways" with the ways of your audience.

Bicultural students writing about topics originating from their backgrounds clearly present compositionists with more complex communicative and rhetorical situations. My students' collections of essays are quite notable in this regard and are indeed collections of papers of honor — *papeles de honor* — because, having discovered their common ground after dancing their passing theories of communication with and by one another, they then saw themselves as a community of writers. More important, they better understood themselves and where they came from culturally, and, after collaborating, they more earnestly sought to share with one another the essays describing their families' festive occasions. As future health professionals, these students' understanding of their varied cultural backgrounds will serve them well as astute and critical citizens, because they will better know who they are, where they come from, and how their identities are constructed. Through their comparative epistemologies of what constitutes culture in their extended families and through a transculturally negotiated understanding of one another after sharing their essays, they will better respect their differences as well as the common ground we all share as members of our communities.

Working with these community college student writers has taught me what the process paradigm in composition fails to accomplish. For students to gain agency and see themselves as a community of writers as well as a part of a larger community, they must share a common set of beliefs about how they write as members of a community with shared values. In composition classes, these beliefs should situate students with a common purpose and earnestly call them to communicate what is most important in their lives. But we should also remember that this concept of community operates collaboratively, which Vélez-Ibáñez, Esteva, and Prakash see as originating locally — from within our families and communities and not from without.

All too often, we as compositionists cast our students of color as isolated and culturally bereft individuals entering our classes without significant, culturally based behaviors they might use to advance their literacy skills. I would prefer to cast our students of color otherwise. Composition teachers should admit to, and understand the full implications of, many of our ethnic minority students' cultural backgrounds. If we recognize these backgrounds, based on important kinds of local knowledge, as transcultural epistemologies, we can then allow our students to enact, through collaborative behaviors instilled at home, a shared sense of agency that our educational practices have too often worn away or utterly ignored. Allowing our students to engage in such a shared sense of agency will better prepare them to be the astute and critical citizenry Professor Gilyard wisely calls for.

Notes

1. Esteva delivered a lecture at the University of Texas at Austin and visited with graduate students there; both events were videotaped and passed on to me by Jordana Barton from the Center for Mexican American Studies at UT-Austin.

2. See chapter four of *Border Visions* (Vélez-Ibáñez 1996: 137-181), "Living in *Confianza* and Patriarchy: The Cultural Systems of U.S. Mexican Households."

3. This grant program is the Health Careers Opportunity Program, or HCOP, which has now completed its final year.

4. Dobrin documents Kent's epigraph from his "Paralogic Hermeneutics and the Possibilities of Rhetoric."

References

Burke, K. (1950). *A Rhetoric of Motives*. Berkeley: University of California Press.

Dobrin, S.I. (1999). "Paralogic Hermeneutic Theories, Power, and the Possibility for Liberating Pedagogies." In *Post-Process Theory: Beyond the Writing-Process Paradigm*, edited by T. Kent, pp. 132-148. Carbondale: Southern Illinois University Press.

Esteva, G., and M.S. Prakash. (1998). *Grassroots Post-Modernism: Remaking the Soil of Cultures*. New York: Zed Books.

Geertz, C. (1983). *Local Knowledge: Further Essays in Interpretative Anthropology*. New York: Basic Books.

Gilyard, K. (2000). "Literacy, Identity, Imagination, Flight." In *College Composition and Communication* 52(2): 260-272.

Kent, T. (1999). "Introduction." In *Post-Process Theory: Beyond the Writing-Process Paradigm*, edited by T. Kent, pp. 1-6. Carbondale: Southern Illinois University Press.

Olson, G.A. (1999). "Toward a Post-Process Composition: Abandoning the Rhetoric of Assertion." In *Post-Process Theory: Beyond the Writing-Process Paradigm*, edited by T. Kent, pp. 7-15. Carbondale: Southern Illinois University Press.

Vélez-Ibáñez, C.G. (1996). *Border Visions: Mexican Cultures of the Southwest United States.* Tucson: University of Arizona Press.

Critically Self-Reflexive Interpretive and Pedagogical Practices for an African American Literature Course

Shelli B. Fowler

> There is a timbre of voice
> that comes from not being heard
> and knowing you are not being heard
> noticed only by others not heard
> for the same reason.
>
> — Audre Lorde (1993)

When the fact that I, a white woman, teach African American literature courses comes up in a conversation, I am often asked by white colleagues and strangers alike: "Oh . . . and what do the black students in your classes think about *that*?" I reply that I am treated as suspect until proven otherwise, and that is exactly how it should be. Most colleagues are a bit taken aback by that response, but *being suspect* is, I think, still an unavoidable part of the white teacher's role in the dynamics of race and racism that still inform our classrooms, including our "gateway," introductory African American literature courses, in the beginning of the 21st century. The historical (and ongoing) issue of white appropriations of black texts, the failure of most disciplines in higher education to actively engage in antiracist analyses of dominant ideologies and discourses, and the covert and overt racism that occurs daily on campuses across the nation mean that any teacher of ethnic texts — and in particular any white teacher of African American literature — is suspect until her or his interpretive and pedagogical practices prove otherwise.

In many university literature classrooms across the nation, the usual suspects are still predominantly white teachers in predominantly white classrooms. For many students of color in those classrooms, how the subject of race is engaged, or not, can determine whether they push open the gates and enter the discipline of English or walk the other way, uninterested and excluded. Although the American literary canon has undergone significant revision in the past two decades and though the scholarship in African American literary study (a field developed by African American scholars) has provided literary critical tools for reading the previously marginalized texts of black writers, much of this scholarship has not seemed to have made an impact on the critical reading and pedagogical strategies of many white teachers of African American literature. This is a troublesome fact for all students in literature classrooms, but it is especially problematic for students of color, who expect something different from a universal approach to literature that speaks to (and for) all humankind. And rightly so. In the 1980s, Audre Lorde took issue with white women who said "I can't possibly teach [b]lack women's writing — their experience is so different from mine" by asking in return "how many years have you spent teaching Plato and Shakespeare and Proust?" (1984: 43-44). And a decade later, Ann duCille (a black feminist scholar and critic) continues to lament the state of affairs regarding appropriative — rather than appropriate — readings of African American texts. Her warnings about "the dangers of a critical demeanor that demeans its subject in the very act of analyzing it" (1994: 612) — and, I would add, of teaching it — have yet to be heeded. Though duCille's focus is on black women writers, her assertion that "much of the new-found interest in African American women that seems to honor the field of black feminist studies actually demeans it by treating it not like a discipline with a history and body of rigorous scholarship and distinguished scholars underpinning it, but like an anybody-can-play pick-up game performed on a wide-open, untrammeled field" (603) has widespread applications for the entire canon of African American literary works taught in classrooms today. In 2002, many teachers of African American literature still have not studied either a broad range of primary texts or much (and sometimes any) of the secondary works in the field of African American literary theory and criticism, including black feminist criticism. Not doing so, I would argue, makes it next to impossible to teach the texts of African American writers appropriately and well. Without studying the field, it is difficult for any teacher to begin to acquire the "cultural literacy and intellectual competence" deemed necessary for the task of teaching these texts (duCille 1994: 603). It is not an "anybody-can-play pick-up game"; there are rules for engagement that anybody can and everybody should learn before joining the game.

Having said all that, I realize that there are practical limitations in the real world of the contemporary academy. Limited budgets at various institutions often translate into the hiring of a single multicultural literature specialist, one individual who is expected to know all and teach all under the rubric of *ethnic literatures* — plural. Some institutions, facing budgetary crises, have been unable to hire new faculty, so that faculty many years away from graduate school, faculty who did not have the opportunity to read any literature or criticism by writers and scholars of color in their program of study, have found themselves trying to retool and broaden their areas of expertise to include writers of color. Other faculty have tried to follow the lead of new anthologies and have revised their American literature survey courses to be more diverse and inclusive. Many of these faculty read widely in the critical theory before deciding how to teach the texts, and many are critically self-reflexive about their own location in relation to both the text and the classroom. But all too often, for one reason or another, some of us teach the texts without thinking much about, or talking much about, race and the difference race makes. In spite of the constraints on faculty time and increased workloads (in teaching and service arenas), we need to recognize the importance of adopting critically self-reflexive reading strategies and pedagogical practices for all teachers of African American literature. Discovering those reading strategies begins with an exploration of the African American literary theory and criticism that informs the primary texts we choose to teach. And our study of the critical approaches to African American literature must go hand in hand with figuring out how to address, pedagogically, the difference race makes in our classrooms.

Reading Accurately

A particular lyric in the En Vogue song "Free Your Mind" captures for me the essence of the issue at hand. The lyric, "Before you can read me, you gotta learn how to see me," suggests that understanding difference begins with the ability to recognize, and "see" clearly, the significance of those differences. The ability to understand how racial (and other cultural) differences impact our perceptions is crucial. Following En Vogue's order of things, learning to see differently allows us to read differently — crucial steps for white readers of African American texts. We need to learn how to recognize and understand how this tradition differs in specific and significant ways from other literary traditions.[1] Unfortunately, however, discussions about how African American literature is best taught (through questions of race politics, racial positioning, and appropriate scholarly methodology and critical approaches to the texts) continue to be viewed by some white academics as unnecessarily political. Ignoring the significance of race and racism continues to be something that many of us seem quite comfortably able to do. Yet for those of us who are white teachers of African American literature, continually attending to, and actively engaging, the politics of race should always already be a central part of our task as cultural workers in the discipline and in the classroom.[2]

It is important to note here that African American literary critics are not suggesting that only African Americans can read and understand African American texts. Since the mid-1970s, African American critics, such as Larry Neal, have argued that white scholars can learn to read the differences inherent in black texts: "The sign of critical competence lies not in the race or face of the critic but rather in the work he or she produces" (quoted in Awkward 1995: 61). The point is that learning to read effectively "is gained by academic activity — 'by studying' — in the same way that one achieves comprehension of the cultural matrices that inform the work of writers like Joyce, Yeats, and e.e. cummings." It is not an impossible task, because "the means of access for all critics, regardless of race, is an energetic investigation of the cultural situation and the emerging critical tradition" (1995: 61). An "energetic investigation" alone, however, is not in and of itself enough. If it were, we would not still be having conversations about appropriative misreadings of African American literature. There must be, combined with that scholarly investigative process, a critically self-reflexive awareness of how one's location, as a white reader and teacher who resides outside the culture, may limit our initial perceptions; that is, we are very likely to read and investigate through a dominant cultural lens, and we need to work hard to learn how to change that habit. A good part of that work begins with recognizing our unexamined assumptions, assumptions that stem from privilege. Wrestling with the blinders that accompany racial privilege and learning to see how that privilege may easily distort our vision is crucial. As Michael Awkward has argued, "Racial privilege may create interpretive obstacles or, more important, points of resistance that color, in racially motivated ways, the effects of an exploration of blackness" (1995: 60). He warns us (and signifies on us in the process) that a "caucacentric (that is, Caucasian-centered)" perspective is not useful in examining the complexity of African American literature and culture (1995: 11). In other words, readers who rely on traditional literary criticism (that is, European American literary theory) to try to make meaning of African American texts will miss much — and may well misread the text altogether. Such misreadings, to recall Ann duCille's warning, comprise a "critical demeanor that demeans the subject in the very act of analyzing it" (1994: 612).

Race matters in interpretive readings. As we study the culturally specific nuances of the African American literary tradition, we must simultaneously study the ways in which our own positioning (and dominant cultural perspective) affects our ability to grasp those culturally specific differences. By way of example, it might be helpful here to briefly examine how our insistence on seeing through a traditional lens can prevent us from reading a text effectively. I have in mind a reprinted and anthologized article by Elizabeth Fox-Genovese, one that I often discuss with students when teaching Zora Neale Hurston to explore this issue with students. In "My Statue, My Self: Autobiographical Writings of Afro-American Women" (1988), Fox-Genovese's reading of Hurston's autobiographical text *Dust Tracks on a Road* exemplifies for us the very kind of problematic reading that we need to work to avoid. Admittedly, *Dust Tracks* is not a simple autobiography — Hurston messes with, and reinvents, the autobiographical genre throughout her narrative. In her analysis, though, Fox-Genovese misses, or misreads, the culturally specific nuances of Hurston's text, wants the text to conform to traditional autobiographical conventions, and, unfortunately, diminishes the significance of Hurston's autobiography as a result.

With what seems to be an awareness of some of the major theoretical concepts that inform readings of African American texts, Fox-Genovese initially seems to recognize the "multiple — and intentionally duplicitous — self-representations" (1988: 63) of Hurston's autobiography as a textual strategy that is central to the African American literary tradition. She argues that Hurston "continually challenges us to rethink our preconceptions" (1988: 64); yet, although Fox-Genovese can name Hurston's challenge, she cannot seem to meet it. Part of the problem, I would argue, is Fox-Genovese's own inability to challenge herself to rethink her own critical preconceptions. She acknowledges "the tension between condition and discourse," which implies some understanding of the unique "ways in which black women writers have attempted to represent a personal experience of condition through available discourses" and subtly subvert those discourses, as well (1988: 65). But Fox-Genovese cannot seem to hang on to that notion of difference and tension and, instead, goes on to contradict herself in her assertion that "the special relation between the autobiographer and the final text outshines all other considerations, especially referential considerations, and reduces specific aspects of the individual history to accidents. There is no theoretical distinction to be made between Jean-Jacques Rousseau's *Confessions* and Zora Neale Hurston's *Dust Tracks*" (1988: 67). The erasing of the cultural and material historical differences between Rousseau and Hurston (as well as the significance of black feminist theory's articulations of those differences) with the sweep of a sentence steers Fox-Genovese into a wrong turn, and she seems unable to recover.

In an earlier essay, Fox-Genovese seems well aware of the kinds of resistances that African American women writers wrote against: "There is no argument about the ways in which [traditional] discourse has treated black writing, especially the writing of black women: shamefully, outrageously, contemptuously, and silently" (1987: 165), but in her critical evaluation of the text, Fox-Genovese's inability to *see* Hurston's skillful signifying keeps her from being able to *read* the text effectively. On the one hand, Fox-Genovese claims to recognize the encoding of cultural difference, yet on the other, she unwittingly dismisses the importance of that difference. She appears to be aware of the significance of signifying, of intentional indirection, in the African American discursive tradition (via her citations), and she acknowledges, but is simultaneously uncomfortable with and frustrated by, that very strategy of intentional indirection in Hurston's multiple self-representations. In the following assertion, Fox-Genovese appears to posit a critical awareness of the various ways the African American woman writer has worked to (re)create and (re)define herself in opposition to, and in subversion of, the dominant cultural definition of the black female as a disempowered entity: "Hurston does not simply 'tell it like it is,' does not write directly out of experience. The discourses through which she works — and presumably expects to be read — shape her presentation of experience even as her specific experience shapes the ways in which she locates herself in discourses" (1988: 64). Yet Fox-Genovese's apparent understanding of how Hurston "works" those discourses is severely limited by her reliance upon, and move back to, a traditional (caucacentric) literary critical view. Although she recognizes that "like the trickster of Afro-American folk culture, [Hurston] speaks with a double tongue" (1988: 65), she is impeded in her analysis of Hurston's text by her own desire for Hurston to stop changing the joke and slipping the yoke. At the same time that she applauds Hurston's propensity to speak with a double tongue, she chastises Hurston for her slippery self-representation: "Although Hurston wrote much more in the idiom of Afro-American culture, even of folk culture, . . . her text does not inspire confidence in the 'authenticity' of her self-revelation. . . . Hurston, like the storytellers on the porch whom she celebrated in *Mules and Men*, delighted in 'lying'" (1988: 78). We cannot have it both ways; if we are celebrating the idea that Hurston functions "like the trickster of Afro-American folk culture," we cannot also expect her text to conform to an unproblematized, traditional definition of an "authentic" self. Fox-Genovese's refusal to acknowledge one of the very significant cultural differences of Hurston's text — the practice of indirection and "self-concealment" — leads her to conclude that "there is nothing in *Dust Tracks* to suggest that Hurston trusted her readers" (1988: 79) and to imply that this is a weakness, a flaw, in the text. To assume that Hurston would or should "trust" her readers is to misunderstand the specific historical and cultural context within which the racially marginalized voice speaks and the intercultural context of which Hurston was both well aware and quite capable of subverting, precisely because she did not assume a bond of trust between herself and her readers. Fox-Genovese's evaluation ultimately cannot *see* the differences between Hurston and Rousseau and thus fails to *read* Hurston's autobiography with the "cultural literacy" required to avoid "demean[ing] its subject in the very act of analyzing it."[3] So along with the studying of the African American literary theory that should inform our readings of texts, we must also pay close attention to the problem of interpretive slippage, to our sliding back into the comfort zone of reading through a dominant cultural lens.

Teaching Effectively

Although the first part of the difficult work is to study the primary and secondary texts in the field with attentiveness to our location as outsiders in order to garner critical competence as readers, the ways in which we teach the texts in the classroom, our pedagogical strategies, rarely are discussed. A critically self-reflexive pedagogy is also important, arguably at all times, but particularly when teaching literatures of color. Such a pedagogy requires white teachers to be critically aware of our positionality but to do so without making the classroom all about *us*. Often that is more difficult than we might think. The privilege of whiteness, for example, has continually placed us at the center of things, with all "others" on the margins. Intellectually, in our work and in our presentation-of-self in the classroom, we often intend to disrupt the centrality of dominant cultural norms, only to find that we quickly reinscribe them at the first sign of tension or discomfort. Sometimes our response to that tension is to shut down the conversation and move completely away from the difficult topic; even worse, we might unintentionally seek affirmation from the students of color in the room that we are doing the right thing — so that *we* might feel better. Both are responses we need to avoid.

Critically self-reflexive teaching means that, first and foremost, we need to have undertaken our own in-depth analysis of the ways in which diversity issues function systemically and structurally; second, we need to engage our students in systemic analyses of race, gender, class, sexual orientation, physical ability, and nationalisms, whether the room appears to present a diverse group of students or not. A class that appears to be visibly white and straight and middle class and able-bodied is very often not. More important, though, is that engaging all students in such critical analyses is the best way to attend to the differently raced, gendered, classed, sexually identified, and abled bodies in our classroom. One of the ways to facilitate the tearing down of the gates of our "gateway" courses is by not focusing solely on the one, three, six, or 16 students of color in the classroom when we talk about race and other diversity issues. Very often, our well-intentioned but misguided attempts to make students of color feel welcome in our classes make those same students feel unwelcome, singled out for scrutiny, and often wishing that the topic of race had not been broached at all. Discussions of race should be broad and inclusive and should, for example, focus on whiteness as a racial category, on the complexities of biracial and multiracial identities, and the intersections of cultural identities.

Although some may be wondering what all this has to do with an introductory African American literature course, I would argue that *all this* is the necessary framework, the critical framing, that must be examined and discussed before (and throughout) the teaching of African American literature. It is this critical framework, focused on systemic analyses, that takes the issues, including discussions of race and racism, off the shoulders of the differently raced bodies in the classroom. The topics of race and racism, for example, are no longer simply individual problems that can be solved if we each, as individuals, agree to not be racist anymore (which is the most popular end point for many white students). It focuses on the persistence of structural inequities that perpetuate divisions across racial lines. It is the kind of framework that does not preclude students' sharing of personal experiences, but it does not make the disclosure of personal narratives, the admissions of guilt, or the declarations of "I'm not racist, but . . ." central to the task. It works to help students critique the it's-a-level-playing-field-now ideology that constitutes the received wisdom under which most of them still operate. This kind of framework for exploring how race (as well as other cultural identities) matters is essential as a foregrounding tool for reading literature by writers of color appropriately and well. We cannot expect students to have a critical analysis of race relations historically or currently when the curricula in most secondary schools in the United States (and, unfortunately, much of their postsecondary coursework) do not include such analyses, or even address diversity issues.[4] Although different students of color bring different kinds of experiential knowledge about race-based inequities and racism to the classroom, it is an error to assume that all students of color automatically enter our classrooms with a complex understanding of the structural issues that bolster the racism they have experienced. It is our job to pedagogically create learning environments in our classrooms that foster a critical consciousness about how race matters to and for all of our students — both of color and not of color.

There are likely a number of ways to go about this, and there are probably a variety of pedagogical methodologies that allow us to work with students, and learn from students as they learn from us, in the process. My preference, however, has been to attempt to apply some of the central philosophical tenets of critical pedagogy, particularly Freirean pedagogy, to accomplish this teaching task. I use the phrase *attempt to apply*, because I am wary of using the phrase *critical pedagogy* at all. As we know, *critical pedagogy* has become an overused, catchall descriptor that can mean anything from a pedagogical praxis that is informed by the works of Freire, Giroux, McLaren, Macedo, and Sleeter, among others, to the term adopted by those who, after reading Chapter Two of *Pedagogy of the Oppressed*, have begun to "allow" discussion to occur in their classrooms for the first time. The difficulty of defining and practicing critical pedagogy in a U.S. context has been an ongoing problem.[5] As Freire (1998b) told his colleague, Donaldo Macedo, "I don't want to be imported or exported. It is impossible to export pedagogical practices without reinventing them. Please tell your fellow American educators not to import me. Ask them to re-create and rewrite my ideas" (xi). One aspect of trying to develop a critical pedagogical praxis that is clear is that it is not a methods pedagogy — a methodical pedagogy that once established is static and fixed. It is a praxis that should be re-created and reinvented for each specific site in which we teach. My particular interest in critical pedagogy is that it asks us to attend to the fact that the specificity of the sociopolitical context and terrain in which we teach should directly inform our educational praxis. The process of rethinking and re-creating pedagogical praxis in relation to our sociocultural and geopolitical location grounds one in a self-reflexive, critically engaged, political, and ethical action. Freirean pedagogical philosophy asks of the educator the ability to facilitate interconnections between the specific subject matter being taught and an understanding of ourselves (students and educators) as historical, political, social, and cultural beings who are shaped by the societal context in which we study the subject matter and who, simultaneously, have the critical capacity to shape the society in which we live. It is the Freirean focus on a problem-posing education that works to foster a critical consciousness that creates the possibility of transformative social change.[6] Although discussing this issue in more extensive detail is beyond the scope of this essay, I would like to attempt to make as clear as possible my qualified and careful use of the phrase *critical pedagogy* to describe the kind of pedagogical praxis I think is most useful in developing and maintaining critically self-reflexive teaching strategies.

Some of the current debates about whether or not a critical pedagogy is actually in operation in our classrooms have focused on the issue of how power relations in the classroom are played out. The notion of how dialogue actually functions has been of particular concern.[7] Guenther and Dees, for example, argue that Peter McLaren's definition of how dialogue should work in the classroom places too much emphasis on what McLaren calls the *emancipatory power* that teachers have as they mediate between the historical and contextual power relations upon which students' realities are built and exercise "an ideological interpretation of these realities" (1999: 33). They go on to ask, "By presenting teachers as the 'great emancipators' over the 'power-structure' created student realities, . . . are we truly repositioning the power structure of our society or are we just inverting the power structure to our own theoretical/ideological perspectives by controlling classroom dialogue and ideology?" (34). Although I agree that McLaren's use of *emancipatory* is potentially problematic (if it is defined solely as a unidirectional process), I do not think it is so easily and simply the case that dialogically engaging students in a critical examination of the ideological underpinnings and seemingly invisible power relations that undergird their "'power-structure' created" realities means that we are merely "inverting the power structure" to enforce uniform agreement with our personal ideologies. At least not if the collective deconstruction of "'power-structure' created" realities is focused on fostering a critical consciousness about social inequities and social justice in our culture. That is, those who undertake the development of a critical pedagogical practice do so from a shared critical consciousness about social inequities (and the resulting discriminatory oppressions within U.S. and global cultures) that their pedagogy attempts to illuminate. It is not the case that the end result of students' dialogic wrestling with the exposure and deconstruction of U.S. dominant ideology is to simply pick a replacement ideology from a grab bag. In part, Guenther and Dees seem to have the answer to the dilemma they pose embedded within the following question (in which they articulate what they see as the challenge of adopting a critical pedagogical practice):

> How could we create meaningful shared experiences within our own classroom space that allowed for the "free interchange of varying modes of life-experience" from which our students could learn from each other and we could learn from them, while simultaneously remaining sensitive to the racist, sexist, ablest, and homophobic agenda that pervades much of our American culture? (36)

It is the teacher's job to do just that, to frame the dialogue and to negotiate and contribute to the interchanges, in order to disrupt "the racist, sexist, ablest, and homophobic agenda" whenever it rears its head. Again, that is the teacher's responsibility in the specific site of the U.S. classroom. I think this kind of pedagogical practice is, perhaps, possible to accomplish if we are careful to avoid control-and-contain dialogue (which is actually closer to a monologue by the teacher with periodic close-ended question prompts). Instead, we should focus on actively facilitating and negotiating a critical engagement with the social justice issues and inequitable relationships of power, a critical engagement that is a necessary precursor to students' "repositioning of the power structure of our society."

A critical pedagogical practice is one that, according to Freire, must be reinvented in and for U.S. contexts. So although the specific pedagogical methods may (and I would argue, should) vary depending on the site (within an institution of higher education — urban or rural, two year or four year, public or private, HBCU or predominantly white campus — within a community-based literacy campaign, within a political organization, and so forth), the goal of those methods is very similar: to foster *conscientization*. Our job as teachers is to facilitate the development of a *critical consciousness* from which one can critically analyze and "read" the ways oppression works in U.S. culture. Freirean pedagogical philosophy makes it very clear that "educational practice, whether it be authoritarian or democratic, *is always directive*" (1994: 79, italics added), but that is one crucial aspect of a Freirean praxis that I think is so often overlooked or forgotten. In our efforts to create a nonauthoritarian, student-centered learning environment, we fail to remember the site in which we work and our role as the teacher in the classroom. Sometimes, in trying not to create what Guenther and Dees call a "controlling classroom dialogue," we step almost completely out of the picture and then wonder why and how the discussion got so far off track, why and how the conversation was distressing by several students' accounts (or even worse, offended some of the students in the class). Abandoning our role as the teacher in the classroom and failing to be directive in a dialogic pedagogy is not part of a Freirean critical pedagogical practice.

> Dialogue between teachers and students does not place them on the same footing professionally; but it does mark the democratic position between them. Teachers and students are not identical, and this for countless reasons. After all, it is a *difference* between them that makes them precisely students or teachers. Were they simply identical, each could be the other. Dialogue is meaningful precisely because the dialogical subjects, the agents in the dialogue, not only retain their identity, but actively defend it, and thus grow together. Precisely on this account, dialogue does not *level* them, does not 'even them out,' reduce them to each other. Dialogue is not a favor done by one for the other, a kind of grace accorded. On the contrary, it implies a sincere, fundamental respect on the part of the subjects engaged in it, a respect that is violated, or prevented from materializing, by authoritarianism.
> (Freire 1994: 117)

To be directive and to engage with students in the dialogue but to do so not in a unidirectional hierarchy of power, to view students as teachers and the teacher as a learner (without relinquishing the role and responsibility of the teacher), are all necessary components for a critically self-reflexive pedagogical practice that attempts to apply some of the central philosophical tenets of critical pedagogy.[8]

The Freirean model of dialogue also includes the idea that the teacher should present, or frame and initially introduce, the specific topic to be discussed. "Pedagogical dialogue implies not only content, or [a cognizable] object around which to revolve, but also a presentation concerning it made by the educator for the educands" (Freire 1994: 117). In introducing the topic, by beginning with an "introductory exposition, the teacher challenges the students, who thereupon question themselves and question the teacher, and thereby share in plumbing the depths of, developing, the initial exposition" (118). Embracing this notion of a content-laden pedagogical dialogue introduced or framed by the teacher does not mean that one is buying into the notion of a static hierarchy of knowledge and knowing that places the teacher always already above the students. Although having the teacher introduce the topic acknowledges the kinds of knowledge and learning that the teacher (by training and study within a discipline) should bring to the classroom (via the role of the teacher), it does not negate the importance of the varied and diverse kinds of knowledge(s) and ways of knowing that students bring to a dialogue on the topic. Students' diverse experiences and understandings contribute to "plumbing the depths of" the topic at hand and of broadening and affecting the teacher's initial understanding, as well as their own, of the topic being discussed.

I believe, then, that it is as important for us to self-reflexively think about the ways in which we frame and introduce a topic for collective dialogue as it is for us to attend to the *how* in how we engage students in a dialogue (which determines whether it is controlling and authoritarian or not). Both these considerations are part of what constructs a critically self-reflexive pedagogical practice. Constructing a critical framework, staying vigilantly aware of the significance of our own cultural location and positionality as we focus on being democratically directive in the classroom, and facilitating students' development of a critical consciousness are necessary pedagogical strategies for creating a classroom site in which students may move far beyond the acquisition of critical-thinking skills, beyond the exhibition of problem-solving skills, and toward a *problem-posing* educational practice that recognizes students as producers of knowledge.

In what follows, I would like to focus briefly on some of the pedagogical strategies I employ at the beginning of the introductory African American literature course I regularly teach at Washington State University, which is a predominantly white institution (approximately 12 percent students of color and international students) in rural southeastern Washington state. (In an African American literature class of 35 students, there are usually about eight students of color.) Our classroom practices should enable us to provide a critical framework for discussions of race and racism, effectively negotiate student resistance(s) to such discussions, and actively facilitate an antiracist approach to the study of African American literature — all of which are crucial components in changing the way many students of color perceive our discipline.

Rather than beginning the course immediately with readings from the anthology, I spend the first week or two introducing the topic of cultural identities and helping students learn to critically engage the topic of race.⁹ I talk about my own racial location as a white woman teaching African American literature and ask them what difference they think that does or does not make. I begin this process of constructing a critical framework for the course by telling students that talking about race and other diversity issues is a difficult and sometimes uncomfortable task, mainly because we are not encouraged or taught how to do so in our schools or within the larger society. In fact, most of us operate under the notion that talking about difference divides. I make it clear early and often that examining the complexities of race, class, gender, sexuality, and disability is not about making anyone feel guilty or defensive or put on the spot. I also make it clear at the start that the information I will present examines the inequities of race, class, and gender stratification and that I am coming from the viewpoint that we do not yet have social justice in American society. I tell students that they do not need to agree with my viewpoint, that they do not have to change their views, but that they do need to engage the course material, even if only to disagree with it. Because the information that I introduce in the first part of the class does not represent, for most of them, the normative view of our society with which they are familiar (usually a mainstream view that uncritically celebrates the status quo), telling them out loud that they need not agree with the alternative views presented actually allows them to be a little less defensive. This very often works to create, for many students, the intellectual space to begin to critically examine what stereotypical assumptions they do or do not hold and what resistances they do or do not harbor toward the process of talking about race and diversity. Perhaps because they are reminded that they are free to disagree, many white students seem to lose the need to do so automatically. Many of the white students, who seem initially reluctant to participate in dialogues that center on critical analyses of race and racism in contemporary culture, are less likely to feel compelled to voice the kind of knee-jerk, defensive disagreement that stems from a fearful need for self-preservation. And for many of the students of color, there is much less anxiety about whether or not to contribute to the dialogues when they realize that they will not be asked (directly or indirectly) to serve as spokespersons for their race.

I also repeat, early and often, that it is no one's fault in the room that inequities and discrimination exist in our society: No one in the classroom created the social structures in which we live. I work to take the discussion off the individuals in the room as I introduce the concept of examining the issues systemically. I have found that students can move from the systemic level back to the individual level with much more productivity than the other way around. Focusing on structural inequities also helps curb the sharing of what bell hooks calls *confessional narratives* merely for the sake of sharing confessional narratives; that is, without a critical framework within which to examine and evaluate their individual experiences, students very often remain entrenched in the ideology of individualism as part of their sharing of, and listening to, personal narratives. Although I agree with bell hooks's assertion that an "engaged pedagogy" empowers students and teachers alike, I disagree with the idea that an engaged pedagogy should focus on asking students or teachers "to share, to confess" (1994: 21). Although confessional discourse has its place in other settings, I do not think the classroom is necessarily one of them. The classroom in higher education functions best, I think, as an intellectual and analytical site where the personal can and should be engaged at moments, but where the personal or confessional narrative is not the primary way of knowing.

Following this setting of a context in which issues of race and racism will be examined, I talk about the power of language in shaping how we think about cultural issues. As a class, we collectively focus on the ways in which derogatory language constructs and sustains racist stereotypes. I then ask students to identify the dominant cultural values for the identity markers we have listed, and they have no difficulty doing so. For the dominant culture's valuing of racial identity, they list white; for gender, they list male; for socioeconomic class, they list upper middle class; for sexuality, they list heterosexual; for ability, they list able-bodied. Students often also suggest that Christianity is valued as the dominant religion and that youthful and fit serve as the dominant values for the identity marker of age. We talk about the social construction of cultural identities and the points of intersection that can occur within the list of identity markers they have created. At this point, it is often useful (particularly with a predominantly white classroom) to discuss the ways that an individual may garner unearned cultural privilege because of one or more of the dominant cultural identities she or he possesses but may simultaneously experience a lack of cultural privilege, or discrimination, based on her or his possession of one or more of the identity markers not valued in the dominant cultural ideology. I ask students to describe an individual who may have racial privilege but may not necessarily have other cultural privileges. Students are quick to talk about how that works and usually offer up several examples in which a white individual may lack class privilege, or gender privilege, or may not be heterosexual, able-bodied, or Christian. It is important, though, to try to avoid playing what is sometimes referred to as *oppression olympics*, an event in which racially privileged students (usually as a way to ease the discomfort around examining how unearned racial privilege is gained at the expense of those without access to such cultural privilege) want to focus exclusively on how they, too, have been oppressed in other ways. It is also helpful, in attempting to facilitate a critical awareness about how the social construction of identities operates, to ask students why class privilege, for example, will not always guarantee freedom from discrimination. I ask for an example, and students are often familiar with the existence of racial profiling and how such profiling may mean that an African American male of upper-middle-class economic standing may be pulled over while driving in the wealthy suburb where he lives simply because of the racist assumptions that inform the officer's decision to stop him. Students work to explore the ways in which not all cultural identities and cultural privileges function in exactly the same way.

After constructing this much of a critical framework for our dialogues, we watch a short video, *Talking About Race, Parts I and II*, which consists of selected footage from the much longer documentary *Skin Deep*. It is important to introduce the video before viewing it. Students should know ahead of time that the film consists of a racially diverse group of college students, very close to their own age, who volunteer to go on a retreat and talk about race with one another. In the video, students voice very different opinions, and a couple of heated moments occur in the large- and small-group conversations. In the clips, we follow six or seven students through their processes of learning to talk about race. I ask my students to pay specific attention to the different views being expressed and to note whether there are any noticeable changes in any of the students we follow through the retreat.[10] After watching the video, we have our first extended discussion. To get as many people as possible involved in the conversation, I begin by having students in small groups of two or three, each with the task of discussing the strengths and weaknesses of the position of one of the individuals in the film. We then reconvene as a group and begin our collective discussion. Because we have already established a critical framework for examining diversity issues and have primarily focused on discussing systemic issues (rather than personal opinions and experiences), students tend to analyze the different student positions in the video by referring back to our discussions on the power of language, the ways we "read" race and "are read" racially (whether or not we intend to be), and so forth. I initiate a dialogue, and am directive, for example, by periodically problematizing a comment further. The focus, however, is on encouraging the students to wrestle with the issues raised in the video themselves. I work to engage *with* them, rather than present more information *to* them.

I am the first to admit that I had to learn the hard way about the importance of providing a critical framework *before* asking students to engage with such a fraught topic in our contemporary culture. The first time I used this video in a class, I did not initially create a critical framework or set up or introduce the film before we watched it. I thought that the video would somehow magically do the work that I was not sure how to do in initiating a discussion about race. The effort had disastrous results. In that class, after the video was over, one of the white students felt empowered to voice his personal opinion that, in his experience, racial discrimination does not really exist anymore and individuals of color who complain are just trying to get ahead without working as hard as others have to. This comment was quickly followed by an emotional outburst from another white student, who vehemently disagreed with his view. My attempts to intervene and redirect were not very successful. The classroom tension was palpable, and students were defensive and resistant as well as fearful of engaging the issue at all. The belief that everyone is entitled to his or her own opinion seemed to be the prevailing sentiment. I had not provided any critical context for trying to understand the range of sentiments expressed on the video. Pedagogically, I had inadvertently and quite unintentionally created the opportunity for further entrenchment on the part of white students, who for the most part had no desire to think about racial inequities, and I did nothing but further alienate (and irritate) the few students of color in the class. I attempted to decipher and explain what I thought had occurred, and we went on to reading the literature, but we never really collectively recovered during that semester.

The next important transition requires moving from the broader, critical cultural analyses to the more specific interpretive readings of African American literature. Before providing some background information on some of the specific literary traditions and interpretive theories that inform African American literature, I assign two short stories. The first is Charles W. Chesnutt's 1899 story "The Passing of Grandison," and the second is Toni Morrison's 1983 story "Recitatif." Students are asked only to keep in mind the question, "What difference does race make in reading African American literature?" Otherwise, students bring whatever interpretive skills they have learned in previous literature courses, as well as their unexamined assumptions about racial differences, to the texts.

We begin with Chesnutt's short story. In "The Passing of Grandison," Charles Chesnutt signifies on Colonel Owens as the Southern slaveholder who believes so fiercely in the institution's paternalistic mythology of the happy and loyal slave that he is unable to recognize, and "read," the ways in which Grandison subtly and repeatedly outwits him. Yet he also signifies on any reader who, like Colonel Owens, cannot see beyond the dominant cultural mythology that defined slaves as docile, childlike, and in need of protection.[11] Chesnutt's text challenges his reader (both the reader of 1899 and the contemporary reader) to recognize Grandison's agency throughout the story, while he portrays Grandison's character as menial and diffident. Fooled, perhaps, by the passive construction in the story's title and also, perhaps, by their unexamined assumptions about both the dialect in which Grandison speaks and a lack of awareness about various kinds of slave resistance, some number of students do not, on their first reading, see that Grandison has outmaneuvered both Dick Owens and his father, Colonel Owens. As different interpretations of the story are voiced during the discussion, the issue of why Chesnutt would confuse or trick his readers often arises. I ask students whether they think an awareness of race and racism might be of importance in trying to understand this short story, and very often at least one student (either a white student or a student of color) will respond that maybe Chesnutt is intentionally drawing the readers' attention to the racist assumptions we may hold about a slave's ability to outsmart a white slaveholder. After reading and talking about Chesnutt's story, I ask students to read the introductory chapter of the anthology for our next class session. The introductory essay gives a broad overview of some of the unique and defining features of the African American literary tradition and, by showing the significance of, for example, the African American text that "talk[s] black" and in doing so, "talk[s] back" (Gates and McKay 1997: xxviii), provides students with background information for a more detailed presentation on the signifying practices that inform the literature they will be reading for this course. I have found that it is usually more productive to begin with the Chesnutt story and then talk about specific African American literary practices than it is to come at it the other way around. I think because the Chesnutt story catches some readers off guard, more of the class seems to be curious, engaged, and more attentive to a discussion about African American literary theory *after* they have experienced reading Chesnutt's story.

Before we focus on some of the theories that inform our reading of the literature, though, we also talk about Toni Morrison's short story. The students are often eager to jump from 1899 to 1983 and generally feel much more comfortable and confident with their interpretations of "Recitatif." It often surprises them to discover that not everyone shares the same "read" of the text. "Recitatif" is the story of two women, Roberta and Twyla, who meet in the St. Bonny's shelter when they are eight years old and who periodically encounter each other through their late 20s. When Roberta and Twyla meet, Twyla tells us "we looked like salt and pepper standing there and that's what the other kids called us sometimes" (1983: 423). Other than this reference that indicates that one of the girls is white and one is black, there are no other racial markers to clarify who is white and who is black.[12] Most readers assume they know who is who almost immediately. Morrison, however, very intentionally messes with the reader's unexamined cultural assumptions about race and racist stereotypes throughout the text. For example, when Twyla first meets Roberta, she tells us, "Mary, that's my mother, she was right. Every now and then she would stop dancing long enough to tell me something important and one of the things she said was that they never washed their hair and they smelled funny. Roberta sure did. Smell funny, I mean" (422). Students often cite Twyla's remark as one that proves Twyla is white and Roberta is black. A student who disagrees with that pronouncement will often point to the place in the text where Roberta and Twyla meet by chance for the second time to argue that Roberta is the white character. Twyla tells us that Roberta

> was waiting for me and her huge hair was sleek now, smooth
> around a small, nicely shaped head. Shoes, dress, everything love-
> ly and summery and rich. I was dying to know what happened to
> her, how she got from Jimi Hendrix to Annandale, a neighborhood
> full of doctors and IBM executives. Easy, I thought. Everything is
> so easy for them. They think they own the world. (429)

Yet when asked what evidence supports these interpretations, students quickly realize that they are relying on a racist stereotype or an unexamined assumption about race and class to make such assessments. At this point, most of the students are confused and desperate to know once and for all which character is white and which is black. This, of course, is exactly Morrison's point in not clearly marking the racial identity of each character. Driven by our need to know, we run right up against the racism and classism we harbor, which, again, is Morrison's point. Once students figure out that there is (intentionally) no answer to their questions about the racial identity of the two main characters, they get very interested in pointing out where and how the story makes readers examine their assumptions. And, again, they tend to do that work with an attentiveness that they have already begun to develop through their work in engaging diversity and social justice issues structurally and systemically rather than only from the context of personal experience. Reading these two stories (following the critical framework with which the course begins) makes students much more critically aware of ways to engage the question of what difference race makes in the reading of African American literature. They are able to hear that question differently from the way they do initially — it is not a question of biology determining reading ability but of a cultural competence that is formed by critically analyzing (and disrupting) the dominant cultural ideology that informs their understanding of race, racial identities, racial inequities, and racism.

One of the best ways to tear down the gates that surround our discipline is to develop critically self-reflexive interpretive and pedagogical strategies that are context-specific to the sites in which we teach. If the complexities of race, class, gender, sexuality, and disability are effectively and competently raised and engaged in all our classrooms (regardless of the demographics), we will change the learning experience for both "traditionally marginalized" and "traditional" students so that the normative pedagogical praxis in each of our classrooms works to break down such distinctions and fosters dialogic learning and critical consciousness for all the students we teach.

Notes

1. Although the En Vogue song also suggests that we should be "color blind," the effort to ignore race usually results in a shallow (and inaccurate) assessment that declares contemporary U.S. culture a level playing field and then attempts to move beyond multiculturalism to a postethnic America where we do not need to recognize difference. The desire to see one another only as members of the human race is an admirable one, but if that goal is to be achieved, it must follow our struggle to understand how racism is perpetuated systemically and our efforts to eradicate racial inequities.

2. See, for example, Giroux 1992. Giroux suggests that rather than defining the work teachers do "through the narrow language of professionalism," we should redefine teachers as cultural workers who not only "need to unravel . . . the ideological codes, representations, and practices that structure the dominant order" but also need to "acknowledge 'those places and spaces we inherit and occupy, which frame our lives in very specific and concrete ways, which are as much a part of our psyches as they are a physical or geo-

graphical placement.' The practice of social criticism becomes inseparable from the act of self-criticism; one cannot take place without the other" (78-79). For discussions about white privilege and pedagogical practices, see Rodriguez and Villaverde 2000.

3. For examples of more useful, "culturally literate" interpretive readings of Hurston's autobiography, see Hemenway 1977, who notes that the text was "written self-consciously with a white audience in mind" and recognizes that Hurston's text does not fall within the traditional boundaries of the autobiographical genre (278). See also "Autoethnography: The An-Archic Style of *Dust Tracks on a Road*" (Lionnet 1989: 97-129).

4. See Loewen 1995.

5. For an in-depth analysis of the problem with misreadings and misapplications of Freirean pedagogy, see Villanueva 1991.

6. The discussion of transformative social change is not meant to suggest that educational practices alone will generate such change. As Freire has said, "It is true that education is not the ultimate lever for social transformation, but without it transformation cannot occur" (1998b: 37).

7. See Burbules 2000 for an extensive discussion of the problematics of dialogue that exerts "a kind of hegemonic dominance that belies its emancipatory rhetoric" (251).

8. For further discussions of the concept of teachers as learners, see Freire 1994 (particularly Chapter Two), 1998a, 1998b (particularly pp. 55-68); Macedo 1994 (particularly pp. 99-124).

9. Attempting to facilitate students' critical awareness and examination of the political economy of race and racism is not always an easy task. As James Charlton suggests in his examination of disability oppression, "The greatest challenge in conceptualizing oppression of any kind is understanding how it is organized and how it is reproduced" (1998: 29). Focusing students' attention on how racial groups are positioned in relation to "economic production and exchange" as well as in relation to "political power and privilege" (1998: 23) is an effective way to direct their intellectual attention toward structural and systemic issues and away from the desire to view race and racism solely as a unique, individual experience.

10. For teachers interested in these video clips, Iris Films provides a facilitation guide with the purchase of the video. See Reid 1995.

11. Even though Chesnutt's text seems at points to very clearly show the gullibility (and even stupidity) of the slave owner, some students continue to focus on a literal reading of Grandison's actions rather than question Colonel Owens's interpretation of events. For example, in the following passage, Colonel Owens tells his son, Dick, what explains Grandison's four-week-long absence from the Kentucky plantation. Although Chesnutt does not intend for the reader to take Grandison's telling of events as the literal truth, very often a few students will not question Colonel Owens's belief that Grandison is telling the absolute truth.

> I was coming along the road three miles away, when I heard some one call me from the roadside. I pulled up the mare, and who should come

> out of the woods but Grandison. . . . I was never more astonished in my life. You could have knocked me down with a feather. He seemed pretty far gone, — he could hardly talk above a whisper, — and I had to give him a mouthful of whiskey to brace him up so he could tell his story. It's just as I thought from the beginning, Dick; Grandison had no notion of running away; he knew when he was well off, and where his friends were. All the persuasions of abolition liars and runaway niggers did not move him. But the desperation of those fanatics knew no bounds. . . . They actually kidnapped him — just think of it! — and gagged him and bound him and threw him rudely into a wagon, and carried him into the gloomy depths of a Canadian forest, and locked him in a lonely hut, and fed him on bread and water for three weeks. . . . Grandison escaped, and, keeping his back steadily to the North Star, made his way, after suffering incredible hardships, back to the old plantation, back to his master, his friends, and his home. (1899: 543)

12. Toni Morrison talks about how language is so predictably "racially informed" and that "Recitatif," the only short story she has written, "was an experiment in the removal of all racial codes from a narrative about two characters of different races for whom racial identity is crucial" (1993: xi).

References

Awkward, M. (1995). *Negotiating Difference: Race, Gender, and the Politics of Positionality*. Chicago: University of Chicago Press.

Burbules, N.C. (2000). "The Limits of Dialogue as a Critical Pedagogy." In *Revolutionary Pedagogies: Cultural Politics, Instituting Education, and the Discourse of Theory*, edited by P.P. Trifonas, pp. 251-273. New York: RoutledgeFalmer.

Charlton, J.I. (1998). *Nothing About Us Without Us: Disability, Oppression and Empowerment*. Berkeley: University of California Press.

Chesnutt, C.W. (1899, 1997). "The Passing of Grandison." In *The Norton Anthology of African American Literature*, edited by H.L. Gates, Jr., and N.Y. McKay, pp. 532-544. New York: W.W. Norton & Co.

duCille, A. (1994). "The Occult of True Black Womanhood: Critical Demeanor and Black Feminist Studies." *Signs: Journal of Women in Culture and Society* 19(3): 591-629.

Fox-Genovese, E. (1987). "To Write Myself: The Autobiographies of Afro-American Women." In *Feminist Issues in Literary Scholarship*, edited by S. Benstock, pp. 161-180. Bloomington: Indiana University Press.

———. (1988). "My Statue, Myself: Autobiographical Writings of Afro-American Women." In *The Private Self: Theory and Practice of Women's Autobiographical Writings*, edited by S. Benstock, pp. 63-89. Chapel Hill: University of North Carolina Press.

Freire, Paulo. (1994). *Pedagogy of Hope: Reliving Pedagogy of the Oppressed*. New York: Continuum Publishing Co.

———. (1998a). *Pedagogy of Freedom: Ethics, Democracy, and Civic Courage*. Lanham, MD:

Rowman & Littlefield Publishers.

———. (1998b). *Teachers as Cultural Workers: Letters to Those Who Dare Teach*. Boulder, CO: Westview Press.

Gates, H.L., Jr., and N. McKay, eds. (1997). *The Norton Anthology of African American Literature*. New York: W.W. Norton & Co.

Giroux, H.A. (1992). *Border Crossings: Cultural Workers and the Politics of Education*. New York: Routledge.

Guenther, D.E., and D.M. Dees. (1999). "Teachers Reading Teachers: Using Popular Culture to Reposition the Perspective of Critical Pedagogy in Teacher Education." In *Popular Culture and Critical Pedagogy*, edited by T. Daspit and J.A. Weaver, pp. 33-54. New York: Garland.

Hemenway, R. (1977). *Zora Neale Hurston: A Literary Biography*. Urbana: University of Illinois Press.

hooks, b. (1994). *Teaching to Transgress*. New York: Routledge.

Lionnet, F. (1989). *Autobiographical Voices: Race, Gender, Self-Portraiture*. Ithaca, NY: Cornell University Press.

Loewen, J.W. (1995). *Lies My Teacher Told Me: Everything Your American History Textbook Got Wrong*. New York: Simon & Schuster.

Lorde, A. (1984). "The Transformation of Silence Into Language and Action." In *Sister/Outsider*, pp. 40-44. Trumansburg, NY: Crossing Press.

———. (1993). "Echoes." In *The Marvelous Arithmetics of Distance*. New York: W.W. Norton & Co.

Macedo, D. (1994). *Literacies of Power: What Americans Are Not Allowed to Know*. Boulder, CO: Westview Press.

Morrison, T. (1983, 1995). "Recitatif." In *Ancestral House*, edited by C.H. Powell, pp. 422-436. Boulder, CO: Westview Press.

———. (1993). *Playing in the Dark: Whiteness and the Literary Imagination*. New York: Random House.

Reid, F., producer and director. (1995). "Talking About Race." Berkeley, CA: Iris Films.

Rodriguez, N.M., and L.E. Villaverde. (2000). *Dismantling White Privilege: Pedagogy, Politics, and Whiteness*. New York: Peter Lang.

Villanueva, V. (1991). "Considerations for American Freireistas." In *The Politics of Writing Instruction: Postsecondary*, edited by R. Bullock and J. Trimbur, pp. 247-262. Portsmouth, NH: Boynton/Cook.

Coalition Pedagogy
Building Bonds Between Instructors and Students of Color

Charise Pimentel and Octavio Pimentel

In this essay we hope to illustrate both theoretical and practical means of creating an antiracist classroom, which is ultimately thought to contribute to the success of students of color in higher education. The pedagogy we explore in this chapter is called *coalition pedagogy*. It largely builds upon Freire's critical pedagogy while addressing the many difficulties professors have encountered when implementing critical pedagogy in diverse and predominantly white classrooms. Through the use of coalition pedagogy in freshman-level writing classes, we hope to show that students gain a greater understanding of their political circumstances and a more developed skill level in writing, despite being in a classroom that is predominantly white.

Coalition Pedagogy

In our implementation of coalition pedagogy, we attempt to address the issues of inequities in diverse and predominantly white classrooms. For a student of color in a predominantly white class, we recognize that this student may not want to assert him or herself in the face of white students who may reject and denounce his or her comments. We believe that this is not a far-fetched possibility, as people of color are shunned on a daily basis for their beliefs, cultures, and languages. In fact, Shor (1992) confirms this reality when he discusses his remedial writing course, stating that despite encouragement, the few students of color in his class remained relatively silent.

With coalition pedagogy, we provide the reading and direction for class discussions for about the first five to six weeks of the semester. Much different from Shor's implementation of critical pedagogy, in which he begins class discussions with *generative themes* — themes "about things students already know and talk about *uncritically* every day" (58), we begin with what Shor refers to as the *topical theme* — "an original and critical conversation about social issues not yet being discussed in daily life, not being studied critically in the standard syllabus and not being reported meaningfully in the media" (58). Thus, during the initial part of the semester, we have students read articles and book chapters that address critical issues on oppression. Some of these readings include excerpts from Kozol's *Savage Inequalities: Children in America's Schools* (1991), Villanueva's *Bootstraps: From an American Academic of Color* (1993), Du Bois's *The Souls of Black Folk* (1989), Takaki's *A Different Mirror: A History of Multicultural America* (1993), and Nieto's

Affirming Diversity: The Sociopolitical Context of Multicultural Education (2000). During these first five or six weeks, we as instructors voice our political viewpoints through the readings themselves and verbally in class discussions. By voicing our political viewpoints, we begin to identify with and build coalitions with students who experience oppression on an ongoing basis, many of whom are students of color. Relationships are built with these students so that they will feel comfortable to voice their own opinions later in the semester. The coalition that we build with our students is often fostered by similar critical viewpoints on oppression that may be shared between the student and the instructor. We recognize that a critical perspective is in large part a reflection of one's firsthand experiences with oppression as a result of being Latino, lesbian, female, etc. In coalition pedagogy then, instructors are encouraged to make both their identities and viewpoints evident so that students who share these similar backgrounds can start exploring a potential relationship with the instructor. For example, as instructors in our writing classes, we have created relationships with students in these classes by seeking and exploring the similarities in viewpoints we share with our students. We have found that the relationships we have built in our classes based on these similarities in experiences and perspectives are pivotal to the trust that is needed for oppressed students to eventually feel safe in our classrooms to voice their opinions. In this sense, we concur with Ellsworth when she states, "We [the students and professor] agreed that a safer space [in the classroom] required high levels of trust and personal commitment to individuals in the class" (1992: 108).

We also recognize that although we are making our critical perspectives evident through our readings and verbal stances we make in our classes, we are not creating openings for white and/or conservative students in our classes. We understand that these students may be unaware of the issues we raise in class and as a result may remain quiet or voice uncritical perspectives in class. Even though white and/or conservative students may not participate fully at the beginning of our classes, we have not found that these students shut down or hold grudges toward us or the students of color in our classes. In fact, we constantly try to connect with the white and/or conservative students in our classes on a one-on-one basis to assess how they are processing the information being presented in our classes. In these conversations, we actually find that white and/or conservative students, although initially verbally inactive in class, are learning from the critical perspectives being presented in our classes. For example, because our first five to six weeks are dedicated to a critical curriculum on oppression, we find that white and/or conservative students are more likely to choose topics in subsequent assignments that are also critical. Indeed, we do not provide a space for students to write uncritical essays on topics such as assimilation or English-only legislation. As a result, many white and/or conservative students end up choosing topics later in the semester that are critical issues — issues that they have not likely taken up before in research projects. In this sense, we feel that white and/or conservative students learn a great deal when they explore and research critical topics that are new to them. We also feel that the white and/or conservative students' learning experience is enhanced when the students of color in class express their critical viewpoints on the topics being explored by the white and/or conservative students.

An important aspect of coalition pedagogy, then, is a push for a critical curriculum on oppression. Researcher Grace Scering (1997) writes that critical pedagogy is an excellent teaching style because of the focus on the political and value-oriented contexts of educational practice and because of its questioning the dominance of economic and cultural formations concealing the instrumental connection of society and schools. Coalition pedagogy aims to expose those systems that are responsible for our ongoing oppression. Coalition pedagogy also encourages, whenever possible and if the class is willing, a teaching pedagogy where students become active participants in their learning. Students are encouraged to speak up in class, and, as will be seen in the next section, they become responsible for picking topics for their essays and presentations at the end of the semester. In this sense, students are not fed information without being able to respond to it, as in banking education. In fact, especially at the beginning of the semester, we encourage students to voice their opinions, critical or not, as these comments often provide opportunities for us as instructors to openly agree or disagree with viewpoints and thus make our political stances evident.

We have found our conception of coalition pedagogy to be successful in our classrooms. In the following section, we share some of our classroom experiences to demonstrate our success.

Coalition Pedagogy in the Classroom

To illustrate the effectiveness of coalition pedagogy in increasing the likelihood that a student of color will have a successful experience in a class, this section shares our experiences in using coalition pedagogy in the freshman-level writing classes that we teach at the University of Utah. As stated in the previous section, we begin our classes by providing the students with critical readings on oppression and leading the students in discussions on these readings.

During the third week of one of Octavio's classes, Octavio led a discussion on the effects of English-only legislation. In this class session, Octavio made it very clear to his students that he believed that all English-only movements are racist and that restricting the language of a people is against our civil rights. During this discussion, Octavio also did a little *code-switching* in English and Spanish so that the students would remember that he was a Spanish speaker and so that he could identify with the two Mexicanos in the class, who were also bilingual in Spanish and English. Octavio's code-switching involved only a word here and there in Spanish and primarily consisted of words that could be easily translated (i.e., *el gobierno, los Mexicanos, Mexico, Inglés*, etc.) as a way to not lose those in the class who were not fluent in Spanish but also to make it evident that bilingualism is something that he values. To Octavio's surprise, about one-fourth of the class was fairly fluent in Spanish, as they had lived in Latin American countries for two years while serving their missions for the Mormon Church.

The issue of English only was definitely a controversial one in this class. Despite many students' being bilingual in either Spanish and English or other languages, nearly half the class argued that English-only legislation was the best way for immigrants to fit into the American culture and have access to the American dream. Many students drew on their mission experience to argue that they had to learn the language of the country they visited and that the same ought to occur here in the United States. It became evident to Octavio during this discussion that Leticia, the only Mexicana in class, disagreed with the English-only comments being made by students. She squirmed in her seat with discomfort and often shook her head back and forth as a way to nonverbally disagree with the comments being made. Finally, toward the end of the class hour, Leticia spoke up for the first time. She argued to the class, "As Americans, we should be forced to learn other languages instead of asking ethnic minorities to learn English. Learning other languages could help eliminate the racism that exists in the United States." Leticia's comment sparked much discussion in the class, as many students questioned Leticia's premise that racism still exists in the United States and implicitly suggested that racism was a thing of the past. Octavio intervened at this point and asked the class whether they could name some ways that racism still exists in our society. Leticia, another Mexicano, a Chinese American, and other white students testified to ongoing and current manifestations of racism. Leticia, for example, talked about how she had been placed in special education classes because of her last name and because English was her second language.

Octavio's intervention here in the class discussion was critical, because it moved the conversation away from a theme that suggested racism was a social ill of the past and instead moved the conversation to present-day forms of racism. Important here is that Octavio's question asked not whether racism still exists but in what ways does it still exist. This wording allowed students who knew racism still exists an entry into the discussion that was being dominated by conservative viewpoints. When several students confirmed that racism does exist by providing personal examples and by turning to the readings for additional examples, a moment of contradiction occurred for the students who were denying the existence of racism. Many of these same students who were denying racism later, in subsequent class discussions, shared their recent experiences of witnessing racism. As the semester progressed, Leticia became a more active participant in classroom discussions, which facilitated Leticia's as well as many white students' understanding of the role oppression plays in their lives. Thus, in this class, Leticia's interaction with the larger class was influential in developing a critical consciousness about oppression.

Octavio's subtle invitation to include Leticia and her viewpoints as part of the class discussion was appreciated by Leticia, as was evidenced on the morning of the next class session, when she arrived in class before any of her classmates to deliver Octavio a jalapeño bagel with cream cheese. In addition to the bagel, Leticia delivered a verbal "thank you" to Octavio for making her feel welcome in the class. Octavio talked to Leticia for a little time before class in Spanish, telling her that he agreed with the statements she made in class and that he appreciated her having the courage to state them. During this conversation, Leticia revealed to Octavio that she felt very intimidated by all the *gavachos* in the class but felt that she had to speak up to them.

For Charise, a white woman, it is especially important that she find ways to demonstrate to her class that she is a "border crosser" — that is, bilingual in Spanish and English, bicultural in Mexican and white American cultures, and very aware of the many ways in which race plays out on a daily basis. These aspects of Charise are not readily evident to students from her appearance alone, so Charise tries to make these qualities evident in class discussions. In other words, Charise tries to prohibit students from making the assumption that she is an ally to those who have conservative viewpoints. Ellsworth notes the importance for white teachers of making their critical perspectives evident to students when she discusses how her own class could have done this better:

> White students/professors should have shared the burden of educating themselves about the consequences of their white-skin privilege and to facilitate this, the curriculum should have included significant amounts of literature, films, and videos by people of color and white people against racism so that the students of color involved in the class would not always be looked to as "experts" in racism. (1992: 108)

We further argue that it is important not only to relieve students of color and antiracist whites from doing the majority of teaching in class about issues of racism but also for teachers to create entries into class discussions for students of color who are overwhelmingly silent in the classroom. In the second week of Charise's writing class, she was able to provide one of these entries for participation. The class was discussing some readings from Kozol's *Savage Inequalities*, focusing primarily on the poor physical education programs and facilities in inner-city schools that Kozol writes about. For example, we talked about how the students at one of the schools in Kozol's study had no gymnasium or outside fields, so the students ran track in the hallways of their school building. Many students in class talked about this issue on an economic level, attributing low academic achievement to low-income students and their families. During this discussion, Charise changed the focus of the discussion by introducing the construct of racism. She expressed her viewpoints about the decisions that are made regarding the services and supplies many inner-city schools receive and stated that these decisions are largely based on racist beliefs that inner-city students are undeserving of a quality education. Charise's discussion on racism provided an entry point for students to talk about other forms of racism, such as that which occurs in the National Basketball Association. At this time, Lewis, the only African American student Charise had in the class, stated that he sees the NBA as racist, because the players are predominantly black and the coaching staff, with few exceptions, are white. He further told the class that he thought the players were objectified as entertainers for the white man and further objectified by being restricted from leadership positions, such as that of a coach. Lewis later thanked Charise for allowing him to make those comments in class and for not disagreeing with him, something he explained that often happens in his other classes.

These examples from our classes were the beginnings of relationships with students of color that later developed into a trust that was needed for the students to become more vocal in our classes. These initial conversations, where we voiced our political positions and identified with students of color by pursuing the commonalities in our critical perspectives, helped set the foundation for students to choose critical topics for their final projects.

For the final group research paper, we specifically asked students to pick critical topics that were currently affecting their lives. We explained to the students that critical topics involve those that are somehow related to oppression. We also provided possible topics that have been successful in previous classes we have taught — bilingual education, standardized testing, the misrepresentation of women and people of color in the media, gay and lesbian rights, among others. This project is assigned during the seventh week of the semester, and we hope by this point that the students feel comfortable enough to pick a topic that is not only critical but also important to them.

In our classes, we began the process of choosing topics by using class time to let students brainstorm ideas in small groups. Many of the topics that came out of this brainstorming activity were critical and included such topics as storing nuclear waste on Indian reservations, images of women in music videos, the unequal distribution of wealth, immigration and border control, and same-sex marriages. Not all the topics students came up with were critical. Some of the uncritical topics included the efficiency of fuel injectors over carburetors in cars, the benefits of playing sports, the dangers of mountain biking, and things to do in a big city. As students discussed possible topics in small groups, Charise and Octavio visited each group, helping students define what a critical topic is and why some of their topics were not considered critical. Once students identified several critical topics, we wrote all of these topics on the front board and then allowed time for students to state the reasons why they wanted a particular topic. Finally, through a voting process, we had students vote for topics that they would be willing to research and write about, even if it meant giving up their primary choice. Pablo, a Mexicano student in Octavio's class, elected to do a research project that criticized the expansion of the Mormon Church in downtown Salt Lake City. It was definitely a risky topic for Pablo to suggest, given that the majority of the students in the class were members of this church. In fact, when Pablo suggested this topic, many students promptly disapproved, arguing that the church needs to remain the center of the community and that the expansion of the church was a very important project. At this point, Octavio asked Pablo to share some of the reasons why this was an important project to do. Pablo expressed that this project was important to him because he regretted the power that this church has on city decisions and that he did not support the environmental hazards the church was willing to pursue in its efforts to expand.

Despite the controversy that arose from Pablo's elected topic, his explanation of the importance of this project influenced several students, including a Mexicana, to vote for his topic and thus form a group. Later during the semester, when Pablo and his group presented their findings to the class, there was once again much controversy. In this group presentation, the students claimed that they thought it was unfair that the church was able to buy a city block for its expansion project. They also reported that the church wanted to use the same rock type it had used in the original building of the church, which can be found only in a local canyon where wildlife lives. More specifically, the group reported that the construction crew wanted to remove rock from the canyon and also build a road to the canyon to facilitate the process of removing the rock. The group finally claimed that various wildlife animals would be lost in the process and that they did not support the church expansion project. At the end of the presentation, the many church members attending the class once again objected to the presenters' viewpoints, stating that they were willing to sacrifice wildlife in the pursuit of the church expansion.

At this point, Octavio opened the discussion up to the larger issues that were learned in this presentation, namely issues of domination and oppression. When Octavio asked the class what they had learned from the presentation, some of the inactive white students in class stated that they learned that the Mormon Church often makes decisions that benefit it without regard to the rest of the community. In response to this statement, another student asked, "In what ways are other community members affected by decisions made by the Mormon Church?" The student responded by stating that she used to enjoy walking down the street in question because it gave her easy access to the mall and now that the street is owned by the church, she is prohibited from walking and parking on the street because she is not a member of the church. This student's comments allowed many students in class to recognize that despite their support for the church expansion project, it was a dominating move made by the church that was at the expense of many nonchurch community members.

When it came time to choose research topics in Charise's class, Lewis, the African American student discussed above, elected to do a project on gangs. There was little interest from the class in doing this project, so Lewis made several statements to the class, telling them that he thinks that many people have wrong conceptions of gangs and that he wanted to change that. Students remained uninterested and joined many other groups on other topics. Despite the lack of interest the class showed toward Lewis's topic, Charise asked him to continue voicing his interest in a project on gangs. At last, students who had not yet found a group joined with Lewis and decided to research gangs. The two members who joined Lewis, Michael and Kevin, were white, middle- and upper-class students. Lewis and his group ended up giving one of the most effective presentations, which was well received by those who had initially rejected the topic. The group was very informative, providing information on the type and number of gangs, the meaning of graffiti, and the reasons why youth join gangs. One of the group's main points was that gangs are not as violent as popular media make them out to be and that membership in a gang often protects youth from the harshness of the streets, including racism.

Both these examples from our classes show that the students of color were willing to stand up to disagreement from the larger class. Both of the topics that Pablo and Lewis decided to pursue were risky, as each larger class did not support their topics. Even though Pablo was able to find group members to join his group rather quickly, the remaining class, for the most part, disagreed with the group's project and its claims. Lewis, on the other hand, had a difficult time convincing others to join his group, but he continued to promote his issue and did not give in to joining a group with a different topic. We like to think that the courage to stand against the thoughts of a class was fostered in part by the implementation of coalition pedagogy, that our intentional efforts to identify with the students of color in our classes and to let them know that they do have a space to voice their opinions in our classes made a difference for these students of color.

In both Lewis's and Pablo's self-evaluations and in our own evaluation of the impact they had on their classmates, it became clear that they played critical leadership roles in their groups. Pablo said, "I think I held the group together," and Lewis said, "I was more or less considered the reference man" (because of his first-hand knowledge); it was apparent that these students had an influential voice in their groups. This is of course much different from the traditional banking education that Freire critiques, where students are not allowed to voice their opinions or assume leadership positions within the classroom. Interviews with the white students who were in Lewis's and Pablo's groups confirmed that they each did play an influential role in his group. We asked these white students about who seemed to be knowledgeable in their groups and what they had learned as a result of being in their groups. In an interview with Kevin, a member of Lewis's group, Charise asked him, "Who seemed most knowledgeable about your topic?" Kevin replied:

> Definitely Lewis. He had previous knowledge. He lived in Las
> Vegas for a while and knows a lot about gangs. He has many

> friends that are in gangs or used to be in gangs. He was able to
> get an interview with one of his friends that used to be a gang
> member, and we were able to use that as a source for our paper.

When Jessica, a member of Pablo's group, was asked the same question, she replied:

> To be honest, I think Pablo was. He made me think about the
> church and the things they are doing in a way that I have never
> thought before. Now I am really aware of any little thing that comes
> out in the paper or the news about the church.

We then asked the white group members what they had learned as a result of being in their groups. In an interview with Michael, another member of Lewis's group, he stated:

> More than anything, I think my awareness changed. Before I was
> only aware of maybe two gangs, the bloods and the crips. Now I am
> aware of up to 30 different gangs. I never realized that gang prob-
> lems existed outside the big cities. Now I am aware that they are
> here . . . and I recognize the many reasons why kids turn to gangs,
> including the racism they experience in their schools and in society.

With this statement made by Michael and the previous statement made by Jessica, we recognize that there is some real learning going on for these students, learning that may have been lost if Lewis or Pablo were not in their groups or if, as group members, they were unwilling to express their opinions. Jessica states that she is now thinking of the church and its influence in a whole new way, and Michael states that he was never aware of the pervasiveness of gangs or how schools and society play a role in constructing gangs as outlets for youth. Both these statements demonstrate an increased knowledge and awareness on critical issues. As a result, we want to emphasize the point that not only are the students of color seeming to have a positive experience with our implementation of coalition pedagogy, but the white students are becoming more critical in their viewpoints. We feel that both these findings are essential to our ongoing project of fighting the inequities that occur in our society.

Conclusions

In this essay, we have proposed coalition pedagogy, a teaching methodology that aims to build trusting relationships with students of color early in the classroom experience. We believe not only that coalition pedagogy encourages students of color to be open and truthful about their beliefs and experiences but also that privileged white students are pushed to become more critical in the process.

In our own freshman writing classes, we have implemented coalition pedagogy and have found positive results for all students involved. We have been able to create relationships with students of color who voiced their critical perspectives, primarily by our identifying with them in terms of similarities in ethnicity, language, and political viewpoints. Students of color in our classes during interviews stated that the relationships we had with them made it easier for them to investigate research topics they were interested in and to verbalize critical political stances, even if it did mean going against the beliefs of the rest of the students. Because students of color were able to voice their opinions about these topics, the white students also had a positive learning experience. These students relayed to us through interviews that they had become more aware and are thinking differently as a result of their working with the students of color in our classes.

Ultimately, we believe that the most significant outcome of coalition pedagogy is the success experienced by our students of color, for without their successes, many white students would remain uncritical about issues of oppression. More important, though, our students of color would be more likely to experience failure in their freshman writing courses. Because freshman writing is a gateway course to many other courses that are needed for a degree and because it is one of the first classes a student takes, we feel that it is crucial to create positive and welcoming atmospheres in these classes. We realize that many students of color often feel unwelcome and criticized on their college campuses and in their classrooms, which often contributes to a decision not to continue their college educations. Coalition pedagogy has been helpful in our classes in creating an environment that fosters success among students of color. We anticipate that if coalition pedagogy were more widely implemented, more students of color would experience success.

References

Du Bois, W.E.B. (1989). *The Souls of Black Folk*. New York: Penguin Books.

Ellsworth, E. (1992). "Why Doesn't This Feel Empowering? Working Through the Repressive Myths of Critical Pedagogy." In *Feminism and Critical Pedagogy*, edited by C. Luke and J. Gore, pp. 90-119. New York: Routledge.

Kozol, J. (1991). *Savage Inequalities: Children in America's Schools*. New York: Harper Perennial.

Nieto, S. (2000). *Affirming Diversity: The Sociopolitical Context of Multicultural Education*. New York: Addison-Wesley Publishing Co.

Scering, G. (1997). "Themes of a Critical/Feminist Pedagogy: Teacher Education for Democracy." *Journal of Teacher Education* 48(1): 62-69.

Shor, I. (1992). *Empowering Education: Critical Teaching for Social Change*. Chicago: University of Chicago Press.

Takaki, R. (1993). *A Different Mirror: A History of Multicultural America*. Boston: Little, Brown & Company.

Villanueva, V., Jr. (1993). *Bootstraps: From an American Academic of Color*. Urbana, IL: National Council of Teachers of English.

Liberating Vampires and Transforming Desires

Critical Reflexive Rhetoric for an Age of Globalization

Rory Ong, Albert H. Kim, and Dorothy Graber

"The story began long ago," Trinh T. Minh-ha writes as she opens her discussion in *Woman, Native, Other*: "The story never stops beginning or ending" she continues, "it appears headless and bottomless for it is built on differences" (1989: 1-2). Trinh's notion that narratives have perpetual beginnings and endings, "built on difference," can be a frustrating concept for many students and teachers alike. Difference obscures the clarity for origins that we often seek and complicates the desire for an undeniably sharp reality of *my* story, *our* story, or *their* story in the cultural crossings, intersections, and struggles over hybrid and contradictory narrative identities. Students and teachers grappling with diversity find too often that the commonplace of "multiculturalism" simply does not work in the transcultural and transnational climate of the new globalized millennium. In spite of the wealth of scholarship on multiculturalism, what is too often missing from these discussions is a critically complex articulation of culture given the current concerns over globalization. Christine Sleeter and Peter McLaren raise this very issue, pointing out that multicultural education must include an analysis of the "global capitalist hegemony that has become increasingly ambiguous, elliptical, ironic, and seductive" (1995: 9), a hegemony that can too easily be masked in multicultural agendas. Rather than teaching cultural appreciation (or tolerance, for that matter), the more difficult task is preparing ourselves and our students to engage and critique such intersections that involve complex, well-established, and structurally redundant formulations of social and cultural hegemony. For the burgeoning global age that is upon us, these redundancies are the multivalent legacies of race, patriarchy, heterosexism, colonialism, and imperialism that are concomitant with the invention of the nation-state and the development of local and global political economies. In fact, globalization, or the global spread of democracy through a corporate and consumer capitalism, has become widely promoted in the popular media as the extension of multiculturalism in the new millennium. Globalization has become the new humanism for the 21st century — the "civil" response of the new world order to the social inequities across the globe. It should come as no surprise then that the corporate world seeks newly educated graduates who are eager to embrace globalization as the logical response to the challenge of an international multiculturalism.

Thus, it might be said that the concept of culture that I and my students struggle over (and with) has been laced with a redundant series of power relations and structures. These long-standing systemic arrangements intersect and overlap along theoretical, institutional, spatial, economic, and ideological axes and are intricately woven into our everyday lives as individuals and as U.S. citizens. And they are complicated by the fact that we each occupy a range of competing and contradictory sociocultural locations ourselves that include, but are not exclusive to, race, class, gender, sexuality, nation, and the new global economy. To assume otherwise is to accommodate a romanticized notion of culture as a utopian site where peace and harmony exist. In fact, culture as harmony is the only context where the everyday rhetoric "only when we understand each other's culture can we all get along" makes sense. This definition of culture, as Cornel West reminded us more than a decade ago, is linked to a bourgeois intellectual tradition that sought a new secular humanism "that could play an integrative role in cementing and stabilizing an emerging bourgeois civil society and imperial state" (1990: 21). Our commonsense embrace of culture "as a site of harmony" functions as a hegemony itself that occasions the appearance of equality but in reality masks the difficulties of lived struggle and strife.

Supporting West's claim, David Lloyd and Paul Thomas maintain that this hegemony emerges from pre-Enlightenment and Enlightenment Europe and is reflective of the universal grand narrative that gave birth to immutable constructions of the citizen, the state, the individual, and common sense (1998: 2). When we embrace the idea of culture as a universal convention yet also as a natural function of human difference, it is simply our sociohistorical reflex — what Pierre Bourdieu called a *habitus* (1993) and what Louis Althusser refers to as our *interpellation* (1971) — to the politics of Enlightenment epistemology. On the other hand, if we are to strategically critique the grand narrative that helped to establish culture as a universal category, it will be necessary to understand that the production of the citizen, the state, the individual, and common sense all work together as the reflexive vehicle, what I would call a *dominant rhetoric*, that continues to function ideologically in our government, schools, popular culture, families, and personal relations (Lloyd and Thomas 1998: 14). To challenge this dominant rhetoric, we need to theorize an alternative practice, a counterrhetoric, that critiques the reflexive quality of this hegemony to bring our students, and ourselves as instructors, to crisis — to cultural dystopia — if we are to interrupt the cultural hegemony of a new global multiculturalism.

Theorizing a Critical Reflexive Rhetoric

Like those of many educators, my pedagogical practice and critique of cultural hegemony have been influenced by Antonio Gramsci and Paulo Freire. Both these thinkers have been influential in shaping current discussions around the formation and empowerment of new critical citizen-agents and the role they can play in transgressing and transforming social, political, and cultural arenas. What I especially like about them is something that often is overlooked: their caution that even new critical agents can become unwitting participants in oppressive practices and discourses. This is even more the case when teaching first-world middle-class students from a pedagogical framework that was developed for third-world peasants with little or no education, as in the case with Freirean pedagogy. In their zeal to be one with the underclasses, first-world middle-class students and their teachers are all too often ready to claim themselves as one with the subaltern and critics of the dominant hegemony without first considering their own relation to the power and privilege that go into creating both. In fact, it is the reflex action of first-worlders to naturally assume their absence from the drama of sociohistorical and political contexts that maintains the cultural oneness that we should seek to problematize. Therefore, it is important to develop a theory that underscores our reflexive relationship with hegemony and that provides for a transformative practice so we can attempt to address the presence of empire in our daily lives.

Both Gramsci and Freire provide some insight into such an analysis by advancing an understated critical turn of this reflex in their assessment of "organic intellectuals" and "liberatory subjects." They articulate these "new cultural agents" as critical practitioners of culture who, operating out of an alternative epistemic framework, (re)consider and (re)think their relation to power and privilege and thus (re)value their own relation to hegemony. For Gramsci, this alternative is linked to the organization of cultural education and involves "the discovery that the relations between the social and natural orders are mediated by work" (1989: 34). Work, as the mediator between "social" and "natural" fields of knowledge (i.e., as sites of politically arranged meaning), keeps epistemological production in tension with human action. Freire echoes Gramsci's focus on human action but also recognizes that the oppressed, who are involved in struggles for power, can also become complicit with the hegemonic structures that surround them. "The very structure of their thought," he writes, "has been conditioned by the contradictions of the concrete, existential situation by which they were shaped" (1989: 29-30). But to alter their condition, Freire continues, the oppressed "must recognize its causes, so that through transforming action [it] can create a new situation, one [that] makes possible the pursuit of a fuller humanity" (1989: 31-32). By including *work* in the rationale for cultural education, Gramsci situates human action as the hinge between social convention and the natural order. Freire, on the other hand, points to a human action that is transformative, one that understands the structure of hegemony and can thereby invent its alternative. The central location of Gramsci's human actor involved in a sociopolitical drama along with Freire's transforming action provide at least two sides of a theory in which to situate the everyday reality of human intervention in relation to lived struggle and critical transformation.

But Gramsci and Freire are only part of the theoretical puzzle here. They are speaking, as Victor Villanueva (1991) reminds us, to human communities that are mired in limited situations because of the hegemony of colonial or imperial forces: a consideration for Western instructors employing their theories. That is, it begs the question "How does this critique apply to our first-world students whose nation status, global economic prowess, consumer capitalist ideology, not to mention military dominance, give them such power and privilege despite the competing threads of their own difference (race, class, gender, sexuality, etc.)?" Gayatri Spivak responds to this dilemma quite well, it seems to me. She expands this critique of power and privilege to include first-world subjects. One way to understand this, she writes, is to recognize how the relation of human subjectivity to culture is always spatially centered and not necessarily dispersed, and thus not fully or completely resistant or functioning as a pure alterity, no matter how interstitial or diasporic its location (Spivak 1999). Any political analysis or program (or curriculum, for that matter) that forgets this centering process "runs the risk of declaring ruptures in the place of repetition [or redundancy] — a risk that can congeal into varieties of totalitarianism, often irrespective of ostensible political positions" (323). "Our task," she adds, "is to look at the two strategies: culture as a battle cry against one culture's claim to Reason as such, by insider as well as outsider; and culture as a nice name for the exoticism of the outsiders" (355).

One possible way to challenge these two strategies, Spivak explains, is to rethink Western subjectivity as an agent of exploitation rather than as a victim of it. She makes this unorthodox recommendation based on the critical turn Marx scripted for the proletariat. That is, Marx wanted the proletariat to be identified as an agent of production and not as a victim of capitalism. However, as hard as Marx sought to establish it, capitalists today have become the benefactors of that ideology: They are identified as the ones who create jobs for workers, while workers who are out of work and on welfare are identified as living on the dole (Spivak 1999: 357). She parallels this turn to the current impact of the privatization of markets on the economic restructuring of globalization with the privatization and restructuring of the burgeoning global Western subject. That is, "there is a broad stroke change in the global economy — a new attempt to impose unification on the world by and through the market":

> It is now more than ever impossible for the new or developing
> states — the newly decolonizing or the old decolonized nations —
> to escape the orthodox constraints of a "neo-liberal" world eco-
> nomic system that, in the name of Development, and now, "sus-
> tainable development," removes all barriers between itself and
> fragile national economies, so that any possibility of social redistri-
> bution is severely damaged. In the new transnationality, "the new
> diaspora," the new scattering of the seeds of "developing" nations
> so that they can take root on developed ground, means: Eurocen-
> tric migration, labor export both male and female, border cross-

ings, the seeking of political asylum, and the haunting in-place
uprooting of "comfort women" in Asia and Africa. (357)

Spivak compares her analogy of the invention of the Western subject as a
strategic agent produced by the unification and globalization of markets and labor
with Marx's critical turn of the proletariat. Given the processes of unification
through global markets, she suggests that hyphenated Americans, both insiders
and outsiders, might consider themselves as agents of exploitation rather than its
victims so that the place they call home might take on a different meaning:

> Then the idea that the nation-state that they now call home gives
> "aid" to the nation-state that they still call culture, in order to con-
> solidate the new unification for international capital, might lead to
> what I call "transnational literacy." Then our multiculturalism, or our
> use of the word "culture," will name a different strategic situation
> from *only* our own desire to be the agent of a developed civil soci-
> ety. Which we need not give up; but let us want a different agency,
> shift the position a bit. (357-358)

Spivak's alternative Marxian analogy here establishes a critical reflexivity on
our understanding of the words *culture* and *multiculturalism*. Not only does she
locate culture within the complexity of the global marketplace, but also she argues
that any critical cultural agency must occur from a "different strategic situation,"
an altered sense of "home," one that recognizes its relation to exploitation, rather
than from the location of a one-dimensional subject of a "developed" society. She
insinuates that this alternative subject must be strategically "re-invented" (as
exploiter) and "re-located" (home as empire) in relation to the complex and competing realities of the growing global economy. Inventing a strategic agent such as
this opens the possibility of a subject, or a range of subjects, who is/are capable of
engaging in a counterpractice that is critical of imperial cultural hegemony.

The ability to account for the arrangement of competing power relations in
everyday life, their operative discourses and the tensions and conflicts they produce, is particularly important when marking the contradictions in our modern
construction of culture as a passive site of knowledge. What is needed to confront
this dominant rhetoric of empire is a counterrhetorical practice that is both *critical* and *reflexive*, one that functions both as a theory and practice of everyday life
— a praxis that, as Gramsci states, "combat[s] modern ideologies in their most
refined form" and "educate[s] the popular masses" (1989: 392). Such a critical
rhetoric would outline and pattern the contradictions and competitions in lived
experience rather than conflate them into a unified notion of national or global
culture. Rhetoric in this sense would not merely be understood in Aristotelian
terms as "all the possible modes of persuasion" nor as a purely utilitarian technology as a tool for conveying information. Neither would it be the circular study of
discourses or the interplay of metadiscourses as some postmodernists would have
it. In fact, rhetoric would need to be recast as an "always already ideological
arrangement" of historically, socially, politically, and economically shaped tropes,

figures, common places, images, or other forms of representation that circumscribe human imagination, culture, and local and global material conditions. It would constitute a complex set of organizing discursive practices that have been constructed from an elaborate network of variant and competing power relations in everyday material life. Rhetorical practice and production, rather than existing outside material reality, become concomitant with the complexity of material life and its competing relations of power. A *critical reflexive rhetoric* would not only reshape and give texture to culture as a material political practice but also reassociate (rather than disassociate) its practitioners, these new cultural rhetors, with a daily life that is linked to struggles over power, privilege, and legitimization. A cultural praxis such as this would provide the framework for a dynamic alternative paradigm necessary to begin rearranging first-world commonsense conceptualizations of cultural oneness by highlighting the complex matrices of historical material cultural practices in local and global arenas fraught with contestations and contradictions.

Critical Reflexive Rhetoric as a Cultural Praxis in Daily Life

The goal of critical reflexive rhetoric as a cultural praxis in my class, then, is to bring students', and my own, commonsense understanding of culture monism to epistemic crisis. That is, I challenge students to consider the organization of cultural meaning in relation to power and privilege. By acknowledging our relation to power and privilege, we confront a contradiction in our ways of knowing; I am, in other words, asking them to consider how we are actors in a political drama, not just a passive audience. This rearrangement of our relation to the production of cultural meaning as a politics has the potential to transgress our assumptions of cultural practice as something that occurs naturally. Such crises generate productive moments wherein we can unmask our own complicity with dominant hegemonic practices and structures and engage in rethinking and reevaluating those relations. We are, as Alan France points out, "initiating students into a materialist rhetorical practice [as a way of] critiquing the phenomenological world of texts. This critique must begin in the material world of everyday relationships, where the very architecture of daily life is structured in order to conventionalize relationships of power" (1994: 23). This is a crucial step in the process of social change, it seems to me, as dominant cultural redundancies are replete in our everyday experiences. The plethora of culturally hegemonic representations that we meet up with repeatedly on a daily basis (in the form of gender, race, and class relations, media representations, social, political, and economic systems we interact with, etc.) have a value of return that is compounded daily and that accumulates ideologically. We need, therefore, a rhetorical praxis that will critique redundant structures of dominant culture at the level of complex lived life. This critique is not something that will occur once and for all but must repeatedly interrupt our commonsense notion of culture as a harmonious and passive singularity — a counterreflexive action, if you would. We need, in other words, a 21st-century critical rhetoric that engenders an interrogation of the cultural hegemony in the common places of our daily lives where we work, eat, drink, play, involve ourselves in relationships, and even keep our memories.

The site where I most often try to engage students in a critical reflexive rhetoric is in an upper-division course at Washington State University called Seminar on Culture and Power. Even though it is an upper-division undergraduate seminar, I approach it as a gateway class for students preparing to leave the university and enter the responsibilities of daily life as critical citizens. Here I want students to range beyond a fixed understanding of culture as a singular practice that is passively inherited by one's ethnicity, race, gender, sexuality, and/or nation to a more dynamic and complex understanding of cultural practice as a politics in their daily lives. I would also like them to understand that this praxis involves not just an acknowledgment of their relation to power, authority, and domination but moreover a reexamination of the sociopolitical and economic consequences of those privileges, as well. Although the classroom may be the gateway where students enter and are initially introduced to such strategies, as they leave the classroom these can often extend into the postdisciplinary sites of the home, dorm, office space, or, as Patricia Harkin (1991) puts it, the politics of one's "lore." I am most interested, therefore, in having my students and myself venture into critical interrogations of everyday discourse. I think it is at this level of lived experience — the histories we shape for ourselves, our memories, and the mundane organization of our daily lives — where a dominant rhetoric is most seductive and clandestine.

One assignment that has worked very well for me has been to ask students to write a short informal narrative about an everyday event in which they have experienced some form of cultural conflict or tension. Although it is a simple assignment in many respects (one of many), students often carry myopic sentiments of the harmony of their own and others' cultural experience and, even in this upper-division seminar, find the exercise "frustrating." This is primarily because the assignment attempts to have students focus on the contradiction of their cultural location, something they have not yet considered. In particular, I ask them to think about an everyday incident, or memory, one that stands out for them, when they were forced to acknowledge their own racism, sexism, homophobia, able-bodiedness, class or nation privilege, etc. I want them to write it as a tale, as part of their personal lore, so that it becomes a countermyth to the standing mantras of "I'm ok, you're ok" or "I have my culture, you have yours." I want them to confront the dissonance of their own narratives rather than file it away, so that it stands as a contradiction to the dominant rhetoric of universal culturalism. Although students taking this seminar would have been familiar with issues of diversity, they might not have had the opportunity to critically examine their social and historical involvement in competing relations of power and privilege. Many of us often hold to the commonsense belief that cultural awareness translates into equality or the commonplace "now that we understand each other, we can all get along." What is not often realized is how our different histories and experience in terms of race, class, gender, sexuality, and nation may set us apart and place us in contention with one another. This is the problem with certain aspects of multiculturalism and certainly of globalization: Neither provides a critical sensibility about competing cultural differences. Multiculturalism and its global counterpart assume all differences are, in essence, mutually exclusive. Developing a critical reflexive rhetoric about the intersections as well as the contradictions of difference means, however, that we must take into account the competing realities that are maintained "rhetorically" by redundant structures of a dominant cultural hegemony. This reflexivity must translate into a practice that helps us to respond critically to the privileges this redundant hegemony asserts by recognizing how those privileges are ordered and arranged vis-à-vis dominant and oppressive systemic values. A critical reflexive rhetoric that rearranges the meaning of common everyday experiences to account for contradictions of power and privilege encourages students to begin participating in a cultural praxis that breaks the spell of utopia in their daily lives. By way of example, I have included the following two narratives from two students who took the Seminar in Culture and Power with me. Albert Kim and Dorothy Graber were both undergraduates when they first wrote them. They have been revised somewhat for this piece but remain much as they were when first written. Both students rewrite a particular cultural experience where their differences and their privileges met. They are trying to rethink, and yet reclaim, the politics of their personal lore.

ALBERT KIM
DRAWING BLOOD WITH WORDS: MY INTERVIEW WITH A VAMPIRE

During the Spring of 1995 I was approached by a reporter from our student newspaper. He asked if I would agree to an interview about the "Asian" community on our campus. I replied, "Do you mean the Asian American community or the Asian community?" "Is there a difference? And if so, what?" the reporter asked. At the time, I couldn't help but shake my head in disappointment from what I had just heard. As an ethnic studies major I had become aware of the long and rich history of people of color in the United States, but more particularly, of the history of Asian Americans. I came to understand the value of the Chinese in building the [P]acific railroad, the travesty of the internment of Japanese Americans in World War II, and the trouble-laden myth of the "model minority." I also learned to closely examine the various forms of oppression leveled against Asian Americans in this country. I began to tire of hearing about Asians as entertainment, and their relentless identification with food and festival. Rather, I wanted those exposed to higher education at WSU to come away with the fundamental understanding that Asian Americans come from multiple and complex communities with very different histories. So, I agreed to the interview in hopes of clearing up some of the confusion and ignorance that I, as an Asian American, confronted each day.

As the reporter and I sat to start the interview, he asked me what my background was. I replied, "Korean American." "Wait a minute," he said, "I thought you just said that you were Asian American." After a slight pause, I started to explain to him what I thought was the difference of identifying myself first as a Korean American, then secondly an Asian American. I had always thought that one should identify within their particular "ethnic" group before identifying with the broader category. I explained this to the reporter, yet at the time honestly not knowing what it all meant. He also asked me the typical questions for my age group like "What's your favorite band?" "Why did you come to WSU?" and "What's your favorite food?" These were things I didn't really have to think about, because I'd heard them so often. Once the two of us talked more informally, I began to relax.

Then came the more difficult questions, the ones that made me think and pause — or should have. "What's your perception on the differences of the Asian American community and the Asian (international) community?" he asked, and "How do you feel when the mainstream 'white' community lumps all peoples of Asian descent together?" Having read a lot about these issues in a seminar on culture and power made me feel like an expert of sorts. So I responded to his inquiries, and stated my opinions. I told him, "I am Asian American. That means that I am not 'foreign' or 'international.'" I went on to say that Asians did indeed have a history here in the United States, and proceeded to ramble off every significant historical Asian American event and experience I could think of. I was trying to justify to the mainstream "white" community that Asian Americans indeed had a place here in the United States. I was trying to locate a space for Asian Americans in the eyes of this U.S. reporter and the U.S. readers of his columns. I also tried to incorporate other things I had learned throughout my course of study. I talked about the gay, lesbian, bisexual community, compared the Asian American "experience" to other ethnic "experiences," and discussed issues related to the "cultural hegemony" in the United States. I wasn't sure if what I had said made much sense to the reporter, but it didn't matter to me. I was going to impress him with my newfound language rather than clearly articulating my thoughts. The interview lasted for about an hour, and when it was over, I felt good. Asian Americans were finally getting the press that they deserved. No longer were we the "model minority." We were finally being recognized on a predominantly white campus. Or so I thought.

The interview was published a week later. As I turned to the article, I immediately felt awkward. There was a cartoon the newspaper put alongside with the column. It depicted an "Asian American" who had a basketball in one hand, wearing a baseball cap backward and baggy shorts. Next to him was another Asian drawn in stereotypical fashion, wearing what the cartoonist thought were "traditional" clothes, with kimono and slippers, and flashing a peace sign. I then turned my eyes down to read the column. It was titled "Asian Americans not Asians." The writer started off by stating, "Albert Kim is dealing with a double-edged dilemma," adding that although American I am sometimes treated like a "foreigner" in the United States. The reporter continued by pointing out that "because America is infatuated with lumping anyone with slanted eyes and straight black hair into one big group called Asians, Kim's racial identity is slurred together with everyone who shares his physical characteristics." Yes, I did say all those things but not exactly in the order the column was written. Only then did it hit me that all those things I tried explaining to the reporter probably didn't make much sense to him. In spite of this, the column was received well among my friends and peers, most of who were either white or Asian American. "Great interview" and "Finally we get our own page," they would say. I felt as if the insecurities I had experienced earlier were all for [naught]. Maybe the awkward feelings I had imagined were just nerves. Now with the reassurance from others, I was confident.

However, when I walked into my seminar I saw a copy of my interview in my professor's hand and had a premonition that what I said in the article might have been a bit problematic. As all the students came in and took their seats, my professor asked if everyone had read the interview. Everyone said yes, turning to me with their congratulations. He went on to ask if there were any questions, particularly making reference to the cartoon characterizations. I raised my hand and felt obligated to have a disclaimer stating that I did indeed recognize that the article was not the most well-written piece of work and that what I had said was not exactly what I had intended it to be. He pointed out that it doesn't necessarily matter how I intended it to be perceived, but how it might be perceived by others among the campus community. We discussed the article briefly, but for the most part, my classmates liked the piece and I felt pleased. Later that day, I was still reeling from the positive feedback I'd been receiving unaware of any negative implications. Imagine my surprise when I received a message criticizing my interview on my answering machine. It was from a student who had read my article. The message, angry and with a "thick Asian" accent simply said, "Who the hell do you think you are?" A bit taken aback, I thought to myself, "What could this person possibly mean?" I tried to shrug off the message, but I received two more later in the week. Still, I tried to forget them, thinking the calls a hoax.

A few days later, I ran across a letter to the editor that read "Asians not as secluded as some like to believe." Even when I read the headline, I didn't equate it with my interview. Once I began reading, however, I realized the writer was one who didn't agree with my stance on the differences between Asians and Asian Americans. The editorial stated I had been "extremely misleading" and "greatly misinformed." The writer wanted to clarify any confusion he believed I caused about the international Asian community. He went on to say that Asians "are not isolated from the world," believing I had implied that in my interview. He contended that the "drastic disparity" between Asians and Asian Americans I mentioned in my interview had more to do with my "inferiority complex," and that I needed to get over it. He closed his editorial by saying that I should not be out to destroy other cultures. Stunned at what I had just read, I thought to myself, "That wasn't my intention!" Suddenly what we discussed in our class made sense to me. It doesn't necessarily matter what I intended it to sound like, but it matters how it was perceived. I realized I was using language that was distancing myself from the Asian international community, while trying to do a cultural analysis of the label "foreign" that has so often followed Asian Americans. It took a while, but I gradually realized that the spaces Asians and Asian Americans occupy link us in America.

The editorial caused somewhat of a stir in the Asian American community on campus, with three letters to the editor being printed supporting me. Still I couldn't help but feel awkward about the things that I had said earlier in my interview with the reporter. What started out as an innocent interview turned into something that caused me to be more thoughtful about the things I say in terms of identifying myself as an Asian American. I never intended to offend anybody when I did the interview, but that didn't matter now. I had offended someone, and for the first time I had to critically examine the way I positioned myself as an Asian American.

DOROTHY GRABER
LONGING FOR LIBERATION: RECOGNIZING AND RESISTING RACIAL OPPRESSION

A year and a half ago, I decided to leave a 10-year career with the Department of Defense to return to school and begin preparation for college teaching. As a Navy civilian trainer of active-duty personnel, delivering instruction on topics like "Navy Core Values," I became increasingly aware of the tension between the rhetoric of "equal opportunity" and the daily practice of elitism. At one point, I observed a talented young Chicano radioman's career systematically squelched by a white, male-dominated hierarchy. After he finally decided to leave the Navy and return to his home state of Texas to attend college, I began to rethink my own participation in patriarchal practices. His desire to leave an elitist and racist military organization helped me realize that I, too, longed to go on to a more liberatory life.

As I began my studies, I learned that the stories of every racial group in the United States contain multiple narratives of oppression by the dominant culture. I experienced stages of shock and sadness as I read the histories of genocide, colonization, slavery, exclusion, and oppression. I felt guilt at realizing how the U.S. system favors whites with unearned privilege, especially because I had benefited having had complicity with systems of white privilege. As I learned more, guilt blended with anger at being lied to by government, educators, historians, and the media. The process of (un)learning in order to resist was tougher than I had expected. As I experienced these initial reactions, my classes opened the possibility for a transformative process.

One class in particular, a seminar on culture and power, investigated some of the ways that racism works and how discursive practices can be used both to recognize racial oppression and to resist it. The atmosphere in the class was of supportive critique; it challenged us but at the same time was not intimidating. In this classroom space we began to explore how white privilege works and affects everyone. We read and discussed Michael Omi and Howard Winant's explanation of Gramsci's concept of hegemony, whereby "ruling groups . . . elaborate and maintain a popular system of ideas and practices — through education, the media, folk wisdom, etc. — which he [Gramsci] called 'common sense'" (1994: 67). We considered critical questions, like who receives unearned privilege and who is excluded? How has law been used to legitimate oppression? How is racism embedded in our unconscious minds? What do white-centered literature and films mean to whites and what do they mean to people of color? We also learned how people of color are critiquing the way that the dominant culture has affected them. We read, for example, how Gloria Anzaldúa (1987) counters the "dominant norteamerican culture" by creating a new identity, called the "new mestizaje." Anzaldúa combines races, cultures, genders, and sexual orientations creating borders that are meant to be crossed, ones that move, shift, and alter. I found her belief in the power of the new mestizaje an inspiration to me in my own desire for change and liberation. Anzaldúa writes that

> the white laws and commerce and customs will rot in the desert they created . . . [while] los mexicanos-Chicanos will walk by the crumbling ashes as we go about our business. Stubborn, persevering, impenetrable as stone, yet possessing a malleability that renders us unbreakable, we, the mestizas and mestizos, will remain. (1987: 63-64)

In a position paper I wrote on Michael Omi and Harold Winant's *Racial Formation in the United States* (1994), I considered their discussion of the influential role of Thomas Jefferson, author of the Declaration of Independence, in framing U.S. national rhetoric. Who was Jefferson talking about when he said all "men" are created equal? Omi and Winant provide the following insight in the form of a quotation from Jefferson's writings in which he gives his opinion of the intelligence of his black slaves:

> In general their existence appears to participate more of sensation than reflection. . . . In memory they are equal to whites, in reason much inferior . . . [and] in imagination they are dull, tasteless, and anomalous. . . . I advance it therefore . . . that the blacks, whether originally a different race, or made distinct by time and circumstances, are inferior to the whites. (quoted in 1994: 63-64)

I explained in my response paper that I could now see how Jefferson had contributed to both a national rhetoric of "equality" and the unequal racial formation that Omi and Winant described. I also described my dismay that I had felt only a transitory uneasiness when in the past I had been reminded that Jefferson was himself a slave owner, without realizing that the justification of the institution of slavery would have to be an intrinsic part of his philosophy.

I experienced the tension between yearning to entirely escape oppressive cultural practices and actually engaging with the study of oppression while reading Wendy Rose's article "The Great Pretenders: Further Reflections on Whiteshamanism" (1992). Rose's historical account of the colonialism imposed on Native Americans was not new to me. However, I felt personally challenged by her critique of the efforts of "white experts" who benefit economically from the appropriation of Native culture and art (1992: 414). I saw myself as one of those so-called whites who longed to escape from the oppressive legacy of U.S. culture. In class discussion I asked my professor and classmates if they thought I could find a legitimate space of study as a white female. How did they see my position in terms of appropriation or complicity with colonial practices? My classmates responded that it would be important for me to always state clearly, and to be up front about, my own position as a white scholar when researching cultural subjects to which I am not an insider. We also discussed that while individuals do not necessarily deserve the entire blame for the history of cultural dominance, Rose's article illustrated how important it would be for all of us to be critically conscious of the way a contemporary culture continues to ignore the historical processes, and consequences, of racialization while simultaneously appropriating aspects of indigenous cultures that it finds useful and expedient, whether spiritually or economically.

As my transformation progressed, I started to see how the oppression worked on many levels, and how much a part of it I had been in my job with the Navy. I had not realized my own complicity in a military training system that was an integral part of a structure of domination. The training I regularly presented was prepackaged, standardized, and mandatory. Discussion was conducted only as a means of clarifying the message. When it came to equal opportunity, "old-boy" networks of both officers and senior enlisted personnel worked effectively to exclude Chicano/Latinos, Asian Americans, African Americans, women of any race, and especially gay men and lesbians. The only members of these groups who gained promotion to leadership positions were those who participated in the old-boy system on its own terms. Anyone who discussed the existence or incidence of racism or discrimination could expect to have their career derailed. The more I had considered this contradiction between the stated "official" commitment to equal rights [and] my observation of exclusionary practices toward anyone not belonging to or submitting to the dominant system, the more I wanted to find out about how it worked.

My only serious attempt at resistance to this system convinced me that there was much to learn. I had received a directive to inform all personnel that any assault on gay sailors would have to be punished; a thinly veiled qualification said, in effect, that the admiral sympathized with the frustration people might feel at the newly elected president's misguided wishes to accept homosexuals into the military. No standardized text had been provided for this training. Seizing the opportunity, I gained the support of the Executive Officer and the

Senior Chaplain and designed a more positive training text which tied the already understood "Navy core values" of respect and dignity for all personnel to the current situation of anger against "gays in the military." The majority of the senior enlisted leaders who presented the training nevertheless made it clear that they supported the admiral's sympathies, not mine. Although I was not especially surprised, I was disappointed.

Looking back, I can see how heavily the weight of oppression bears upon any attempts to resist. Analyzing my own experiences with the Navy helped me understand the systemic nature of oppression. I now realize that racism is not limited to organizations like the Ku Klux Klan, but that racism gets its real power from the way it becomes institutionalized into systems of government, education, culture, and authorized historical narratives. I began to better understand E. San Juan, Jr.'s definition of racism as "an articulating hegemonic principle that involves both the practices of civil society and state apparatuses" (1992: 57).

As we discussed in our senior seminar, critiques of racism need to occur on many levels. Our hope comes from being able to recognize racism, how it functions, and to embrace our contestation with it rather than erase it by pretending it will simply vanish if we leave it alone. The transformation I spoke of earlier is not something I have completed, or may ever complete. My next step has been to go on to graduate work in American studies where I can continue learning the theories and methods of critique, as well as a critical pedagogy for teaching students to not only "recognize" but to "resist" racism and other forms of oppression, in their academic work, popular culture, and in their everyday lives.

Cultural Crisis and Transformation

When I began writing this conclusion, I was visiting relatives in the rural Midwest. At the time, there was an advertising campaign for "international family planning" running on one of the local television stations. The slogan for this particular ad was "As long as there is a third world, there will never be one world." I was immediately struck by the utopian desire for "one world" especially since it was airing in the heartland of America. The ad left little doubt that the "third world" was in need of assistance. Not surprisingly, the first world remained unnamed in the ad; it was under erasure, refigured, as the universal one world. Because of this erasure, there was never any question that the first world had anything to do with the conditions of the third world. The slogan would never have read "As long as there's a first world, there will always be a third world." Even though the ad promotes international family planning, and is endorsed by liberal agencies such as Planned Parenthood as a way to provide "third world women" more freedom from patriarchal practices, this too is not free from the cultural hegemony we have been investigating. As both Angela Gilliam (1991) and Uma Narayan (1997) point out, to level a critique at global patriarchy while speaking from the point of view of the West, especially without giving thought to national boundaries and differences, not to mention the particular political, economic, and social conditions that inform different national patriarchies, can lead to a conflation of the inequitable and complex power dynamics that different women in different national sites encounter daily. The advertisement assumes a natural equanimity among women across the globe and ignores the fact that "developed" countries, the policies of the World Bank and the International Monetary Fund, and economic sanctions by first world countries are too often complicit with the dire social and political conditions of so-called "developing" countries, all of which complicate "third world" women's lived conditions. So although the ad purports to lend agency to third world women by liberating them from patriarchy, it is neocolonial and imperialist in its universalist trajectory. In fact, the images on the television screen suggest that third world women will become more like the American middle class as they gain economic power and independence. Therefore, not only does it encourage third world women to become part of the global economy without question as to the political economy of gender, race, and nation articulated in the ad campaign, but it also reinforces the dominant/subordinate relationship of third to one (first) world.

Thinking about the neocolonial rhetoric in the advertisement, I wondered whether students coming through my class would recognize the contradictions in its discourse. Would they be able to articulate the problem for themselves, critically and reflexively recognizing that they are most likely the unnamed firstworlders to whom this third world is being represented? Would they recognize the power relations being set up and the political economy of family planning as articulated by the ad? Would they know in what ways to act, to live their lives, in such a way as to interrogate this form of global culture they are being sold? Albert Kim and Dorothy Graber give me some hope. Both students articulated, more or less, the kind of cultural praxis I hope is engendered from a critically reflexive rhetoric. Each of them, at different moments, was confronted with a dystopic reality that contradicted the smooth and uninterrupted cultural practice they were used to or had been seeking. While trying to find his voice as an Asian American, Albert was forced to confront the complexity of national, racial, and social differences that compounded the Asian community on his campus. Dorothy came to the realization that she had benefited from, but also struggled with, the racial and gender inequalities she experienced as a civilian Navy trainer. In his attempt to articulate Asian America on his predominantly white campus, Albert met with opposition from the international Asian community and the diasporic locations they inhabited. Albert had to rethink the binarism of Asian America for a more complex notion of competing and contradictory hybrid locales that involved race, ethnicity, and nation. As a returning student, Dorothy was able to acknowledge her own relationship to hegemony and began to recognize how her own racial privilege, and her resistance to it, was compounded by the systemic limitations of a state apparatus that she had experienced daily. Dorothy not only had to reflect on the restrictive practices she was experiencing but also had to acknowledge the political economics of race, gender, class, and sexual orientation operating in the very materials she was required to teach. She had been participating in a hermeneutics of oppression in her daily life.

Although these students left my classroom and entered civil society from different points of praxis, they each articulated themselves along a spectrum consistent with a critical reflexive rhetoric. One goal is to acquaint students with an alternative rhetorical framework that challenges a simplistic cultural monologism and enables them to confront cultural complexities. But the more reflexive action would be for us to recognize our own complicity with cultural hegemony, account for the systemic forces of its conflation and our involvement with it, and articulate an alternative praxis that interrogates and abrogates the cultural hegemonic redundancies found throughout state-sanctioned and quotidian structural apparatuses. To this end, it is imperative we have a critical mass of cultural workers who are cognizant of the various sociohistorical problematics that confront them. We can do this if we understand that part of our project in multicultural gateway courses is to provide for a dynamic rhetorical framework that prompts all of us, students and teachers alike, to revalue cultural space as contested sites. Rather than reinforce cultural unity, cultural crisis has the potential to transform by the very contradictions that its complications pose.

References

Althusser, L. (1971). "Ideology and Ideological State Apparatuses." In *Lenin and Philosophy and Other Essays*, translated by B. Brewster, pp. 127-186. New York: Monthly Review Press.

Anzaldúa, G. (1987). *Borderlands/La Frontera: The New Mestiza.* San Francisco: Aunt Lute Books.

Bourdieu, P. (1993). *The Field of Cultural Production.* Irvington, NY: Columbia University Press.

France, A.W. (1994). *Composition as a Cultural Practice.* Westport, CT: Bergin & Garvey.

Freire, P. (1989). *Pedagogy of the Oppressed.* New York: Continuum.

Gilliam, A. (1991). "Women's Equality and National Liberation." In *Third World Women and the Politics of Feminism*, edited by C.T. Mohanty, A. Russo, and L. Torres, pp. 215-236. Bloomington: Indiana University Press.

Gramsci, A. (1989). *Selections From Prison Notebooks.* New York: International Publishers.

Harkin, P. (1991). "The Postdisciplinary Politics of Lore." In *Contending With Words,* edited by P. Harkin and J. Schilb, pp. 124-138. New York: Modern Language Association.

Lloyd, D., and P. Thomas. (1998). *Culture and the State.* New York: Routledge.

Narayan, U. (1997). *Dislocating Cultures: Identities, Traditions, and Third World Feminism.* New York: Routledge.

Omi, M., and H. Winant. (1994). *Racial Formation in the United States: From the 1960s to the 1990s.* 2nd ed. New York: Routledge.

Rose, W. (1992). "The Great Pretenders: Further Reflections on Whiteshamanism." In *The State of Native America: Genocide, Colonization, and Resistance,* edited by M.A. Jaimes, pp. 403-421. Boston: South End Press.

San Juan, E., Jr. (1992). *Racial Formations/Critical Transformations.* Atlantic Highlands, NJ: Humanities Press.

Sleeter, C., and P. McLaren. (1995). "Introduction: Exploring Connections to Build a Critical Multiculturalism." In *Multicultural Education, Critical Pedagogy, and the Politics of Difference,* edited by C. Sleeter and P. McLaren, pp. 5-32. Albany: State University of New York Press.

Spivak, G.C. (1999). *A Critique of Postcolonial Reason: Toward a History of the Vanishing Present.* Cambridge, MA: Harvard University Press.

Trinh, T. Minh-Ha. (1989). *Woman, Native, Other: Writing Postcoloniality and Feminism.* Bloomington: Indiana University Press.

Villanueva, V. (1991). "Considerations for American Freiristas." In *The Politics of Writing Instruction,* edited by R. Bullock and J. Trimbur, pp. 247-262. Portsmouth, NH: Boynton/Book Publishers.

West, C. (1990). "The New Cultural Politics of Difference." In *Out There,* edited by R. Ferguson et al., pp. 9-36. Cambridge, MA: MIT Press.

The Color Line

African American Vernacular English and Computerized Grammar Checkers

Janet Bean

The widespread availability of computers and increasing sophistication of word-processing software have profoundly changed the teaching of college composition. As teachers emphasize the processes of revision and editing, students routinely use word processors to reorganize blocks of text, add and delete material, and check spelling, grammar, and style. Because many students own their own computers and most institutions provide computer labs for student use, writing instructors generally assume that their students know how to use them. Word processing has become an invisible literacy, one that goes unmarked because the majority of students possess the basic skills. Yet there is mounting evidence of a divide in computer ownership and use that separates rich and poor, suburban and urban, high school and college educated, Caucasian and African American. In courses such as first-year composition, the advantage that computer literacy provides is real. Because writing instructors expect the polish of a word-processed text and encourage (if not require) multiple drafts, students who know how to manipulate computer technology have a distinct edge over those who do not.

As an English professor at an open-admissions urban university, I have witnessed firsthand a gap in computer literacy among my students. This gap too often falls along racial lines, with African American students — particularly those who attended urban high schools — less likely than Caucasian students to enter the university with strong word-processing skills. Students with limited computer proficiency must divide their attention between the technology and the writing assignment itself. How do you double space? How do you choose a font and set margins? How do you save a document? How do you cut and paste text to revise it? How do you use the spelling and grammar checkers? Unfamiliarity with word processing adds to the already complex set of tasks that college writing demands, with issues of dialect further complicating the composing process for many African American students.

This essay examines how one word-processing tool, the grammar checker, might be better integrated into the composition classroom. Because grammar checkers are now fully integrated into commercial word-processing programs, they have in effect become our students' first readers, offering immediate feedback on grammatical and stylistic correctness. Most composition instructors would agree that grammar checkers are not ideal first readers due to the software's exclusive emphasis on sentence-level correctness and limited accuracy in error diagnosis. The fact remains, however, that any student who sits down to write at a computer equipped with a current version of a commercial word-processing program will encounter the grammar checker's highlighted or underlined passages unless that student knows how to change the default settings of the program and customize its features.

Students should be critical users, not passive consumers, of computer technology. Unfortunately, it is easier for students to view the grammar checker as an authority rather than use it as a tool. If we want students to develop a critical perspective toward text-editing software, we need to make grammar checkers a visible part of our composition pedagogy. So the question for writing instructors is no longer whether students should use grammar checkers but rather how and when they should use them.

This question is particularly relevant for those who teach composition to African American students. As an arbiter of "correct" English, the grammar checker poses special problems and promises for students who speak African American vernacular English (AAVE) in their homes and communities. Therefore, it is particularly important for these students to develop a critical understanding of the limitations and uses of this technology. Grammatical correctness can take on enormous importance for students from diverse language backgrounds, as their success as academic writers can hinge on their ability to produce — or at least to approximate — edited American English (EAE). When used critically, text-editing tools have the potential to help students develop metacognitive awareness of dialect and register. Because grammar checkers raise key issues about authority and correctness, they can serve as a tool to examine language diversity and its connections to broader issues of power and inequity in our society. The green line of the ubiquitous Microsoft Word grammar checker is emblematic of a deeper color line in American culture and its education system.

African Americans and the Digital Divide

In *The Souls of Black Folk*, William E.B. Du Bois writes, "The problem of the 20th century is the problem of the color-line" (1994: 9). These were prophetic words in 1903, yet they seem just as apt at the start of the 21st century when we consider the racial divide in educational and technological arenas. Mastery of computer technology brings economic and cultural power, and African Americans as a group have lagged behind in their access to that power. In its 1999 study *Falling Through the Net: Defining the Digital Divide*, the U.S. Commerce Department found persistent gaps in computer ownership and Internet access based on race, income, and educational level. The divide between those who have access to computer technology and those who do not has widened in the last 15 years, with the computer rich getting richer. Only 32.6 percent of African American households are equipped with a computer, compared with 55.7 percent of white households. Even when adjusted for income, statistics show that computers are more likely to be present in white households (U.S. Dept. of Commerce 2000). There is an even greater divide among families with school-age children, with 73 percent of white children reporting that their families own a computer, compared with only 32 percent of African American children (Hoffman and Novak 1998: 390).

Racial disparities in computer access and use are found not only in our homes but also in our schools. In *Computers and Classrooms: The Status of Technology in U.S. Schools*, Coley, Crandler, and Engle (1997) report that students attending poor and high-minority schools have less access to computer technology than do other students. In schools with fewer than 25 percent minority students, the student-to-computer ratio is 10 to 1; in contrast, schools that have a population of 90 percent or greater minority students have a ratio of 17.4 to 1. This study also found qualitative differences in the computer experiences of white and minority students. Although students from minority groups are more likely to take courses that focus on vocational uses of computers such as data processing and computer programming, they are less likely to have used computers for word processing in English courses or for solving math or science problems. Clearly, experiences that build computer skills in academic core subjects are more likely to enhance students' success in college. There has been a call for libraries and community centers to bridge the gap in computer access (Hoffman and Novak 1998), but demand can outstrip these institutions' ability to provide services. For example, the Cleveland Public Library, which serves a diverse, urban population, had so many requests for computer use during after-school hours that it established a policy that limited students to 15 minutes of use (Schiller 2000).

What these statistics mean for the teacher of college composition is that we cannot take computer access and experience for granted, particularly if we want to open higher education to a more diverse student population. Cynthia Selfe (1999) warns composition faculty about the "perils of not paying attention" to the complex and interconnected issues of technology, literacy, poverty, and race. The use of technology in education has not served to reduce illiteracy or widen opportunities for disadvantaged or at-risk students. Instead, argues Selfe, the expansion of technological literacy has sharpened existing social inequities "because citizens of color and those from low socioeconomic backgrounds continue to have less access to high-tech educational opportunities and occupy fewer positions that make multiple uses of technology than do white citizens or those from higher socioeconomic backgrounds" (1999: 421). Given the issues of race and class that underlie computer access in our society, it is essential that instructors of composition pay attention to the role technology plays in our courses, implicitly and explicitly. We must make technology more visible in our teaching theories and practices and in our scholarly discussions.

Who Should Use Grammar Checkers?

Grammar checkers are perhaps the most controversial of the text-editing tools offered by word processors. Since their introduction as stand-alone programs in the 1980s, composition specialists have questioned their effectiveness as pedagogical tools in the writing classroom. Ruth Goldfine, who recommends that students disable grammar and spelling checkers entirely, argues that using a grammar checker limits students' growth:

> First, students are dissuaded from evaluating and correcting their own grammatical errors. Thus, their ability to reason about writing and to manipulate language is not challenged and, consequently, does not improve. Second, the presentation of a "preferred alternative" implies a single correct way of phrasing a given passage, thereby discouraging or discounting creativity in writing. (2001: 309)

The most vehement objections to grammar checkers, however, involve the issue of accuracy. In their study of journalism students, Fischer and Grusin found numerous errors in grammar checkers' feedback and argue that these programs "still have not advanced to the stage of development where they can be a useful tool in the journalism writing lab. . . . [They] may detract from learning rather than enhance it" (1993: 25). Lorraine Ray compared the responses of WordPerfect's grammar checker, Grammatik, with those of three English professors and found agreement only 12 percent of the time. After "Gramma" missed 78 of 125 errors, Ray concluded, with some humor, that "she's probably more trouble than she's worth" (1997: 96). Alex Vernon found that WordPerfect 9.0 identified 17 of 36 representative errors, with incorrect suggestions for two of them and two errors flagged incorrectly. Microsoft Word 2000 correctly identified 12 of the 36 errors, offering no suggestions for correcting three of them and making no incorrect identifications. This study suggests that grammar checkers will catch a third, perhaps close to half, of the most common errors found in student essays (Vernon 2000: 339-340).

Because grammar checkers are accurate less than half the time, some scholars have suggested that grammar checkers should be restricted to students who already know the rules of grammar. Renshaw (1991) argues that students must have a foundational knowledge of grammar rules to be able to make effective judgments about grammar checkers' feedback. Similarly, Goldfine (2001) claims that students may not find grammar checkers' feedback useful if they do not understand grammar. Willis and Skybis contend that editing tools are "used best by students who have been taught the basics of spelling, editing, and grammar" (1994: 14). This research reflects a concern that many writing instructors share: Grammar checkers may reinforce poor skills through incorrect and misleading feedback, giving students who have a weak understanding of grammar a false sense of complacency about correctness.

Some scholars view beginning or nonproficient writers as particularly vulnerable to the negative effects of grammar checkers. Kozman (1991) argues that "text analyzers should be used carefully with novice writers," because they place undue emphasis on sentence-level issues and distract students from addressing larger and more important problems in their writing. In an article on computers and basic writers, Lisa Gerrard (1989) critiques the use of error-correction software as a teaching tool, suggesting that grammar and spell checkers encourage passivity because students come to rely on the computer to correct their mistakes. Moreover, she points to the detrimental effects that grammar checkers may have on students' attitudes:

> Basic writers do not need additional insecurities. If error identification is not 100% accurate, it will misinform and frustrate these students. . . . At worst, it will affirm a conviction so many students hold: that assessments of their writing are capricious and the computer, like the train of English teachers who preceded it, is yet another "subjective" judge. (102)

Clearly, this goal of 100 percent accuracy has not been — and will not likely be — met, which means, if we accept Gerrard's argument, that basic writers must continue to be protected from grammar checkers.

Although I share many of the concerns that these scholars raise, I would like to make an argument in favor of making grammar-checking technology accessible to *all* composition students. Much of the negative scholarship on grammar checkers has focused on basic, nonproficient, or novice writers, asserting that they either should not use text-editing tools or should use them only under the careful supervision of writing teachers. Because disproportionate numbers of African American students are placed in remedial writing courses, this position in effect becomes an injunction to withhold computer technology from a group of students who may already be at a disadvantage in terms of computer access and experience. The position that only those who already know grammar rules should use grammar checkers is particularly dangerous, because it reflects a bias in favor of students whose home language most closely resembles edited American English. Despite more than three decades of linguistic research on AAVE, studies show that many teachers still believe that AAVE has a "faulty grammar system and that children who speak it are less capable than children who speak standard English" (Ball and Lardner 1997: 473). If we allow the grammar haves in our composition classes to use word-processing tools and restrict access for the grammar have-nots to these tools, we are exacerbating existing racial and socioeconomic inequalities in computer access.

We must consequently ask ourselves whether we want to adopt pedagogies that reinforce the gap in computer literacy that already divides Caucasian and higher-income students from African American and lower-income students. If composition instructors do not teach basic writing students to use grammar checkers effectively, they lose an opportunity to help students learn to manipulate computer technology — and avoid being manipulated by it.

How African American Basic Writers Use Grammar Checkers

Composition teachers have some reason to be concerned that grammar checkers may cause passivity and frustration, particularly in students who are struggling with college writing. To better understand how students actually use grammar checkers and how they affect their attitudes about writing, I studied a noncredit basic writing course at my open-admissions, urban university, focusing on African American students who use vernacular English in their writing and have difficulty writing EAE. Information was collected through interviews, self-reports, and observation of classroom activities in the computer lab.

One consistent finding of my study is students' willingness to concede authority to the grammar checker. Kisha, a basic writing student, is well aware of the discontinuity of her speech and academic writing and trusts the grammar checker more than her ear: "If the computer gives me a green squiggly line, then I change it 'cause I know it's right. Because I write the way I talk, and that's not good." When she reads the solutions offered by the grammar checker, she uses the following strategy: "If it sounds wrong to me, then I know it's right. 'Cause I talk ghetto fabulous." In her study of basic writers, Mina Shaughnessy shows how academic writing is a "trap, not a way of saying something to someone" (1977: 7), an act that reveals errors and vulnerability rather than a process that communicates ideas. The basic writer

> is aware that he leaves a trail of errors behind him when he writes. He can usually think of little else while he is writing. . . . For every three hundred words he writes, he is likely to use from 10 to 30 forms that the academic reader regards as serious errors. Some writers, inhibited by their fear of error, produce but a few lines an hour or keep trying to begin, crossing out one try after another until the sentence is hopelessly tangled. (1977: 7)

When a student uses a grammar checker, especially when it is set on the default check-grammar-as-you-type option, the fear of leaving a trail of errors is reinforced with each green line that appears on the screen. I have seen students sit at a computer for 45 minutes and produce two lines of text, the process of writing degenerating into a series of starts and stops. Because it is difficult to negotiate the grammatical systems of two dialects, students often concede absolute authority to computer technology and judge their first linguistic inclinations as wrong.

The strategy used by most of the students in my study was to eliminate the green and red lines as soon as they appeared — the faster, the better. It seems that fear of the red pen has been replaced by fear of the green line. Tia reflects on her use of editing tools: "As I am typing a paper and lines appear on the screen, I quickly correct it." She feels that making the lines go away is even more important than discerning whether or not the feedback is correct. "If a green line appears on the screen," she says, "whether I know it's right or not I change it anyway." Similarly, Michael wants to "get rid of the green lines" as quickly as possible. "Otherwise," he says, "they stay on there the whole time you write your paper." Clearly, these students do not like seeing green lines on their screens and are willing to interrupt their drafting process to eliminate them. Although this strategy allows students to take advantage of the advice of text-editing tools, it concedes all authority to the computer. In addition, it prevents students from having stretches of uninterrupted drafting and keeps their attention focused on sentence-level issues.

A smaller group of students used a different approach, ignoring the grammar checker entirely. It is interesting to note that two of the strongest writers used this approach. Jonathon wrote lively, engaging arguments that had many surface errors. He had no proofreading strategies other than to "read it over" and never paid attention to the green and red lines on his computer screen. "They are everywhere," he says, "so I ignore them." Likewise, Romelle paid little attention to the grammar checker's marks and dismissed its feedback as inaccurate. Unfortunately, she threw out the good advice with the bad, missing opportunities to reduce the number of errors in her essays. On the positive side, Jonathon's and Romelle's strategy does allow them to draft without interruption; however, it prevents them from using the available tools to polish their texts.

Neither of these strategies helps these students use grammar checkers effectively. Whether they concede total authority to the software or disregard it entirely, they do not critically engage the grammar checker. It becomes a voice of authority — to be obeyed or ignored. In contrast, experienced writers who use grammar checkers often separate the drafting and editing processes, postponing the use of grammar and spell checker until the end of a section or the end of a document. They use the tools when and if they want them, sometimes ignoring them, sometimes turning them off, sometimes checking grammar as they go. Most important, they constantly make judgments about the feedback and are often skeptical about the suggestions offered. They see the grammar checker as a tool, not as an expert.

The Logic of Error: Grammar Checkers and AAVE

It is easy to understand why African American basic writing students might find it difficult to challenge the authority of grammar checkers. When Jonathon, Kisha, Tia, and Michael write academic essays, they find the rules about language that they have internalized as speakers are often at odds with the rules of "correct" writing. In negotiating the differences between AAVE and EAE, they may introduce elements of their spoken language into the target language or produce *inter-language*, which David Bartholomae defines as "an idiosyncratic grammar and rhetoric that is the writer's approximation of the standard idiom" (1980: 259). As a result, the text may be riddled with errors and the student judged incompetent or indifferent. Mina Shaughnessy (1977), however, argues that even the most incoherent-looking text has an internal logic, and she has identified underlying patterns in student error that show that basic writers do operate under a rule-governed system. Writing teachers may find it difficult to recognize these patterns, Mike Rose warns, because "class and culture erect boundaries that hinder our vision [and] blind us to the logic of error" (1989: 205).

Grammar checkers have the potential to help students identify patterns of error in their own writing. But how accurate are they at identifying errors that are rooted in dialect difference? The following section examines the response of Microsoft Word's and WordPerfect's grammar checkers to sentences from student essays that contain features of AAVE. I should note that grammar checkers' performances can vary in different contexts. I am using Word 2000 and WordPerfect 9.0 set on the check-grammar-as-you-type option and have only noted feedback relevant to the target error.

- **Subject/Verb Agreement**
  I have an uncle that laughs so hard that his face **look** like it is coming off and his eyes look like they will pop out his face.

Word:	[no flag]
WordPerfect:	"faces look" or "face looks"

- **Past Tense and Past Participle**
  I have **experience** some **prejudice** people before, and it all **happen** my senior year of high school.

Word:	[no flag]
WordPerfect:	"experienced," "happens"

- **Plural and Possessive**
  The shoe stores were crowded the most [with people] buying new **shoe** for the weather changes.

Word:	[no flag]
WordPerfect:	[no flag]

- **Negation Concord ("Double Negative")**
  I **don't** think that there **wasn't** any racial insensitivity, just a lot of parent with nothing better to do, then to accuse this well intentioned teacher of racism.

Word:	[no flag]
WordPerfect:	[no flag]

- **Zero Copula (Deleted "to Be" Verb)**
  I guess **it cause he the** youngest.

Word:	[no flag]
WordPerfect:	[no flag]

Overall, the grammar checkers' performances were disappointing. Microsoft Word did not identify any of the target errors, and WordPerfect, while effectively identifying some errors in inflectional endings, let the other constructions slip by undetected. Not surprisingly, the grammar checkers did not recognize errors that were based in syntax, such as negation concord or zero copula. Based on the data presented above, one might think that grammar checkers offer little to students whose writing contains errors based on transfer of AAVE. In practice, however, students do improve their writing through the use of text-editing tools.

Even though grammar checkers may miss significant errors, they do identify a host of other grammatical and stylistic issues, forcing the student to slow down and reconsider the sentence. This interruption, which can be distracting in the drafting process, is just what students need when they edit. Grammar checkers can reinforce the recursive nature of the writing process, teaching students to pause and reread. This pause can be particularly productive if students understand the limited accuracy of grammar checkers. In the example of negation accord above, WordPerfect's grammar checker highlighted "a lot of parent" and suggested "many parent." Rereading the phrase, the student may notice the unmarked plural and add the "s." Perhaps the student may even reread the entire sentence and catch the double negative.

Time and time again, I saw students encounter green lines or highlighted passages and find errors that had not been identified by the grammar checker. And often, they focused in on what Muriel Harris (1981) calls "status-marking errors," those that indicate affiliation with less prestigious social groups and are judged more serious by teachers. For example, a student might see a passage highlighted to show that a comma is needed after an introductory element and end up correcting an error in subject/verb agreement. Of course, the benefit here is somewhat random: If a sentence containing an AAVE error does not happen to get flagged for another reason, then that error may not catch the student's attention. Still, grammar checkers can help students identify at least some problems in their writing and reduce the overall number of errors in their essays. Most teachers have a critical threshold for error, and the grammar checker may help push a student into the acceptable range.

Implications for Teaching

My research suggests two things: First, students who are learning to move between AAVE and EAE are likely to grant grammar checkers a great deal of authority. When a student feels she cannot trust her ear, she may be more reluctant to challenge the advice given by text-editing tools. At least for Kisha, who says, "If it sounds wrong to me, then I know it's right," the fact that a grammar checker's advice conflicts with her own linguistic understanding is further proof that the computer is right. Second, grammar checkers have limited effectiveness, particularly in identifying the kinds of errors that AAVE speakers may make as they learn to write in EAE. Because students may follow the advice of grammar checkers without questioning the software's accuracy, the shortcomings of these tools become even more problematic.

How then can we use grammar checkers effectively in our teaching? I have already argued that requiring students to disable their grammar checkers and demanding that students understand grammar rules before they can use these tools are not the answers. Instead, we must help students develop a critical perspective about grammar checkers and issues of correctness.

At the most basic level, students need to understand that grammar checkers are not foolproof. Composition instruction can encourage a healthy skepticism in a variety of ways. Patricia McAlexander asks her students to "test" Microsoft Word's grammar checker and rate its effectiveness by typing in a series of error-ridden sentences. When students see the range of correct identification of errors, from 71 percent of fragments to 25 percent of errors in parallelism to 0 percent of missing commas in compound sentences, they better understand the limitations of text-editing tools (2000: 137). Alex Vernon holds contests that pit human checkers against one another and the computer in identifying a particular error such as subject-verb agreement. He suggests other exercises such as writing "bad" sentences to see whether the grammar checker is triggered or fooled and comparing the advice of the grammar checker at different style settings (2000: 346).

Students should also understand that grammar checkers — particularly when set to "formal" style — work from rules that are quite conservative and restrictive. To show that good writers often break these rules, I select passages from highly acclaimed texts that have features that I know will be flagged, such as long sentences, use of dialect, or presence of first person pronouns or contractions. I ask students to type these passages on a word processor and evaluate the grammar checker's response. After seeing a grammar checker find fault with the Declaration of Independence, Alice Walker's Pulitzer Prize-winning novel *The Color Purple*, Frederick Douglass's *Autobiography*, or Geneva Smitherman's "It Be's Dat Way Sometimes," students are ready to engage in critical discussions about what constitutes an error and who gets to decide.

To use grammar checkers effectively, students must know when to trust the computer's judgment and when to trust their own. Assignments that draw on students' expertise in their home languages can help students develop confidence in their abilities to discern rhetorical purpose and correctness. For example, I ask my students to write personal narratives that incorporate dialogue. When they edit their prose, I ask them to notice the advice the grammar checker gives and use it only when it fits their goals as writers. Perhaps the description should be written in EAE, but it may be more appropriate for dialogue to be written in AAVE. As part of an assignment on storytelling and culture, I have students interview a family or community member and try to capture the flavor of his or her storytelling style, which encourages the use of dialogue and dialect. In addition, they must use an academic style to analyze the story and the function it serves in the community. My colleague Arthur Palacas asks students to examine a slang word that is common among their friends or family or in their community, such as *dogg, tight, hooptie, awesome, skankie,* or *dweeb*.[1] To complete this assignment, students must move between everyday and academic language as well as study their own language use and its social contexts. As students write essays that require conscious shifts between dialect and register, they develop metacognitive awareness of language — an awareness that will help them increase their confidence in their own linguistic abilities and develop a sense of how language difference can be used to create rhetorical effects.

From this perspective, a grammar checker becomes not an arbiter of absolute right or wrong but a tool that can help students write a particular *kind* of English. Like any tool, it can be manipulated to meet their needs. Instead of relying on the default settings, students should understand the program's features and how to set preferences. For students who have trouble writing fluently, it can be immensely helpful to draft without a grammar or spell checker's interrupting the flow of thought. The first thing I teach students is how to turn off the check-grammar-as-you-go function. Grammar checkers offer a range of style checking, including informal, standard, and formal in WordPerfect and casual, standard, formal, technical, and custom in Word. In the custom style, writers can selectively activate classes of errors. Those writing social science papers, for example, may want to turn off the identification of passive sentences, and those who want more freedom with style can turn off a range of options, including the identification of contractions and sentences that begin with *and* or *but*. WordPerfect allows users to further customize settings such as the maximum number of consecutive nouns or prepositional phrases.

Teaching a limited number of comma rules to students can help the grammar checker work more effectively. Because grammar checkers use a parsing system to identify errors, they work best when they can easily identify independent clauses. I teach two basic rules: the comma after an introductory element and the comma preceding a coordinating conjunction that joins two independent clauses. Because human checkers are consistently better than grammar checkers at applying these particular rules (which is a lesson in itself), students work on a hard copy of their draft, circling any preposition or subordinating conjunction that falls at the beginning of a sentence and making sure they have placed a comma at the end of the phrase or clause. Next, they underline each conjunction and check to see whether it is connecting two complete sentences. Once students have set off independent clauses, the grammar checker does a better job of identifying errors. For example, the following sentence came through Word and WordPerfect grammar checkers unflagged: "After my decision my mother and I wasn't on speaking terms." When the introductory element was set off, however, both programs picked up the error in subject/verb agreement and recommended that the writer change *wasn't* to *weren't*.

Composition instructors do not need to teach in a computer lab to incorporate these strategies in their classrooms. A single laptop computer and projector can bring technology into a traditional classroom. If available resources are limited to an overhead projector, transparencies made from printouts of computer screens can introduce students to the features of grammar checkers. Students can also complete assignments that require the use of grammar checkers as homework and report their findings in class.

The most crucial issue here is access. Teachers of composition should know what computer labs are available to their students and act as advocates to ensure adequate facilities and open access. In addition to physical access to computers, students also need access to critical perspectives on grammatical authority and correctness. Grammar checkers do designate difference as deficiency, yet we must remember that they are *tools* and can therefore be manipulated and used to examine issues of power. If educators want the computer revolution to benefit all Americans, we must work to address existing inequities. The green lines and highlighted passages of grammar checkers may be one place to begin.

Note

1. This assignment comes from Arthur Palacas's unpublished textbook *Write With Ebonics: A Course in Composition, Language Awareness, and Culture.* I would like to thank Arthur for the many productive discussions we have had relating to this project, and Alan Ambrisco, Julie Drew, Lance Svehla, and Caroline Sutowsky for their insightful comments on drafts of this essay.

References

Ball, A., and T. Lardner. (1997). "Dispositions Toward Language: Teacher Constructs of Knowledge and the Ann Arbor Black English Case." *College Composition and Communication* 48(4): 469-485.

Bartholomae, D. (1980). "The Study of Error." *College Composition and Communication* 31: 253-269.

Coley, R.J., J. Crandler, and P. Engle. (1997). *Computers and Classrooms: The Status of Technology in U.S. Schools.* Princeton, NJ: Educational Testing Service.

Du Bois, W.E.B. (1903, 1994). *The Souls of Black Folk.* New York: Dover Publications.

Fischer, R., and E.K. Grusin. (1993). "Grammar Checkers: Programs That May Not Enhance Learning." *Journalism Educator* 47(4): 20-27.

Gerrard, L. (1989). "Computers and Basic Writers: A Critical View." In *Critical Perspectives on Computers and Composition Instruction*, edited by G.E. Hawisher and C.L. Selfe, pp. 94-108. New York: Teachers College Press.

Goldfine, R. (2001). "Making Word Processing More Effective in the Composition Classroom." *Teaching English in the Two-Year College* 28(3): 307-315.

Harris, M. (1981). "Mending the Fragmented Free Modifier." *College Composition and Communication* 32(2): 175-182.

Hoffman, D., and T. Novak. (April 1998). "Bridging the Racial Divide on the Internet." *Science* 17: 390-391.

Kozman, R.B. (1991). "Computer-Based Writing Tools and the Cognitive Needs of Basic Writers." *Computers and Composition* 8(2): 31-45.

McAlexander, P. (2000). "Checking the Grammar Checker: Integrating Grammar Instruction With Writing." *Journal of Basic Writing* 19(2): 124-139.

Ray, L. (1997). "Does 'Gramma-tik' You Off?" *Business Communication Quarterly* 60(1): 92-96.

Renshaw, D.A. (1991). "The Effect of an Interactive Grammar/Style Checker on Student Writing Skills." *Delta Pi Epsilon Journal* 33(2): 80-93.

Rose, M. (1989). *Lives on the Boundary*. New York: Penguin Books.

Schiller, Z. (April 2, 2000). "Bridging Northeast Ohio's Digital Divide: Internet's Virtues Still Less Accessible to Poor, Minorities." *Cleveland Plain Dealer*: 1H.

Selfe, C.L. (1999). "Technology and Literacy: A Story of the Perils of Not Paying Attention." *College Composition and Communication* 50(3): 411-436.

Shaughnessy, M.P. (1977). *Errors and Expectations: A Guide for the Teacher of Basic Writing*. New York: Oxford University Press.

Smitherman, G. (1974). "It Be's Dat Way Sometime." *English Journal* 63: 16-17.

U.S. Department of Commerce. (1999). *Falling Through the Net: Defining the Digital Divide*. [Online at http: ntia.doc.gov/ntiahome/fttn99/contents.html/]

———. (2000). *Falling Through the Net: Toward Digital Inclusion*. [Online at http: ntia.doc.gov/ntiahome/fttn00/contents00.html/]

Vernon, A. (2000). "Computerized Grammar Checkers 2000: Capabilities, Limitations, and Pedagogical Possibilities." *Computers and Composition* 17(3): 329-349.

Willis, T., and R. Skybis. (1994). "Spell Checks Not Foolproof." *Communication: Journalism Today* 28(1): 14-15.

Diversity
An Assignment for Basic Writing Students

Marcia Ribble

> The body will achieve what the mind believes.
> — Elliott County basketball motto

Even something as simple as a paper assignment can increase the likelihood of students from working-class families succeeding in college by assisting them in the processes of imagining the transition from working-class to professional lives. (The entire assignment I use is reproduced at the end of the essay.) The assignment I will discuss here asks students to imagine themselves in a leadership role in a large corporation, creating a diversity plan that will deal with the workplace of the future. The rationale for the assignment is the need students have to imagine entering a world with which they are not familiar. We need to be more sensitive to the issues our basic writing students may be dealing with that can make success less likely, and continue to develop assignments that help them to make that transition. This assignment is only a single scratch on the surface of problems facing working-class students of any color, especially first-generation college students. It does not discuss their past learning experiences, the discrimination they may have suffered, poverty, the reluctance of family and friends to see attending college in positive terms, or the way these issues can put roadblocks in our students' paths.

We need to take seriously and learn from the fears expressed so eloquently by Richard Rodriguez that he would forever be alienated from his family and friends (1982), the sense of sorrow expressed by Victor Villanueva (1993) that he would never find anyone who looked like him in academic roles, the anger in William Penn's (1995) voice because he believed he was despised because he is a Native American, and the political intimidation faced by Mike Rose (1989) as he struggled to articulate why people of color who are poor and from working-class backgrounds deserve to take a place at the same educational table where others are already sitting comfortably.

We have much to do to build up a literature so rich with detail and so overwhelmingly compelling that no one can claim that only a few "exceptional" students from the working class deserve a chance in higher education. Our world has changed, probably forever; it has become more technologically rich, requiring a highly educated workforce. As retention specialist Dr. William Hudson notes, "We cannot afford anymore to leave anyone behind" (personal conversation). Assignments such as this one are a simple, no-cost method for trying to help students from working-class families succeed in college. We can give assignments that form connections between students' old and new lives, including teaching students ways to remain connected with their pasts.

Gilles Deleuze and Felix Guattari (1987) have envisioned the rhizome as a metaphor by which one can see the relationships between the seen and unseen parts of connected realities. I am borrowing their metaphor and applying it here to talk about basic writing students from working-class backgrounds. The rhizome is such a useful metaphor because it helps us to visualize the contiguous relationship between the seen and the unseen of life. When we see one part of life, we have a tendency to imagine the unseen as enormously different and perhaps even impossibly remote from us. For those of us who come from working-class families, what we have seen is what we know, and we often imagine the academic/professional world to be vastly different from our world. It must be the world of people very different from ourselves, people who are everything we are not, people who are qualitatively different and maybe even superior.

The metaphoric image that many people have about the differences between the academic/professional classes and the working class of society is that academics and professionals are "clean" and "aboveground," separated from those who are working class by the line of soil that demarcates the underground root systems from the aboveground foliage, flowers, and fruit. Deleuze and Guattari caution that drawing that line of demarcation is an illusion. The connectedness of the rhizome will not allow that line to hold for any length of time. So what we find when we cross that artificial boundary is more people like us. Yet because our working-class students do not have experience with those seeming aboveground "others," they know only the stereotypes they have picked up over the years. Their stereotypes about people with professional backgrounds are as inaccurate as the stereotypes about working-class people held by many academics, stereotypes that need to change before our students can begin to choose a professional life for themselves.

One of my undergraduate professors told me recently that she had not understood how different it was for working-class students until she watched her own daughter-in-law struggle through the process of obtaining her bachelor's degree. From a working-class family, the daughter-in-law had to work hard to surmount what to my professor had been commonplaces, the simple expectations of life. From infancy, my professor had been expected to do well in grade and high school, attend college, obtain a professional terminal degree. But that had not been the case for her daughter-in-law, and it made even ordinary decisions the sites of challenging and great difficulty.

Using Deleuze and Guattari's rhizome metaphor, we could think about writing instruction not just as about learning to write but also as about learning about a world with which working-class students are unfamiliar, the world of professionals. This learning needs to occur so that our students can gain a more realistic understanding of the people they will be working with and the kinds of writing tasks they will actually be asked to do in their future employment.

Deborah Brandt has another way for us to understand the success of this writing assignment. In her book *Literacy as Involvement*, Brandt argues for a reconceptualization of literacy as always embedded in the "situation bound, practical, concrete, communal, and action oriented" (1990: 124), and she notes that "textual language is always embedded in working contexts of action, driven by the 'aim of pursuit,' its meaning accessible only in reference to the intersubjective enterprises of those who are involved" (125). It is clearly easier for students who come from families where higher education is part of the family's culture to enter into the intersubjective enterprises of college education. Brandt notes on the first page of her introduction that the "working class scholarship student who goes off to school and becomes literate is forever estranged from home, ruined, in a sense, by a new and irreconcilable way of being in the world" (1). She explains the reason for it: Because literacy is a hypersocial activity, "to read and write is to trade heartily — inescapably — on commonality and collectivity" (1). Our working-class students come to us without many of the commonalities that belong to the middle and upper classes. Addressing the lack of this kind of preparation is as crucial to the success of working-class students as the need to learn standard forms of English. But preparation for careers and for professional lives must be done in ways that allow students to maintain the important ties to their old collectivities.

This assignment allows students to spend time not only thinking about and talking about their future careers but also investigating their careers and actually preplanning and problem solving for their careers. In its current form, this writing assignment asks students to go back to their home communities to talk with family and community members about solving the problems of diversity in their communities. Diversity can become an easy metaphor for the problems of religion, class, gender, or other differences students encounter as they move from working-class to professional lives. Thinking about solutions to diversity issues can provide students with ready-made ways to deal with the increasing complexities of their college and postcollege lives.

Such involved inquiry is seldom initially easy or fun. It is deeply challenging for students, and I spend time both in and out of class with my students, helping them to work through the frustrations they often get caught up in as the tasks overwhelm them. Most of the time we talk about their ideas and how to structure the paper so their ideas will be clear and well argued. The students invent diversity problems and resolve them in their papers. Those problems include:

- A male employee's harassment of a female employee through email.
- The desire to do business in the burgeoning Chinese marketplace despite language issues.
- A Muslim employee who asks to be put on the night shift during Ramadan.

- A charter school in inner-city Detroit to rival Cranbrook Academy.
- A hotel restaurant manager with international customers and their varied food preferences.
- The manager of a Brazilian tennis tournament who must deal with international players.
- A Chinese greenhouse in the United States growing Chinese fruits and vegetables.

I ask students to take multiple points of view and discuss them with a great deal of thoughtful reflection on the causes and consequences of their choices. They work to admit to their own prejudices, their own narrow perspectives, and their own faulty logic and to actually hear what was being said about cultures very different from their own.

Mihaly Csikszentmihalyi (1993) explains times such as these as *flow*, when the juices of the mind are running fast and energizing the entire organism of the thinkers. He claims that these kinds of experiences are peak experiences and so deeply penetrating that they actually lead to a process of psychological evolution. Intense intellectual activity is the condition most likely to lead to flow, an experience so pleasurable that people will invest themselves in the activity that resulted in that wonderfully positive feeling and continue to repeat it.

This assignment works because it draws students into the intense pleasure of deeply involved learning, despite the process of learning being both challenging and difficult. It pulls on them to use resources of imagination and creative problem solving they have developed over years of life. It forces them to engage in spirited debate about important workplace issues. It places them actively in the position of managers seeking solutions for realistic workplace problems, as equals, able to agree or disagree as they see fit.

Another explanation for the success of this assignment lies in Walter R. Fisher's (1987) work on narrative. Fisher claims that all thinking is done in terms of storytelling and that all communication has at its heart the telling of stories, stories about how life works that we accept or reject or ignore but that form the foundation for mental activity of many kinds. This assignment places students into the role of storyteller, with the story being their own lives. It puts the navigational joystick into their hands and allows them full creative control over their lives. In response to the assignment, students most often do what I had hoped they would do: They write stories of lives richer and more varied and complex than any stories about them I could possibly have invented. In that process of creation, they placed themselves at the center of their origination myth, made themselves the heroes of their existence, and became able to imagine a different world to live in. At the same time, they were not forced to reject their old lives and often were able to creatively incorporate their old lives into their new versions of reality.

These students — with their visions and dreams of making life better for themselves, their families, and their communities — are not what is typically thought of as basic writing students. In fact, one of my basic writing students designed his webpage in three languages — English, Chinese, and Japanese. These students were basic writers, writers many teachers would chain down to working at the sentence level, doing interminably boring sentence combining or writing awful essays about what they would do if they saw someone cheating in class or some other prompt they cared nothing about; basic writing students are rarely allowed to stretch their metaphysical wings or encouraged to imagine lives beyond the boundaries they know. Sentence-level exercises too often do nothing but further convince students that they are only suited for the factory or the fast-food joint. Good assignments for basic writers need to light the imagination on fire, give students a reason for struggling when the going gets frustrating, and provide students with an introduction to options beyond what many of them have been offered.

References

Brandt, D. (1990). *Literacy as Involvement: The Acts of Writers, Readers, and Texts.* Carbondale: Southern Illinois University Press.

Csikszentmihalyi, M. (1993). *The Evolving Self: A Psychology for the Third Millennium.* New York: HarperCollins.

Deleuze, G., and F. Guattari. (1987). "Introduction: The Rhizome." In *A Thousand Plateaus: Capitalism and Schizophrenia.* Minneapolis: University of Minnesota Press.

Fisher, W. (1987). *Human Communication as Narration: Toward a Philosophy of Reason, Value, and Action.* Columbia: University of South Carolina Press.

Penn, W.S. (1995). *All My Sins Are Relatives.* Lincoln: University of Nebraska Press.

Rodriguez, R. (1982). *Hunger of Memory: The Education of Richard Rodriquez.* Boston: D.R. Godine.

Rose, M. (1989). *Lives on the Boundary: A Moving Account of the Struggles and Achievements of America's Educationally Underprepared.* New York: Penguin Books.

Villanueva, V., Jr. (1993). *Bootstraps: From an American Academic of Color.* Urbana, IL: National Council of Teachers of English.

The Assignment

The basic assignment is to write a paper on diversity in the workplace. The paper is to be a 10 page, typed, double-spaced paper using a size 12 font or some approximation thereof, with a minimum of 10 sources from multiple types of sources, documented using MLA citation formats. This paper was the capstone paper of the course and we devoted the last three weeks of the term to it, working on it in the writing lab in every class period. I broke the paper down into tasks and allowed the students to format their papers in terms of those individual tasks.

Paper Structure

I. Organizational Structure Analysis   1-2 pages

Develop a workplace which would realistically be one you would work in post degree, in your major. You are to take a leadership role in this workplace, with 100 employees under your supervision. You are working directly under the supervision of the Board of Directors for this project which asks you to develop a diversity plan for your particular work situation. Set up the workplace, including a graphic of the organizational hierarchy. This paper will sum up your findings for a report to your Board of Directors, but first you need to understand what kind of organization you are working in, along with being able to visualize internal relationships between employees and management, employee and employee, and employee and customer. It is appropriate to do a short organizational history in this section of the paper.

II. Analysis of Diversity Issues Likely in Our Organization   2 pages

Write an analysis of the particular kinds of diversity issues your organization is likely to experience, given its particular needs and mix of employees. Use information from the 2020 projections about population demographic diversity in the US or in your country to determine what mix of employees you are likely to have. This information is available on the Internet. Try to remember that you will be dealing with other organizations and not just your own organization, so issues of diversity in marketing to, selling to, and serving your clients can also be considered in your diversity plan. Remember that diversity in the workplace has both positive and negative connotations.

III. The Diversity Plan   2-3 pages

Write a diversity plan to take into account the advantages and problems your organization is most likely to experience from the diversity of your employees, your inter-organizational contacts, or even the governments in countries within which and/or between which you will be conducting business. Be sure to include any training sessions you may conduct for your employees to increase productivity and reduce interpersonal tensions.

IV. Implementation of the Diversity Plan   2-3 pages

Now do some storytelling to implement your plan and see how successfully you have predicted and managed to control diversity issues in your organization. In this section it is more helpful to you for your plan to have some flaws than it is for it to work perfectly, simply because a flawed plan will give you more analytical experience as you attempt to figure out how to resolve any problems that may occur in the implementation of your plan.

V. Final Report to the Board of Directors   1-2 pages

This final part of the paper is a summation. It will summarize the findings you have obtained and show how well your plan works, or doesn't work, after implementation along with recommending further action to be taken to proceed with your diversity plan.

Note that I have built in some flexibility into the assignment regarding the lengths of the particular sections of the paper. You may want to balance the parts of the paper differently, for instance, using 4 pages for the implementation or storytelling section, and only one page for your introductory section and only one page for the final report section. But do try to stick to the 10 page paper length, because some of your later professors may impose a sanction on your paper if it is longer than the stated length.

You may put additional information in Appendices which are placed after the Works Cited page in the paper, and these pages are not counted in determining the paper's length, nor are your reference pages. You may want to put an organizational hierarchy chart in an Appendix. Appendices are not numbered, but lettered as Appendix A, Appendix B, and so forth.

Using Assessment Techniques in a Racially and Ethnically Diverse Classroom

Jennifer Rene Young

Students bring a wealth of resources to the classroom. Their age, race, sex, religion, and socioeconomic backgrounds are all factors in their learning process. Faculty may use several classroom exercises to help students develop their critical-thinking, reading, and writing skills. The exercises that follow are otherwise known as *classroom assessment techniques* (CATs). Some of the CATs are adapted from a handbook of some 50 such activities by Thomas Angelo and Patricia Cross (1993), two researchers who study and construct these techniques. Angelo and Cross conclude that pinpointing the strengths and weaknesses of students gives the instructor a better sense of how to organize class time, assignments, and grading criteria. CATs also help the instructor see which students need help and the incentive to do better.

CAT I: SELF-CONFIDENCE SURVEY

This CAT[1] works best in the beginning of the semester when the instructor wants a general idea of her or his students' academic preparation. The questions are designed to "aim at getting a rough measure of the students' self-confidence in relation to a specific skill or ability" (Angelo and Cross 1993: 275). The rating system — none, low, medium, high — is general enough so that students do not feel as though their intelligence is being challenged. The version shown in Figure A, for instance, asks the students how comfortable they are in "editing your own essays" or "the essays of your peers"? Once the students have submitted this CAT, the instructor can implement certain materials and teaching methods based on the results of the survey.

CAT II: ONE-SENTENCE SUMMARY

The One-Sentence Summary is a CAT that is useful in the first quarter of the semester. Administer it at least twice a week so that students continue to practice their critical thinking. The repetition of this CAT teaches students to condense large amounts of information into smaller parts that are easier to process and recall. The One-Sentence Summary has many purposes, yet it is specifically designed to encourage individual thought and creativity.[2] Angelo and Cross

describe this CAT as the discipline of creative thinking. It is "the ability to inter-
weave the familiar with the new in unexpected and stimulating ways" (1993: 181).

Students should review sample summaries before formulating their own
(see Figure B). The One-Sentence Summary answers five questions: Who?
What? When? How? Why? (For instance, Who is the story about? What is the
problem? When does the character realize the problem? How does he solve it?
Why does he solve it that way? In what ways does his action satisfy or not satisfy
the plot?) Such elementary questions are necessary to understand the basic plot
and character structure. It is the students' responsibility to learn the fundamentals
so that they may begin to see what they are arguing for or against. In a class that
is rich with diversity, students are looking for ways to relate the text to their own
backgrounds and interests. One-Sentence Summaries help students create a
sophisticated argument that supports or rejects what they have read.

Once they complete the exercise, ask the students to read their sentences
aloud so everyone can hear a new set of examples (see Figure C). As the students
share their summaries, the instructor may hear what is being retrieved from the
text. More important, students can use this CAT to synthesize information in their
own words.

CAT III: GUIDE TO CRITICAL THINKING

This CAT is taken from Allison King's (1995) research on teaching critical thinking. King found that when students are asked to generate questions on their own,
they usually pose factual rather than thought-provoking ones. Therefore, she suggests that instructors teach students how to generate thoughtful questions. Unlike
the One-Sentence Summary, which shows students how to abstract basic information from a text, this CAT (see Figure D) encourages students to use generic
questions as initiators for their own thoughts. With this CAT, students learn to
formulate specific questions pertaining to the new material (1995: 14).

King suggests that students use the generic question stems and work independently to generate two or three questions based on lecture material and text.
This exercise can be completed in two rounds. In the first round, give students five
minutes to write down their own questions. Once they formulate these questions,
divide them into small groups where they can engage in peer questioning.
Depending on the size of the group, peer questioning can last from five to 10 minutes. It appears to work best when each student asks a question and gets a question in response. For example, one student may ask, "What is a self-made man?"
The other student could reply, "How is Frederick Douglass a self-made man and
how does his life differ or agree with Ben Franklin's?" By answering a question
with a question, students find that they have some of the same questions; they are
also less inhibited because there is less pressure to know the answers.

While the students are still in small groups, move into the second round of critical thinking. In this round, ask students to answer some of the questions raised in their groups. For instance, if one student asks, "What do white women have to do with *Uncle Tom's Cabin?*" it would be up to the group to think of possible answers. They then must pick a spokesperson to report to the rest of the class. This round should take no more than 15 minutes.

When the class rejoins, the representatives share the questions and ideas that arose in their group's discussion. King also suggests that instructors ask probing follow-up questions to effectively extend the discussion. By doing this, students begin to see how they can lengthen and support their own arguments for their own essays. This CAT is a good measure of students' reading comprehension.

Another way to implement this CAT is by having students write questions outside class. At the beginning of class, students can turn in their questions on index cards. The instructor may then shuffle the cards before selecting some to read aloud. The questions can initiate small-group or class discussion. This exercise is a great way to begin class, because students can remain anonymous while showing what challenged and/or interested them. Index cards also require a degree of critical thinking outside the class session.

CAT IV: THE LIST OF WHO CARES

This CAT satisfies many students who cannot see the relevance of your class in their lives. Ask students to take out a blank sheet of paper and draw a line down the center. Writing on the left side of the page only, students have three minutes to list all the negative adjectives and phrases about the assigned passage that they read. It is possible that students will use this exercise to vent their frustrations over having to read certain texts. This CAT warrants such reactions, but it also rids students of flat, unsupported statements early in the session. Writing on the right side of the page only, students then have three minutes to list all of the positive things about the assigned passage. When time elapses, ask for volunteers to be chalkboard or easel scribes as the rest of the students share their negative and positive lists.

I recall one semester at Howard University when I taught Christopher Marlow's *The Tragical History of Dr. Faustus*. A sophomore named Jimmy was one of the few Euro-American students in my class. Jimmy often used class discussion to speak about his Italian heritage. At first, Jimmy's List of Who Cares seemed obscure (see Figure E). His list differed from Serina's, an African American female student, who had equally strong feelings about the text. In his negative list, Jimmy used the words *punk* and *idiot* to describe Dr. Faustus. Jimmy found fault in the fact that Faustus did not see the wicked ways of Mephistopheles. Jimmy also labeled Faustus a nonscholar filled with greed and one-mindedness. Jimmy felt that Faustus's doom was "predictable." Likewise, Serina called Dr. Faustus "worse than the devil himself" and a "fake holy person." Serina also wondered why there were few "good women" in the play.

From her positive list, Serina was apparently pleased to see the Seven Deadly Sins as characters. She liked the "bouts between Good Angel and Evil" and when "Faustus asks Mephistopheles for a wife." On the contrary, Jimmy liked the "elements of black magic" and the scene when Faustus meets Lucifer. In response, the other students asked Jimmy and Serina to explain their positive and negative lists. Thus, with little interference from me, the students expected Jimmy and Serina to defend their literary interpretations of the story.

By the end of the class period, Jimmy and Serina had several concrete ideas that helped them with their essays. Jimmy, who was majoring in philosophy, wrote on the irony of Dr. Faustus's fatal flaw. He called his essay "Too Smart for Your Own Good." Serina based her essay on her interest in the fine arts. She compared *Dr. Faustus* to Brunelleschi's *Duomo* painting in Florence. Serina saw distinct correlations between Brunelleschi's painting of the seven deadly sins and the seven heavenly virtues. Serina titled her essay "The Seven Heavenly Virtues." She outlined all the errors Dr. Faustus made that distanced him from God.

The List of Who Cares helps students generate responses that also represent their personal interests. For instance, before they shared their lists, Jimmy and Serina had never talked to each other outside class. During class discussion, Jimmy revealed that though he was Italian American, he had never visited Italy. He planned to study abroad there his junior year. Serina, who traveled around a lot with her family, had lived in Italy for almost two years. "Oh, you'll love it," she gasped. "Not to be stereotypical, but as soon as you get off the plane, grab a gelato!" To see the students entertaining themselves in conjunction with 17th-century material is golden. This CAT, however, gets the best results when the students are comfortable with one another and once they begin to grasp the objectives of the course.

CAT V: THE MIDTERM INSTRUCTOR EVALUATION

The Midterm Instructor Evaluation is important not only to assess what a student is learning but also to evaluate whether the student is learning effectively. The evaluation is another measuring tool that helps both the student and instructor think about the progress that is being made (see Figure F).

Conclusion

CATs are great exercises to use in any classroom, because students always bring their distinct learning experiences with them. The CATs help bring out students' differences and similarities while showing them how to apply intellectual reasoning to their literary responses. CATs help students link their critical responses to the text to their diverse backgrounds and experiences.

Notes

1. For the Self-Confidence Survey Form, see CAT 32 in Angelo and Cross 1993.

2. This One-Sentence Summary is based on CAT 13 in Angelo and Cross 1993. The summary helps the instructor assess students' skills in synthesis and creative thinking.

References

Angelo, T.A., and K.P. Cross. (1993). *Classroom Assessment Techniques: A Handbook for College Teachers.* 2nd ed. San Francisco: Jossey-Bass.

King, A. (February 1995). "Inquiring Minds Really Do Want to Know: Using Questioning to Teach Critical Thinking." *Teaching of Psychology* 22: 13-17.

Suggestions for Further Reading

DiPardo, A. (1993). *A Kind of Passport: A Basic Writing Adjunct Program and the Challenge of Student Diversity.* NCTE Research Report. Urbana, IL: National Council of Teachers of English.

Field, G. (April 1994). "Write Type: Personality Types and Writing Styles." *The FBI Law Enforcement Bulletin* 63(4): 27(1).

Roberts, N.R. (Spring 1997). "Notes of a Non-Gendered 'Ecological' Writer." *Women and Language* 20(1): 60-64.

Savory, E. (Autumn 1994). "Wordsongs & Wordwounds/Homecoming: Kamau Brathwaite's Barabajan Poems." *World Literature Today* 68(4): 750-758.

Figure A

Self-Confidence Survey
This survey is designed to help the instructor measure your confidence in your reading comprehension, research, and critical analysis skills. Please indicate your ability to do the various kinds of assignments listed below.

Assignments	Confidence in Your Ability to Do Them			
1. Abstracting essential information from a text	None	Low	Medium	High
2. Finding the central argument in an essay	None	Low	Medium	High
3. Stating and supporting your own argument in an essay	None	Low	Medium	High
4. Creating a research project	None	Low	Medium	High
5. Doing independent research in the library at Howard University	None	Low	Medium	High
6. Doing independent research at libraries on other campuses	None	Low	Medium	High
7. Researching on the Internet or with other technological tools	None	Low	Medium	High
8. Editing your own essays	None	Low	Medium	High
9. Editing the essays of your peers	None	Low	Medium	High
10. Giving an oral presentation of your research	None	Low	Medium	High
11. Compiling a "Works Cited," "Bibliography," and/or "Annotated Bibliography"	None	Low	Medium	High

Figure B

One-Sentence Summary
Notice this example of a One-Sentence Summary of Charles Dickens's novel *Great Expectations* that has come from answering the 5 W's and one H:

1. **Who** is the story about?	A poor boy (Pip)
2. The boy does **What?** or **What** happens to the boy?	A rich suitor grooms him
3. **When** does this happen?	When he meets an old rich lady
4. **How** does it happen?	She financially supports him and educates him (though it is a secret)
5. **Why** does the old lady do it?	Her own heartbreak vexes her to break the boy's heart by leading him on to think her daughter likes him.

In Sentence Form:
When a poor boy meets an old rich lady, she secretly decides to groom him and educate him in a high society, simply because she wants to mold the boy into something he is not in order to mislead him and leave him heartbroken.

Figure C

One-Sentence Summary Practice
The task is to summarize the information provided throughout the novel *Song of Solomon* by Toni Morrison in just one sentence. The matrix below is designed to help guide you toward your sentence form. Answer each question, so that you have the proper components to complete your sentence.

1. **Who** is the story about?
2. The _____ does **What?** or **What** happens to the _____?
3. **When** does this happen?
4. **How** does it happen?
5. **Why** does this happen?
6. Now combine your answers into **sentence form**:

Figure D

Guide to Critical Thinking

Generic Questions	Specific Thinking Skills Induced
What are the strengths and weaknesses of...?	Analysis/Inferencing
What is the difference between.... and....?	Comparison-contrast
Explain why... (Explain how....)	Analysis
What would happen if....?	Prediction/hypothesizing
What are the implications of...?	Analysis Inferencing
What do we already know about...?	Activation of prior knowledge
What does... mean?	Analysis
How could... be used to...?	Application
How does.... affect....?	Analysis of relationship (cause-effect)
How does... apply to everyday life?	Application to the real world
How are... and ... similar? different?	Comparison-contrast
What is the counter argument for.....?	Rebuttal to argument
What is another way to look at....?	Taking other perspectives

Figure E

Jimmy's List of Who Cares
(F stands for Dr. Faustus)

Negatives
F is a punk
An idiot
Greedy
One-minded
Not a doctor; not a real scholar
Cowardly
He had a predictable doom

Positives
Elements of black magic
F meets Lucifer
The coveted book of spells

Serina's List of Who Cares
(F stands for Dr. Faustus)

Negatives
F is worse than the devil himself
F is a fake holy person
Where are all the good women?
How did F expect to get a good woman?

Positives
7 deadly sins as characters
Bouts bet. Good Angel & Evil
F asks Meph for a wife?

Figure F

Early Semester Questionnaire
Please do not put your name on this sheet

	Disagree			Agree
I think the readings are helpful and pertinent to this course	1	2	3	4
I understand the importance of participation	1	2	3	4
I think the reading assignments are too long	1	2	3	4
I think the reading assignments are too short	1	2	3	4
I am keeping notes in my journal over the reading assignments, class discussion, current events, and cultural activities.	1	2	3	4
I prefer small group discussion to big group (class discussion)	1	2	3	4
I prefer big group discussion to small group discussion	1	2	3	4
So far I have learned something from the readings and/or discussion.	1	2	3	4
I understand the significance of this course	1	2	3	4
Class lectures are interesting and clear	1	2	3	4
The instructor is helpful in answering my questions	1	2	3	4
I feel that the instructor is easily accessible	1	2	3	4

In Our Own Voices
Liberating Race From the Margins

Judy Massey Dozier

Introduction to Literary Studies is a gateway literature course that focuses on a variety of genres from diverse racial and ethnic groups. An American literature survey or a women's literature course may also provide excellent classroom environments for the following pedagogy.

Rationale for a Liberating-Race-From-the-Margins Approach

I continue to be struck by the number of African American students who adhere so closely to "standard" English that any trace of dialect in their articulations is completely erased. And I still bristle when I hear white professors compliment black students (or scholars, for that matter) by stating how "articulate" they are. My annoyance, of course, stems from my knowledge that being "articulate" denotes not only a masterful control of language and a precision with words that promotes clarity but also, when applied to students of color, the suggestion of a level of intelligence. Whether students are conscious of this or not, I fear that dialect for some of them, especially African American students, will come to suggest just the opposite: the lack of intelligence. As black students conform to the demands of education, many move further and further away from the "sound" of their elders. As Alice Walker argues, the "real language" of those family members for whom dialect or black vernacular remains the form through which they communicate may become a source of shame (1988: 6).

My experience in teaching on the college level, however, has taught me that many African American students are outraged by the lack of attention to African American issues in some classrooms. Although the sound of many of these students often suggests total assimilation, they still approach me about their anger at not seeing themselves or their history and culture represented in classroom discussions. And even more outrageous to them is what they consider a distortion of their culture. One of the most salient complaints came from a young African American woman who related a professor's arrogance (as she perceived it) in his inclusion of African American voices listed on his syllabus. She shared with me that in one of her classes where Langston Hughes's poetry was included among a variety of texts by various authors, the white male professor read the poems in standard English, ignoring the dialect and thus literally rewriting Hughes's words.

She was outraged but said nothing until she spoke to me. As I listened to this student express her anger in perfectly articulated standard English, I was sympathetic to her concerns and delighted that she took issue with the dismissal of Hughes's choice of language.

I can only guess at the reasons for the professor's actions. An obvious one might be that he simply did not feel comfortable reading the dialect. Such pronunciations may have been so foreign to him that he feared the ridicule of the class as he struggled through a reading of the poem. Nonetheless, I am concerned about the message his reading sends to his students — that dialect is a substandard form of standard English that may be arbitrarily "corrected" without altering its meaning. It seems clear to me that teaching African American literature this way for whatever reason ignores the cultural distinctiveness of this language. The dismissal of race and the language of the text subjects the work to what I call *literary double consciousness*. According to W.E.B. Du Bois, the "American world . . . yields [African Americans] no true self-consciousness, but only lets him see himself through the revelation of the other world" (1903: 5). Teaching African American literature without attention to cultural distinctions or to the authenticity of the language preserved by these writers allows African American texts to show up in traditional English classes, though they are not allowed to "speak freely" until they are back at home in African American literature courses. The limited number of African American students in the discipline of English suggests that many African American students, like the one above, choose not, as English majors, to witness their own erasure, no matter how they might otherwise conform to the dominant culture's educational standards.

Such a dismissal of the importance of the preservation of language in African American texts does little to change the representation of African Americans in the eyes of our 21st-century students. Thus, forcing dialect into structures of standard English or ignoring the dialectic presence in African American texts undermines diversity in our institutions of higher learning and the mission of the academy to help broaden our understanding of ourselves and our relation to our own cultures and those of others. Let me offer a specific example of my pedagogy to suggest a means of liberating race from the margins in English courses outside African American literature classes.

Language as Resistance

I attempt to get beyond what Toni Morrison argues is "the habit of ignoring race . . . [as] a graceful, even generous, liberal gesture" (1992: 10) by telling students that their use of the racialized terms *black* and *white* is essential to our discussions. Before our analysis of Zora Neale Hurston's novel *Their Eyes Were Watching God* (1937), I inform students of her dual mission as a writer/anthropologist, who wished to preserve her research in African American dialect in her fiction.

Hurston feared that the cultural significance of this language would be lost as more and more rural, black southerners migrated north and assimilated further into mainstream culture. Thus, we explore literature that presents some conclusions derived from Hurston's anthropological work with an assigned reading of her essay "Characteristics of Negro Expression." This essay allows students to begin to identify the distinct rhetorical devices illustrated in black speech patterns (drama, will to adorn, use of metaphor and simile, the double descriptive, verbal nouns, and, of course, the section on dialect itself). This interesting and accessible essay serves to give all students a context for speaking about the use of the dialect we will be reading. In addition, they begin to see for themselves how standard English can become "the mask which hides the loss of so many tongues, all those sounds of diverse, native communities we will never hear, the speech of the Gullah, Yiddish, and so many other unremembered tongues" (hooks 1994: 168).

Next, every student is encouraged to speak the language of the text, to hear the sound of the dialect in her or his own voice. To accomplish this, we read aloud the third act of *Mule Bone*, a play coauthored by Langston Hughes and Hurston (1931). Students volunteer to read a part (if necessary, with my gentle coaxing), even if we are compelled to change actors during the reading many times to accommodate all our voices (I, too, read a part). Students usually enjoy the humorous lines of the play and have fun acting it out. No one is forced into the reading. The rare extremely shy student is allowed to sit and listen.

At this point, the class is comfortable enough with the dialect to begin the discussion of Hurston's novel. I establish the formal aspects of the text: Janie Crawford's position as outsider in the small Florida community, the fact that she is at the end of her story in the beginning of the book, and her decision to relate her journey to her friend and to us, the readers. We speak about the importance of her coming to voice in a text that has been identified as one of the first feminist texts in the 20th-century African American tradition, and the significance of the language through which she tells her story. This discussion is a perfect segue into the relation between orality and status. For instance, Hurston devotes seven pages to the free, indirect discourse that issues from the men who station themselves on the porch of the mayor's store. Close readings of these pages, using Hurston's essay as a guide, helps students gain insight into the relevance of the performativity and creative play of language on acquiring status in the community. The function of *the porch* in Hurston's work is akin to that of the Greek chorus. Yet teaching *the porch* from a tradition that arises from within African American communities brings a distinction to its significance that helps to accomplish the goal of liberating race from the margins of the Euro-American tradition and centering it in a unique American cultural tradition. Additionally, through the voices of the men who assemble on the porch, we as readers are introduced to the morality of this counterculture, the values of the community and its reaction to Janie. Most important, students begin to recognize that Hurston's commitment to this language represents her work as a continuing site of resistance. I point out that historically the vernacular has often embodied a coded meaning derived from its use during slavery. The resistance employed in the use of the spirituals to signal escapes, for example, contained grammatical constructions that continue not only in the speech of the characters in the novel but also in the speech of many blacks today.

The class listens to the sound of this historical resistance in two recordings of spirituals available in most audio/visual departments on campuses: "Go Down, Moses" and "Steal Away to Jesus" (often cited by historians as one of the most popular songs for signaling a planned escape).

Assessment

A brief response paper assignment requires students to examine the language of one of the characters on the porch. Students refer to Hurston's essay on black expression, which helps students to think through the role of language in the text.

Student Empowerment

In many of my classes, my most "articulate" African American students point out that the language they speak in the classroom is often not a language they speak at home with family members or friends. Through our observations of Hurston's use of dialect, many begin to view themselves as bilingual speakers, and as such they bring new insight and dignity to the dialect in Hurston's text. For example, during our discussion of dialect and its significance to our analysis of the text, these students often proudly voice phrases repeated by cherished elders, phrases that bear the distinction of cultural dialect.

Liberating race from the margins will not occur simply by the inclusion of African American texts on syllabi. Years of negative representations, many taken as normal, will not disappear without critical examinations that engage students in the history and cultural traditions of African Americans. An exploration of African American works that avoids rigorous scholarly investigation in favor of dismissing race to fit these works into course themes and approaches is an insistence on reading these works "simply as objects in someone's else's histories" (duCille 1996: 94).

I do not offer my pedagogy as a perfect classroom approach; I am constantly reevaluating my teaching strategies in an attempt to get it "right." I am certain, however, that if we as English professors are committed to making diversity work in the classroom, we must broach controversial subjects such as race, and we must honor the language and the culture of the speakers when we teach African American texts. In this manner, we honor and respect not only the texts themselves but also our African American students as we offer them, and all the other students in our classes, a stake in the change diversity studies offers them. For as Alice Walker sagely insists, "When we hold up a light in order to see anything outside ourselves more clearly, we illuminate ourselves" (1988: 62). Diversity in literature taught in English departments must be more than the inclusion of an "other" text. We must allow these texts to enter our courses using their own voices and culture. It is our job as scholarly investigators to throw light on these cultures in a way that holds the potential for change both within and outside our classrooms.

References

Du Bois, W.E.B. (1903, 1989). *The Souls of Black Folk*. New York: Penguin Books.

duCille, A. (1996). *Skin Trade*. Cambridge, MA: Harvard University Press.

hooks, b. (1994). *Teaching to Transgress*. New York: Routledge.

Hughes, L., and Z.N. Hurston. (1931, 1991). *Mule Bone: A Comedy of Negro Life*. New York: HarperPerennial.

Hurston, Z.N. (1937, 1991). *Their Eyes Were Watching God*. Urbana: University of Illinois Press.

Morrison, T. (1992). *Playing in the Dark*. New York: Vintage Books.

Walker, A. (1988). *Living by the Word: Selected Writings, 1973-1987*. San Diego: Harcourt Brace Jovanovich.

About the Contributors

The Editors

Shelli B. Fowler *(volume editor)* is associate professor of English and comparative American cultures at Washington State University. Her research is interdisciplinary, and she teaches and publishes in the areas of African American literature and critical pedagogy. She has been the recipient of numerous teaching awards, including the Sahlin Faculty Award in Instruction and the William F. Mullen Excellence in Teaching Award. She was named the Lewis F. and Stella G. Buchanan scholar in English at Washington State University from 1998 to 2001.

Victor Villanueva *(volume editor)* is professor and chair of the English Department at Washington State University, where he also teaches rhetoric and composition studies. He is the winner of two national awards for his *Bootstraps: From an American Academic of Color* (NCTE, 1993) and the editor of *Cross-Talk in Comp Theory: A Reader* (NCTE, 1997). The former chair of the Conference on College Composition and Communication and twice cochair of the organization's Winter Workshop, he was named Rhetorician of the Year for 1999. His concern is always with racism and with the political more generally as embodied in rhetoric and literacy.

Carolyn Vasques-Scalera *(AAHE project editor)* is director of diversity initiatives at the American Association for Higher Education. Her work focuses on the intersections of diversity and democracy, social justice education, intergroup dialogue, service-learning, and the sociology of education. She received her Ph.D. in sociology from the University of Michigan, where she was also active in the Center for Research on Learning and Teaching, the Center for Community Service and Learning, and the Program on Intergroup Relations, Conflict, and Community.

The Authors

Janet Bean is assistant professor at the University of Akron, where she teaches undergraduate and graduate courses in composition. She also directs an outreach program that seeks to improve writing instruction in high schools and better prepare urban students for the demands of college writing.

Judy Massey Dozier, Ph.D., is assistant professor and chair of the African American Studies program at Lake Forest College in Lake Forest, Illinois. Her interests include teaching continuities of African traditions in African American literature, the retention of African Americans in predominantly white college environments, and the enrollment of nonblack students in culturally diverse courses. She was voted the recipient of the Great Teacher Award by the graduating class of 2001.

Lisa M. Gonsalves, Ph.D., has been teaching in public urban colleges and universities since 1987. She is assistant professor at the University of Massachusetts at Boston in the Graduate College of Education. The majority of her research focuses on examining cross-racial and cross-cultural (including cross-class) dialogue and interactions between and among educators and students in educational institutions, primarily in urban high schools and colleges.

Dorothy Graber is a Ph.D. student in the American Studies program at Washington State University. Her research interests are in Native American studies, particularly in the politics of artifact collecting, and the discourse of genocide and anti-Indian hegemony in the United States. She received her B.A. in comparative American cultures in 1995 and her M.A. in American studies in 1997 from Washington State University.

Rhonda C. Grego, Ph.D., is associate professor of English at Benedict College, one of South Carolina's historically black colleges. She teaches courses in first-year composition, technical writing, literary criticism, and research writing. Her articles have appeared in journals such as *College Composition and Communication, Writing Program Administrator,* and *English International.* Her work at Benedict College has included two FIPSE grants to explore the teaching of writing and retention issues for diverse college student populations. The most recent grant (with colleague Gwen Greene) examines service-learning as a methodology for writing across the curriculum.

Ana Lucía Herrera is a master's degree candidate at the University of Illinois at Urbana-Champaign and fifth-grade teacher in the Chicago Public Schools. Her interests include creating culturally relevant learning spaces and working for social change.

Michelle Hall Kells is a Ph.D. candidate in discourse studies at Texas A&M University. She is writing her dissertation on the rhetoric of South Texas Mexican American civil rights activist Hector P. Garcia. Kells specializes in civil rights rhetoric, composition theory, and sociolinguistics. She is coeditor, with Valerie Balester, of *Attending to the Margins: Writing, Researching, and Teaching on the Front*

Lines (Heinemann, 1999). A second anthology, *Latino Discourses and the Teaching of Writing*, coedited with Valerie Balester and Victor Villanueva, is forthcoming.

Albert Kim works for a software company in Seattle, Washington. He received his B.A. in comparative American cultures from Washington State University in 1995.

Jaime Armin Mejía is assistant professor at Southwest Texas State University in San Marcos, Texas. His primary academic interests include finding ways to combine Chicano and Chicana literary and cultural studies with rhetoric and composition studies to advance the literacy of all students, especially Mexican American students.

Dan Melzer received his Ph.D. in rhetoric and composition from Florida State University. His interest in pluralistic teaching began when he took a job as an adjunct at Tallahassee Community College, an open-admissions institution.

Rory Ong is associate professor at Washington State University in the departments of English and Comparative American Cultures, where he teaches graduate and undergraduate courses in rhetoric, ethnic studies, and Asian American studies. He is also a member of the American Studies graduate faculty. His research interests include classical and Enlightenment rhetoric, race and ethnicity theory, cultural and critical theory, and Asian American literature. He is working on an anthology, *Of Color: Asian American Literature* (Prentice Hall). Ong received his Ph.D. in English from Miami University in 1992.

Charise Pimentel is a Ph.D. candidate in the Education, Culture, and Society Department at the University of Utah, working on a degree in social foundations with an emphasis on multicultural education. She also teaches first-year writing and multicultural education courses. Her dissertation examines the process white elementary and secondary teachers undergo in their attempts to implement multicultural curriculum in their diverse classrooms.

Octavio Pimentel is a doctoral candidate at the University of Utah in the Education, Culture, and Society Department. He has taught basic writing, first-year composition, and multicultural education courses using the coalition pedagogy described in his essay in this volume. His dissertation uses cultural production theories to examine, through the means of narratives and oral life histories, how Mexicanos achieve success in their diverse settings in the United States and Mexico.

Marcia Ribble is a developmental writing specialist at Morehead State University. She conducts research on writing pedagogy and placement. She earned her Ph.D. from Michigan State University.

Arlette Ingram Willis is associate professor at the University of Illinois at Urbana-Champaign in the Department of Curriculum and Instruction, Division of Language and Literacy. Her research interests include the sociohistorical foundations of literacy, preservice teacher education in English and language arts, and teaching/learning multicultural literature for grades six to 12.

Jennifer Young is a Ph.D. candidate and lecturer in the Department of English at Howard University in Washington, DC. She plans to defend her doctoral thesis, "Marketing a Sable Muse: The Cultural Circulation of Phillis Wheatley," in December 2002. Young gives students the incentive to learn by using cognitive psychology. She encourages students to connect the ideologies of African writers from the 18th century with artists of similar and different ethnic backgrounds in the 20th and 21st centuries.